KU-574-793

your wedding, your way

SOPHIE VINCENZI

EBURY
PRESS

For Simon

First published in the UK in 2003

© Sophie Vincenzi 2003

1 3 5 7 9 10 8 6 4 2

Sophie Vincenzi has asserted her right to be identified as author
of this work under the Copyright, Designs and Patents Act 1988.

All rights reserved. No part of this publication may be reproduced,
stored in a retrieval system, or transmitted in any form or by any means,
electronic, mechanical, photocopying, recording or otherwise,
without prior permission from the copyright owners.

Ebury Press
Random House, 20 Vauxhall Bridge Road, London SW1V 2SA

Random House Australia (Pty) Limited
20 Alfred Street, Milsons Point, Sydney, New South Wales 2061, Australia

Random House New Zealand Limited
18 Poland Road, Glenfield, Auckland 10, New Zealand

Random House (Pty) Limited
Endulini, 5A Jubilee Road, Parktown 2193, South Africa

The Random House Group Limited Reg. No. 954009

A CIP catalogue record for this book is available from the British Library

ISBN 0 09 188395 4

Typeset by seagulls

Printed and bound in Great Britain by Mackays of Chatham plc

Papers used by Ebury Press are natural, recyclable products
made from wood grown in sustainable forests.

www.randomhouse.co.uk

contents

SECTION THREE: IT'S *YOUR* CEREMONY

Deciding what's right for you ... the legalities, here and abroad ...
making every moment meaningful and personal

SECTION FOUR: IT'S *YOUR* PARTY

Style, food, drink and entertainment for the best party you'll ever throw

SECTION FIVE: LOOK FABULOUS AND STAY SANE

The ultimate guide for a gorgeous, happy couple

With contributions from
Emily Vincenzi, Clare Nolan, Simon Cornish

Acknowledgements
I am greatly indebted to a great many people (too many to name) for their help, encouragement, wisdom or enthusiasm, especially the many couples who shared their own wedding experiences with me. For contribution to the book or professional guidance I would like to thank in particular: Ben Fletcher, Professor of Psychology at the University of Hertfordshire; Bishop Jonathan Blake of the Society for Independent Christian Ministry and Open Episcopal Church; British Humanist Association; Bob Grosse, Secretary of the Guild of Professional Toastmasters; Bruno Barton at Sparkling Wedding Speeches; Catholic Marriage Care and Advisory Council; Church of Scotland; Chloe Hardy, Speechtips.com; Clare Nolan; Clare Alexander; Claudia Vincenzi; Doug Showell, Alternative Occasions; Dr Lori Bisbey, Chartered Psychologist; Episcopal Church of Scotland; Elaine Gallagher; Flowers & Plants Association; General Register Office for Northern Ireland; General Register Office for Scotland; General Synod of The Church of England; Graham Pugh and Caroline Thorogood; Guild of Wedding Photographers UK; Kathleen Cox, Clinical Psychologist; Nicki Marsh; Occasional Words; Office for National Statistics; Office of the Chief Rabbi; Ralph Van Dijk; Office of Registrar General for England & Wales; Sophie Lillingston, Lillingston Associates; Tombi Peck; *You & Your Wedding* magazine.

Special thanks to Thomas Wilson, my editor at Ebury Press, Sarah Bennie, for her publicity talents, and to Matthew Parker, with whom the idea for *Your Wedding, Your Way* was first hatched.

Most importantly, though, this book literally would not have happened without the practical (as well as emotional) support of my parents, together with the endlessly cheering interest shown by my three sisters and a sweetly patient and enthusiastic band of friends. But my husband, Simon, and our children, Ollie and Honor, have undoubtedly taken the most on the chin – and I am on my knees with love and gratitude to them for so obligingly taking up the life of a single-parent family so soon after our own wedding!

Credits
Extract from *Captain Corelli's Mandolin* by Louis de Bernières, published by Vintage (May 1995). Used by permission of The Random House Group Ltd.
Extract from *On Green Dolphin Street* by Sebastian Faulks, published by Hutchinson. Used by permission of The Random House Group Ltd.
Extract from *Like Water for Chocolate* by Laura Esquivel, published by Doubleday/ Black Swan. Used by permission of Transworld Publishers, a division of The Random House Group Ltd.

section
one

so you're getting married...

The fun starts here ...

chapter
one

why this book?

BECAUSE IT'S YOUR WEDDING ...

Everyone else can do their wedding how they like – but this one's yours. Doing your wedding your way is simply about making your day completely you. Totally personal. Absolutely unique.

Whether this is your first, second or third wedding, you've probably always known that the conveyor-belt wedding is simply not your style. So what is? A ceremony that means far more than just keeping the vicar happy? Running away to distant shores? A big funky party? Whatever your style, one thing is certain: you don't want it cramped by anything or anyone, when there are hundreds of ways to do a wedding, and the standard white variety is only one of them.

You're going to remember this day for the rest of your lives, so it really is worth holding out for what's right. And if that's something special, unusual or chic, you're in luck: there simply couldn't be a better time to plan your wedding. After decades of image crisis and sitcom ridicule, the wedding is back in vogue. With marriage rates up and divorce rates down for the first time in years, magazines like *Elle* and *Cosmopolitan* are dedicating lots of their glossy pages to super-stylish nuptials, and the celebrity band just can't get enough of them. The choice of place and time, already dramatically improved by the 1994 Marriage Act, will be even better soon, with further reform from Church and State. The wedding industry has really smartened up too, bending over backwards to give couples exactly what they want.

You may not want an 'alternative wedding' (the expression does, after all, have a slightly uncomfortable ring to it, resonating of weird settings and over-extreme dress codes) but still you might look at the conventions … and feel there *must* be alternatives. It could be that all you need are the ideas, and the elbow room, for small but meaningful twists on a classic wedding: like your own children playing leading roles, or a speech from the bride. Or you might want quite a different approach: if the slightest hint of convention is completely alien to you, Vegas or New Age handfasting may be the only way to go! Whatever your vision, every chapter in this book will help you achieve it, and find the alternatives you're looking for. It'll cut down on legwork, costs, stress, anxiety, and hassle, and add to the possibilities with hundreds of ideas (and phone numbers). And hopefully, it'll help you stick to your guns and get what you want. All without upsetting anyone's parents – too much!

IT TAKES TWO

The assumption here is that your entire wedding is a joint effort. There's no law of biology that says women alone plan weddings – in fact I've seen many men prove far more creative, organised, and calm. Traditionally, grooms have been kept out of things until there's no option but to let them in on the act … when they dress up and show up. Which seems a shame. While I wouldn't suggest that every groom should master the art of making sugarcraft roses, you can both contribute your talents, possibly even discover some new ones, and enjoy the teamwork. The workload will be so much less, and you're likely to both enjoy the day a whole lot more, if it's one you've created together (because you want to) than one where the groom does what he's told (for a quiet life). To find out who's *officially* meant to do what, *see* Chapter Fifteen.

GOODBYE MR AND MRS AVERAGE

With so much diversity, and so many choices, weddings in the 21st century are less likely than ever to follow a set path. The latest National Statistics Office figures for England and Wales show that of the 300,000 couples who marry every year:

- About 10% marry overseas.
- In 42% of weddings at least one person has been married before, and in 19% of all weddings, it's the second time for both.
- About 64% of weddings in England and Wales are civil ceremonies.
- Despite a surge in the millennium year, religious ceremonies are still on the decline.
- About 17% of all weddings here are in approved marriage premises, and half of those are away from the couple's home.
- The 'average' age for a first-time wedding is now 30.5 for a man; 28.2 for a woman. But since so many marriages are second time around, there's another 'average' age (for *all* weddings): 34.8 for men and 32.1 for women.

BEFORE YOU BEGIN:
SOME ESSENTIAL WEDDING WISDOM

Fast-track wedding expertise
Originality calls for some fast learning, making a reality of your brilliant ideas, and knowing when to bring in help. Chapter Eleven covers the golden rules for appointing services and suppliers; Chapter Fifteen will help you to capitalise on assistance from friends, family or professionals; and Chapter Eighteen is all about getting organised.

How long have you got?
Whether you have years, months or weeks until you get married, the following key timings will help you decide on the wedding style your schedule allows. There's a complete rundown of what to do when on page 285.

- **Register offices and churches** get booked six months to **a year** ahead, even longer on popular days. If you're short of time, you may get lucky with a midweek booking or a weekend cancellation. *See* Chapter Eight for ceremony choices, logistics and legalities.
- **Venues:** Approved civil marriage venues and reception locations will have some bookings **a year** ahead, and some popular ones have no vacancies whatsoever for even longer! Booking nine months ahead should give you a good choice, and even three months ahead you should find something suitable as long as you can be flexible. *See* Chapter Five for guidance.
- **UK legalities:** You need **at least sixteen days** for most civil marriage preliminaries, up to twenty-one days in Northern Ireland, and longer for most religious ones.
- **Overseas weddings:** Legal preparations can take anything from one day to three or **four months**, other preparations even longer. *See* Chapters Six and Eight.
- **Caterers, musicians, entertainers, florists, photographers** and other suppliers or services: Allow **a few months** at the very least for popular days, up to a year if you don't want any competition. *See* Chapters Ten, Eleven and Seventeen.
- **Wedding gowns: Five months** is the oft-quoted time required to create a made-to-measure dress, but many dressmakers can do it considerably faster, and high street or ready-to-wear just depends on your shopping stamina. *See* Chapter Fourteen.
- **Hire of formalwear:** Go for a fitting and make reservations **a month or two** ahead; ring around first if you're in a hurry.

Etiquette: Good manners, common sense – or a nuisance?

There's a school of thought that says that in certain circumstances – weddings being one of them – a set of rules define acceptable social behaviour. Call it tradition, convention or etiquette, some people (especially older generations) believe it's compulsory, while others find it out of date, tiresome, and sometimes even downright rude – the very thing, of course, that it's intended not to be. The tradition of displaying wedding gifts, for instance,

From the expert: Adjusting etiquette

Bob Grosse, Secretary of the Guild of Professional Toastmasters

'Even as a defender of etiquette and preserver of tradition, I can usually find a precedent and justification for breaking with etiquette. There's no point in a formality if it's going to spoil someone's day, and I can always cite a Lord and Lady Somebody who broke the rules first.'

would now more often than not seem a little tactless, even though it was once considered the height of good manners.

Nonetheless, some of the smartest advocates of etiquette tell us it's simply there to help. It can give a practical structure to the day, be a guide in a dilemma, help ensure that people know what to expect, and feel thought-of and valued at a time when, in truth, there's just *too* much to think about. Looked at another way, it can serve as a reliable reference point, freeing you up to focus on something new, unique, personal or exciting. So see tradition and etiquette as your friends, but not ones you have to stick to like glue; and keep them to hand, without letting them get in the way. 'It's another word for good manners,' says Bob Grosse, Secretary of the Guild of Professional Toastmasters. 'It's not there to spoil anyone's day.' The trick is to approach etiquette intelligently, think it through – then sometimes even dump it.

Real world wedding truths

Before you go any further with your plans, your checklists, your contracts with caterers and musicians and dressmakers, I should tell you about a growing suspicion, amongst recent brides, that there's a conspiracy going on …

Weddings are lovely. Your own wedding is oh, a whole load lovelier than that. Just amazing. But more than a few of the couples who have told their stories for this book (me included) refuse to believe the ones who say their weddings were perfect. That they wouldn't change a thing. Really? Most couples haven't done it before, and they have to go from novice to full-scale wedding planner in the space of a year or less. And which wedding is the test-zone? Their own. It's unlikely they'll get it 110% right first time.

So why the conspiracy? Maybe it takes guts to admit your wedding wasn't perfect and maybe not, in one or two tiny ways, worth all the work and money. And maybe there's an element of jealousy: while the memory of some disappointment is fresh, we might envy the future bride her chance to get it right. Throughout this book are the words of wisdom which you *must* read, fresh from the mouth of a bride, groom, or expert, to prepare you for some mixed emotions, help you avoid disappointment wherever you can. Even if you're skipping a chapter, pick out these icons ☺☹ for not-to-be-missed advice (and regrets). Start with the ones below to help you go in with your eyes wide open!

☺☹ *'The only wedding worth having is a happy wedding – and the bride sets the mood of the day. Whatever your worries, tiredness or last-minute squabbles, be absolutely determined that the only thing that you're going to feel on the day is the sheer happiness of what's happening to you and going on around you.'*

☺☹ *'The day will go unbelievably fast, hours will literally disappear in moments, and time will accelerate throughout the day. Don't make the mistake of thinking you've got loads of time to do what you wanted to do, say what you wanted to say or share a special moment. Do it now!'*

☺☹ *'You'll feel like you haven't spoken to any of your guests all day, which can be quite distressing. It's less of a problem for the groom, because he can get there early and say hello to everyone as they arrive. Build in plenty of time for circulating, keep numbers down, and tell everyone in your speeches that instead of "going away", you'll be staying on and taking up a patch near the door so you can send them off instead!'*

☺☹ *'You're likely to feel quite strange for much of the day. I felt "spaced out" and a bit confused – even though everyone kept telling me how calm and happy I looked! Don't expect anything of yourself except to smile and enjoy as much of the day as you can. Organisation and decision-making may well be totally beyond you.'*

☺☹ *'If you usually like to wear a watch, your wedding day won't be any different – so don't let anyone convince you not to. Not knowing the time can make you feel disoriented and the day will run away with you even faster.'*

☺☹ *'Take a moment, early on in the day, when the two of you stop together, take stock, look on and memorise what you see. You may not get another chance.'*

☺☹ *'Your photos, video and guest book are your memories. When the day is over, they are your wedding for the rest of your life. Invest enough time and energy in them.'* See Chapter Seventeen.

☺☹ *'Tell people beforehand whether you want to be consulted on last-minute questions on the day itself. Some couples want to be kept informed, others want to be kept in blissful oblivion. It's a personal thing.'*

☺☹ *'I just wasn't prepared for the post-wedding day blues. I've heard it described as losing a friend, post-natal depression and worse! Now I see why. Prepare yourself emotionally and practically for the comedown.'* See Chapter Nineteen.

☺☹ *'It's worth realising well in advance of the wedding that The Dress – that wildly expensive and previously most revered and cleanest of things – will almost certainly end up filthy, and may well acquire a few permanent stains. Mine were chocolate, red wine and felt-tip pen in prominent places and quite large quantities. I'm just about over it now!'*

☺☹ *'Obsessing and over-planning don't necessarily make for the best weddings. I worried and worked for months, and I was exhausted by the end of it. But on the day, I didn't have a clue what was happening – I was literally drunk on happiness. I think I could have got away with a lot less of the slog, enjoyed the preparations more, and had just as good a time on the day!'*

Important note: Suppliers and contacts mentioned throughout the book are not tested or recommended. A 'Contacts' section is at the end of most chapters. Costs, where given, provide an indication only, and may increase significantly depending on area and overheads.

chapter
two

a decent proposal...
and telling the world

THE ALL-IMPORTANT QUESTION

Done right, a proposal can be the highpoint of your relationship so far. Right up there with the first time he (or she) said the 'L' word, you're bursting with the kind of happiness Bridget Jones would write a thousand diaries for.

There are hundreds of ways to do it, and if you're meant for each other (we're assuming here that you are) you'll know what's going to work. If you've got as far as reading this book, your proposal may be happily accomplished, leaving you to skim eagerly over to the next chapter. If you've reached the point, on the other hand, as so many 21st-century couples do, where you've chatted casually – or even confidently – about getting married, but got no further than that, the following might inspire one of you to do the thing properly. People will ask you again and again how it happened, so you might as well have a good story to tell.

The expensive or impressive variety

These are the proposals that little girls dream of from the first day they dress up in a fairy princess outfit and sparkly plastic shoes. They're still the only kind that will do for some people.

- Romantic cities (any of significance will do). Keeping an element of surprise could be the challenge here.
- Those magic words drawn in the sky, the sand, or shaped-out rose petals on crisp white sheets.

The cool variety

These are my favourites. Despite being low-key, much style and thought (and therefore love) has obviously gone into them.

- Try hangman: 'We were playing on the beach. He marked out the letters for 'marry me'. I thought he was joking, of course.' Or try Scrabble. Or any other word game.
- Key the words into the screensaver of your loved one's computer (avoiding open-plan offices).
- Have a jigsaw puzzle made to reveal the all-important question (or perhaps a big clue). Do it together, and keep back a few crucial pieces till last! Wentworth Wooden Jigsaw Company can help.

21st-century dilemma: Presenting the ring

Some girls feel a neat little box with something sparkly inside is the only proper accompaniment to a marriage proposal, and would love any ring chosen by their husband-to-be because it has been selected under such special circumstances. Others prefer a chance to choose the ring together, and might even find the 'done-and-dusted' ring presentation a little presumptuous. 'And anyway,' said one bride, 'he wouldn't have known an emerald from his elbow.' One compromise is to give a precious stone, ready for a setting that you'll choose together – which has all the romance without the pitfalls.

The reluctant groom

Brad Pitt wasn't all that keen – at first. So if the urge to wed is a little one-sided, you're in good company. 'I wasn't actually pushing for marriage,' admitted Brad recently, since his wedding to Jennifer Aniston. 'But now I highly recommend it. I'm loving it all.'

The 'not such a big deal' variety

These are usually for the reformed commitment-phobic. Proposing properly doesn't have to mean making a big fuss, if that's not your style. This is the real world, after all, where men and women sometimes take a while to see eye-to-eye on the subject of getting married and some of us are happy (ecstatic, even) with a resoundingly unromantic declaration that the love of our lives has 'come round to the idea'. No need to hold out for a fairy tale – as long as you know she/he loves you.

- Let your children take the initiative: '"Daddy," said three-year-old Oliver in the car one day, "why has Mummy got a different name from us?" Less than a year later we all had the *same* name!'
- Say it ... but don't say it: 'It had been a bit of an issue in the past, but lately we'd been getting on fantastically. I'd resisted mentioning the "M" word for weeks, but how much more laid-back was I going to have to be? One day, walking through park, he stopped and said, "Whatever you want, I want you to have." And that was it. I was happy with that, believe me. And he was 100% enthusiastic about the wedding from then on.'

Can a woman propose?

Of course, and not just in a leap year:

- It's not such a radical idea; in fact it's quite old-fashioned. The tradition for women to propose on 29 February is an ancient one.
- Some of the happiest marriages have followed a woman's proposal.
- I've asked around and, if they like the idea, most men tell me they'd prefer low-key, rather than hearts and flowers.
- If you're not sure, could a friend do some subtle background research for you? He could be planning the same thing ...

Etiquette issue: Should the bride's father be asked?

When a woman was 'owned' by her father, and traded on to her prospective husband by arrangement between the two, a father's permission was more necessity than courtesy. Now, of course, it's entirely up to the couple, unless you're lucky enough to have some serious inheritance at stake. You might like the idea – or have reservations, either on the grounds that a woman is not a chattel to be given from one man to another, or because you feel it's a decision between the two of you alone. There is a pragmatic alternative: the groom can inform the bride's father, at a private moment, of your wedding plans – and express the hope that he will give them his blessing. The demonstration of respect and the nod to tradition are there, but certain more contemporary principles have been upheld.

GOING PUBLIC

Until you have a very clear idea of how you want your wedding to be, secrecy is wise. The weeks or months when you keep your plans to yourselves are exciting and romantic, and the best chance you'll have to decide what to do, without interference.

As soon as you're ready, your own children, if you have them, should be the first to be told, enlisting the support of their other parent if relevant, and possible. After that, the bride's parents are traditionally the first to know, then the groom's. If your parents are divorced, leave as little time as possible between telling each. Then tell immediate family and closest friends. Your boss and workmates should be told soon, too, followed by more general announcements to the rest of your world. If it's appropriate, try to introduce the two sets of parents as well.

Tell people properly, if not formally: You may feel that you don't want to make a fuss of your engagement, or you might want the whole world to know. Either way, people can feel hurt that you didn't tell them yourselves, so don't rely on the grapevine. Personal notes and phone calls are considerate and a chance to talk: you to your friends and close family and each set of parents to their friends, siblings and so on. The informal route allows you and your parents each to make announcements as they wish – just make sure they don't hand out the pledge of a wedding invitation at the same time.

A formal newspaper announcement is usually worded in the third person:

> *Mr A. Groom and Miss C. Bride*
>
> *The engagement is announced between Adam, eldest son of Mr and Mrs Benjamin Groom of Haywards Heath, Sussex, and Clare, second daughter of Mr and Mrs Donald Bride, of Teddington, Middlesex.*

Where divorce and remarriage are involved, the variations are the same as for invitations, *see* page 291. Check the newspaper beforehand as some have a set form of wording you may need to follow. If the information doesn't appear in the paper itself, call (or check their website) for rates and booking details. (*See* **Contacts** on page 22.)

Real world proposals

'I couldn't see what was the big deal about proposing, so to prove it I said, "It's easy to say, listen: Will – you – marry – me?" Deliberately misunderstanding me, he came back with, "Can I have a month to think about it?" He actually made me wait the full thirty days before he said yes (although I knew he would)!' Bride, 27.

'She proposed to me, but I wished she hadn't, because I was just getting up the courage to do it myself ...' Groom, 34.

'He did it – unshaven, unwashed, and with a gun against his head. He wrote it on a napkin!' Bride, 27.

'He did it all properly: got down on one knee in a restaurant. And I just laughed. I thought he was joking. It took him a year to forgive me and try again.' Bride, 30.

Don't give anyone cause to label you Smug (nearly) Married: You're going to need plenty of support in the next few months. Even if you've been living together for ten years, or you're the last in your pack to go legal, there'll inevitably be some mixed feelings.

Ex-partners should be told personally, if the split has been quite recent, or you have children together.

Don't announce your wedding plans while one of you is still married: You may feel it's important to tell people privately, but avoid a printed announcement.

Don't let people assume that they'll be invited: It's much easier to make it clear that the wedding will be small, or family only, when you announce your engagement, than later on when expectations have grown.

If reactions are not so good, *see* Chapter Sixteen.

THE RINGS

What exactly is a carat, anyway? 'The very least you should accept, my dear,' said one friend. I accepted rather less, in fact, and love it just the same.

There's an unpleasant commercial aspect overtaking the tradition of giving a ring. For the record, the idea that an engagement ring should cost at least a month's salary is not a romantic tradition: it appears to have originated through the advertising campaign by a well-known diamond corporation. So don't let that influence you, and don't be pressurised into overspending for any of the other 'traditional' reasons, either. Precious jewellery is not necessarily a great investment, despite what the marketeers might tell you, as the relatively lower price of second-hand and antique rings would indicate. For all but the most significant pieces, a well-managed savings account would probably give a better return. As for security, perhaps it would be nice to have something valuable on your left hand, if you think your betrothed might leave you in the lurch, but that kind of thinking is one wedding tradition most brides would rather be without.

People talk of engagement rings (or rather the diamonds within them) in terms of the 'Four Cs' (Cut, Clarity, Carat and Colour) but I prefer to think in

21st-century dilemma: 'I don't want to wear an engagement ring'

If wearing a sparkly ring makes the bride-to-be feel, in the words of one, 'like a reserved sticker has been slapped across my forehead', there's certainly little point – or pleasure – in it. Or it might just feel a little clichéd. A problem arises only if your partner doesn't sympathise, or even feels hurt. I think most men would feel that wearing a natty pair of cufflinks etched with the words 'I'm engaged', would make them uncomfortable – so some empathy might be elicited with that thought. An alternative piece of jewellery may be a solution (you could wear a necklace, earrings or bracelet). The meaning is more private, and possibly more sentimental as a result. If you're taking a really modern view, the groom-to-be should be given a gift, too, so why not give each other engagement gifts, such as some art or books. As for friends and family who find the absence of a ring difficult to deal with, try saying cheerfully that 'we decided against it.' It'll just be a taster of how proficient you'll become, over the next few months, at politely telling people that you plan to do things your way.

terms of the 'Two Ls': that your engagement ring should Last (because the stone and metal are durable enough) and that you should Love it forever (and you can rely on your own good taste for that). It makes sense to order your wedding ring at the same time.

For an engagement ring to last a lifetime ...

Choose a durable stone such as garnet, amethyst, diamond, aquamarine, emerald, pearl, ruby, peridot, sapphire, opal, topaz or turquoise.

And a hard setting such as gold or platinum, but don't wear them next to each other – the gold will wear away.

If you're choosing a diamond, you might want to know about the 'Four Cs'; each of these quality indications should be detailed by independent certification accompanying the stone: **Cut, Clarity, Carat** (weight) and **Colour**.

An insurance certificate should accompany the ring. If the ring is very expensive, get an independent valuation, too.

ENGAGEMENT PHOTOGRAPHS

Most couples are wary of cheesy engagement photos. Still, you might consider pictures if you know the photographer is fantastic (some engagement pictures are lovely) or can afford to use the episode to test one or two photographers for the wedding itself. If you have children, it's a timely trigger for a set of family photos, and a chance to get them used to being photographed. *See* Chapter Seventeen.

Money-wise: What to expect
Engagement announcement in a national daily newspaper: about £100
Engagement ring, average spend: about £1000
Wedding ring, average spend: about £300

Contacts
Daily Telegraph: 020 7538 5000; www.telegraph.co.uk
The Guardian: 020 7278 2332; www.guardian.co.uk
The Independent: 020 7005 2000; www.independent.co.uk
The Times: 020 7782 7347; www.timesonline.co.uk
Wentworth Wooden Jigsaw Company: 01666 840033;
    www.wooden-jigsaws.com

21st-century dilemma: What to call each other once it's official
If you're happy with 'fiancé', then that's wonderfully convenient because it's the easiest term to use and everyone knows what you mean. There are many alternatives – not forgetting, of course, that you could just continue to use each other's names: the listener invariably knows you're referring to the person you're going to marry, whatever you call them! For me, through a decade of cohabitation and two children together, I had amused myself by referring to my (previously) non-committal man as 'my current boyfriend', especially at the school gates. Now the church bells may not have been ringing, but the register office computer was bleeping, and 'fiancé' seemed too green, 'partner' too business-like, 'wife/husband-to-be' too politically correct. We finally settled on 'betrothed', although I did like to tell people, 'He's going to be my first husband!'

section two

it's *your* wedding

Possibilities, inspiration … and big decisions

chapter
three

oh, happy day: what's it to be?

Your wedding is obviously one of life's defining moments. People will tell you that committing yourself to the person you love is the *most* important thing about it, especially when you're fretting disproportionately over a precise shade of pink ribbon or a late delivery of stationery. And it is, just ... but *how* you make that commitment is vital, too. If it feels right, it'll be a wonderful, happy start – and probably the biggest public statement you'll make about yourselves, ever.

So what's it going to be? The decisions you need to make about where and how you get married, when and with how many guests, are intrinsically entwined and may swing from one extreme to the other. One moment, A Few People Somewhere Very Chic seems the perfect solution; then the next, A Huge Crowd Having The Time Of Their Lives is the only way to go. And inevitably there will be a moment, however brief, when you say, 'Let's just run away.'

The solution will be the combining and compromise of three things: first, your options (explained below); second, your main considerations and the big decisions you make about them; and finally, your vision (there are some ideas to help inspire you later in this chapter).

THE OPTIONS

A wedding is, of course, classically made up of two parts: the ceremony, and the celebrations afterwards. From the point of view of choice, celebrating is the easy bit. There's not a corner of the world that won't match someone's idea of the perfect post-marriage party, nor any way of celebrating that can't be achieved (funds aside) … It's the legal and religious elements – of actually *getting married* – which typically limit your options.

Here in the UK
The legislation that once restricted weddings to a local approved place of worship, or local register office, is long gone. Now, of the 270,000 marriages in England and Wales each year, only about a third take place in the local parish church. Since 1995 couples have had far greater scope: they can also marry at any 'approved' civil marriage premises, and in any register office, countrywide. And in Scotland, a minister has the authority to conduct a religious wedding at *any* 'suitable' venue.

The result today is a choice of literally thousands of beautiful, romantic, chic or wacky locations – where less than ten years ago most couples were restricted to two or three rather ordinary ones. For a building to be 'approved' for civil wedding ceremonies, it has (amongst other things) to be a permanent structure, open to the public, and the ceremony must take place between 8am and 6pm. The full rundown on where and when you can wed is in Chapter Eight.

The scope may be extended still further over the next few years: legislation is currently under review relating to both the location and time that marriages can take place. In the next few years, couples may be able to marry at a church other than that of their parish, if they can demonstrate a strong connection to it, or have a civil marriage at almost any time or location, by arrangement with the registrar, as long as it is 'solemn and appropriate to the occasion'.

Until then, what is there for the many people who would dearly love to marry at home, or on a hilltop, or at night? Or who wish to express beliefs that fit neither with recognised religions nor civil authorities. They're such ordinary wishes, yet the law currently prevents it. More extreme, but no less heartfelt by some, is the ambition to marry in the sky or underwater, via the Internet, or on horseback, which even new legislation is unlikely to facilitate.

Good news, right now

People who are already planning their wedding don't have to wait for the law to change: if you'd like to get round the restrictions, a change in approach can allow you to marry any way you choose. 'Who says that the legal and the ceremonial aspects of getting married have to happen simultaneously? The British have traditionally done it that way, but most Europeans have not,' says Bishop Jonathan Blake of the Society for Independent Christian Ministry and the Open Episcopal Church. On the Continent, couples take care of the paperwork in their local town hall or register office, and then have a 'spiritual', religious, or personal vow-exchange wedding ceremony shortly afterwards. Adopting that approach in this country opens the door to almost any kind of wedding you want.

There are many wedding celebrants in the UK (religious and secular), who will conduct a spiritual, non-legal ceremony wherever and whenever you choose: in your own garden, beneath the stars, on a beach, or in a forest. All you need to do is take care of the legalities in a minimal way in a separate register office ceremony. For the subsequent, 'main', wedding, you might choose an independent celebrant, or one from an organisation such as the Society for Independent Christian Ministry, the Open Episcopal Church or the British Humanist Association. Such a ceremony is serious and sincere, but warm and informal, and created almost entirely around your personal choices and beliefs. The celebrant or minister can either lead the ceremony, or enable you to lead it yourselves. Second marriages, mixed faith and same-sex relationships are welcomed, and the format can be quite traditional, with an aisle, music, reading and vows – or it can be created in an entirely original way. As Bishop Jonathan Blake puts it, 'I love to say yes. I've overcome my fear of heights to marry a couple in an aeroplane, and now I've

Two-stage weddings

Zoe Ball & Norman Cook *took care of the legalities at Bath register office, then went to hip Babington House in Somerset for a blessing and party with all their friends.*

Jemima Goldsmith & Imran Khan *followed a brief Parisian ceremony (conducted in Urdu) with a civil ceremony at Richmond Register Office.*

Sir John & Lady Mary Mills *finally enjoyed a full church ceremony recently, sixty years after a snatched war-time civil wedding at a Marylebone register office. He said, 'The first sixty years are the worst, so we're hoping to push on from here.'*

agreed to conduct the first wedding in space.' It's simply down to you to choose the format and celebrant that's right.

For those who feel that a wedding isn't 'proper' unless the legalities form part of it, the legal and personal aspects can be seamlessly dovetailed together: at an approved marriage premises, the minimal civil ceremony is conducted by the registrar, then, when everything is signed and the officials have left, ministers like Bishop Jonathan Blake or a humanist celebrant will enter the room to lead the next part of the ceremony. 'This can be frowned on,' explains Bishop Jonathan, 'but even if some of the content is religious, it's entirely legal.' It may take more organisation and persuasion on everyone's part, but could be well worth the effort.

Overseas

Many countries outside the UK have less restrictive wedding legislation, so if you're willing to travel, the options are wide open. Most nations will welcome you and your wedding party with open arms, but keep in mind that some others make it a *little* more difficult, to say the least.

For venues, *see* Chapter Five; for a full explanation of the choice of ceremonies, the legal procedures and paperwork you'll need, *see* Chapter Eight. For locations and logistics of planning a wedding abroad, *see* Chapter Six; for legalities and residency requirements of many more countries worldwide, *see* Chapter Eight.

CONSIDERATIONS AND BIG DECISIONS

As you begin to dip a toe in the water of wedding world, you'll be hit by the slightly daunting realisation that the main decisions have to be made right at the start. The business of wedding planning is typically an early one, with bookings a year or so in advance. Chapter One lists key timings that might affect your choices; a detailed countdown to the day is on page 285. While prompt action is always a good idea, be wary of suppliers who have a tendency to exploit your anxiety about time in order to secure a booking before you're ready. Give yourselves as much elbow room as possible to get the right location, ceremony and suppliers, by making the following decisions as soon as you can:

- **When:** With so much to take into account, from work commitments and the sporting calendar to your own impatience, settling on a date can be a challenge. To help you decide, *see* Chapter Four.
- **Where:** If your dream is the local register office, you've got it easy. If it's the vineyards of Tuscany, then don't be deterred. For locations, venues, travel and organisation, *see* Chapters Five and Six.
- **How much you plan to spend** and where it's going to come from. Money is covered in Chapter Seven.
- **Numbers:** From the legal minimum of four people (the two of you, plus two witnesses) to a massive party. Many people combine the two, with

Etiquette issue: When your parents have other ideas

So what happens now, when you realise that you and your parents have very different dreams for your wedding? Weddings were traditionally a family occasion, largely orchestrated and paid for by the bride's parents, and celebrated at their home. If you accept your parents' money, it's only fair to accept their traditions and expectations, too. If you want complete freedom, be ready to pay your own way – and to be patient while they get used to the idea! Most families strike a happy compromise, but problems can arise when people want to have their cake and eat it.

a few people present at the ceremony, and many more at the reception; others have a large ceremony and drinks for everyone, then a quieter celebration later with close friends; others may prefer to take a minimal group away somewhere, followed by a bigger party when they get back home. Numbers obviously influence choice of venue, so get this clear early on. For more on guest lists, *see* Chapter Four.

- **Ceremony:** Religious, civil or both, *see* Chapter Eight.

INSPIRATION

- What's your style? Low-key or flash? Trendy or classic? Conformist or irreverent?
- How would you get married if you had absolutely no limitations: financial, practical or otherwise? A chateau in France, a snowy New England chapel, an achingly trendy restaurant – these could all be more realistic than you allow yourself to think.
- What are your talents and pleasures? Throwing a party? A way with words? Creating, making, sewing? Relaxing and enjoying yourself while everyone else does all the hard work? Build them into your vision.
- Seek inspiration from all around you: holidays, experiences, homes, books and parties.
- What's your heritage? Bring in family or national traditions.
- The following are just a taste of what you might do, here or abroad; there are more ideas for themes, looks and styles on page 131.

UK wedding ideas
Rich in culture and style, you couldn't find a better backdrop – just make your peace with the weather! How about:

- **The best of summer:** Garden ceremony, picnic lunch or afternoon tea, fruit punch, croquet, puppet show for the children, and a jazz band. Eastwell Manor in Kent has a gazebo in its walled garden that's licensed for marriages: as close as you'll currently get to a legal outdoor ceremony.
- **A castle:** Hot for celebrities lately, a castle ceremony and banquet will

give you every excuse to live a day-long fairy tale. The most beautiful include Highcliffe Castle in Dorset and Highclere Castle in Berkshire.

- **Low-key and last-minute:** An off-season booking (or short-notice cancellation) for your ceremony, a ready-to-wear white trouser suit, a table for you and your closest friends in a fave restaurant, a hastily made bouquet from the florist on the way to register office and a riotous chocolate cake ordered from a patisserie the day before.
- **An elegant evening:** Five o'clock ceremony, evening dress, a formal dinner in a magnificent hall followed by witty speeches and toasts.
- **Surprise:** Invite close friends to a special party, but hand them a wedding invitation only as they arrive.
- **Urban:** Marry at London media hotspot Soho House, follow with drinks and canapés on their roof-deck bar, book a fleet of black cabs, and blag your way on to the guest list of the club of the moment.
- **Cheap and chic:** A register office in a big metropolis like Manchester or Glasgow, a little white dress and kitten heels from that boutique to the stars, Topshop, and a cluster of flowers straight from the garden. Followed by cocktails in one of the grand hotel bars. The drinks aren't cheap, but the trimmings are worth it: choose killer cocktails which will take all night to drink, and enjoy the poshest of bar snacks thrown in, too.
- **Vanilla classic:** Village church, white tulle, and a close family reception at your parents' home with lots of romantic touches.
- **Small-scale country weekend:** Take your friends to a cosy, country hotel with just a handful of rooms and a licence for weddings.

Doing what matters

'Only two things mattered at our wedding: that it was an incredibly special, meaningful, emotional day; and that it was the most brilliant social gathering – all the people we love best, coming to one place to celebrate a big part of our life. A real show-off! In fact, we got married in two places last year: once on the beach in my native New Zealand, and then a few weeks later (wearing deepest red) at Chelsea Register Office. Both followed, of course, by big, funky parties! It was twice the stress, and twice the fun.' Bride, 29.

Keeping it neat

'We wanted to be married, but we didn't really want a "wedding". We booked into the Malmaison Hotel in Edinburgh, and into the register office, too, and I nipped down to Calvin Klein one lunchtime to buy a little white summer dress, before we sneaked up to Scotland for the weekend without telling a soul. The hotel was fantastic, really helpful and excited for us, and the receptionist and her sister came along to be witnesses. Neither set of parents was very happy about it, but we knew our wedding was going to be stressful, whatever we did – and they got over it, eventually! I do love weddings, but as a guest, and since I have a tendency to get depressed, I wasn't sure I could deal with the come-down once a big wedding was over. As it was, we just went back to work on the Monday and told everyone. It was fun, and special, but comfortingly normal. We went on a fantastic holiday six months later, and even then, I really enjoyed the fact that we were a married couple, without the cliché of being labelled "honeymooners".' Bride, 27.

- **London parks:** Pump House Gallery in Battersea Park and The Orangery in Holland Park make stylish city weddings. Add a funky floral dress code.
- **Underwater:** Literally, with sharks swimming overhead, at Deep Sea World in Fife.
- **House party:** Chances are that your favourite country house hotel has a licence for weddings: fill it with your friends for 24 hours, or take over an entire private country seat, like Silchester House in Berkshire.
- **A day at the races:** Newmarket Racecourse is licensed for ceremonies; schedule it for a race day and you've got instant atmosphere.
- **A Midsummer Night's Dream:** Turn your garden into a dreamy stage-set and exchange moonlit vows there. Decorate awnings and scatter simple flowers everywhere. Hire musicians and costumes, too.
- **A three-day event:** Make the most of it, by adding the American tradition for a wedding-eve meal, and the European one for a brunch or gathering the day after.

☺☹ *'Write down your most instinctive wedding wishes before you read or hear too much wedding "advice". We ended up having lots of things we'd originally said we didn't want – from buttonholes to a "first dance" – simply because we forgot!'*

Worldwide wedding ideas

One of history's most romantic couples, Elizabeth Barrett and Robert Browning eloped to Italy in 1846. The paperwork might be more complex now, but the miles are much easier to negotiate.

- **Zambia safari:** Ceremony and celebrations under the mahogany trees overlooking the Zambezi river.
- **Rustic Provençal:** A blessing in a French country chapel, followed by sunlit drinks in the courtyard and dinner at the long banquet tables of a chateau.
- **Uluru/Ayers Rock:** Make your vows as the sun sets over Australia's spiritual monument.
- **Disneyland, California:** Kitsch is cool, after all.
- **The beach:** From Bali to Bermuda, Mexico to Mauritius, Turkey to Thailand, Seychelles to Sri Lanka, you can walk a sandy aisle just about anywhere.
- **Venice:** After a romantic wedding, take gondolas on the canals to drink Bellinis at the celebrated Hotel Gritti Palace.
- **Winter white:** From the turreted castles of Germany's Black Forest to Sweden's Ice Chapel, there are some magical backdrops for a fur-trimmed white cape and horse-drawn sleigh.
- **Greece's idyllic fishing villages:** Arrive by speedboat for a church ceremony at the tiny islet of St Nicholas at Kefalos; celebrate later in traditional plate-smashing style.
- **City style:** New York, Rome, Sydney ... Be prepared to compromise if your hearts are set on Paris, though – they don't make it easy!
- **Elope ... to Vegas of course:** The instant wedding venue. Just show up (or drive thru), choose your Elvis (or don't), and be married. Follow with a night at the casinos.
- **Glitterati:** Book a fully staffed Bajan mansion and host a wedding house

party with more than a hint of glamour. Swim with turtles in the afternoon and celebrate at the fashionable Lone Star Restaurant.

● **Tuscany:** A town-hall wedding amid the towers of the walled town of San Gimignano, then a classic Italian feast, served at long trestle tables shaded from the sun by gauzy white canopies.

Money-wise: What to expect

UK wedding, total average spend: about £14,500
Overseas wedding, total average spend: about £4,500
Basic register office ceremony: about £100+
Basic church ceremony: about £200+

Contacts

Venue details for UK weddings can be found in Chapter Five.
Travel agents for weddings abroad can be found in Chapters Six.
Ceremonial contacts are on page 111.

chapter four

dilemmas, dilemmas: dates and numbers

DECIDING ON A DATE

Just when you thought (probably with a degree of relief) that dates were a thing of the past, you become utterly preoccupied with them – in another form. All things considered, Naming The Day will probably call for compromise in one way or another … but you're getting the message on that one. It goes without saying that if you'd like a Saturday in June, you've serious competition on all fronts. The factors affecting date-setting include:

- **How much time you want to spend planning and prepping:** A year – or more – is not too long for an elaborate wedding; three months is a minimum for something formal; three weeks the least you'll need for basic legalities, unless you're off to Vegas. There's a case for keeping the planning stage short: things may be manic, but the wedding won't have the same chance to take over your life/get you sacked/lose all your friends because, frankly, they couldn't care less about the organza versus tulle debate … As wedding planner Sophie Lillingston puts it, 'All brides obsess about something, and the longer they have, the more obsessive they get.'

- **The religious calendar:** Sundays are very rare for a Christian ceremony, but only because they are busy days for a church; Lent may prohibit a Christian ceremony; weekdays are less common but usually possible. Jewish weddings may not take place on Fridays and Saturdays.

- **The sporting calendar:** Even if you don't care about the FA Cup Final, or the Rugby World Cup, lots of people will – and the division of loyalties could dampen some spirits. Avoid key sporting fixtures if you can. Most are at weekends in the months/years shown below:

Six Nations Rugby	January to April (fortnightly)
Oxford v Cambridge Boat Race	March/April
Grand National	April
FA Cup Final	May
Test Cricket	May, June, July and August
The Derby	June
Royal Ascot	June
Wimbledon final	early July
Start of football season	August
British Grand Prix	July
The Open (golf)	July
Lions Tours (rugby)	summer four-yearly; next 2005
Rugby World Cup	summer four-yearly; next 2003
Cricket World Cup	summer four-yearly; next 2003
Football World Cup	summer four-yearly; next 2006
European Football Championships	summer four-yearly; next 2004
The Olympics	summer four-yearly; next 2004
Winter Olympics	February four-yearly; next 2006

- **The seasons and the weather:** A sunny wedding is most people's ideal. If you're mathematical, or optimistic, you may want to take account of the following: the highest-ever recorded temperature here was in August, (the lowest was in January); May, June and July have the highest average sunshine hours in the UK; but rain comes fairly steadily all year round – every third day, on average – with a far from guaranteed decrease in the summer months.

Winter weddings are a lovely idea, but the only weather that's less predictable than sunshine is snow. There are hazards associated with a snowy wedding, blocked roads being just one of them. Short daylight hours will restrict outdoor photography.

Marry abroad and you'll have the luxury of choosing your location according to the season – but rain may still come wherever you are. If you're prepared to go slightly off season, you could bag a bargain. Best for weather:

Antarctica:	November to March
Australia/NZ:	October to February
Bahamas:	December to June
Bali:	April to October
Barbados:	December to May
California:	spring and autumn
Canada:	June to August
Canary Islands:	February
Caribbean:	December to February
Cuba:	December to April
Cyprus:	June to September
Far East:	December to March
Florida:	November to March
France:	May to July, September
Greece:	April to June, September, October
Hawaii:	December to April
India:	October to June
Italy:	April to October
Jamaica:	November to April, July to August
Kenya:	July to March
Las Vegas:	September to June
Mauritius:	April to June, September, October
Mexico:	December to March

New England:	spring and autumn
Seychelles:	May to September
St Lucia:	December to May
South Africa:	October to May
South America:	January, March, April, November
Spain:	March to June, September and October
Turkey:	July, September
Virgin Islands:	December to June

- **Your chief helpers:** As well as being free on the day itself, you may need close family and friends to be around to help you a *lot* in the weeks before, so it's in your interests to choose a date which suits them.
- **High days, holidays and Saturdays:** Christmas, New Year and bank holiday weddings can be fantastic, but plan carefully around the fact that suppliers, accommodation and the roads will all be very busy. Even Saturdays – the classic wedding choice – are becoming a little competitive.
- **Availability of venues and suppliers:** The perfect venue can be hard to find – and may offer you the seventh Wednesday in November as the only available date. If someone or somewhere is absolutely crucial to your peace of mind, check out their availability right from the start.
- **Costs:** Venues and suppliers may offer reduced rates at the following times:
  - Off season – usually between late October and 1 March, with the exception of Christmas and New Year.
  - On less popular days; Monday to Thursday should always be a bargain; Friday and Sunday weddings cheaper than Saturdays.
  - In early spring, your florist's bill may be a fraction of its winter equivalent.

SETTING A TIME

Currently, the limitations are:
- A legal ceremony in England and Wales must normally take place between 8am and 6pm, be it civil or religious. A wedding in Scotland can take place at any time as long as the registrar or minister agrees.

- Register office weddings must take place during office hours: usually 9am to 4pm Monday to Friday; 9am to 1pm on Saturday.

Bear in mind:
- The earlier the wedding ceremony, the more time left for eating, drinking and partying.
- Guests who are travelling to your wedding – or just getting dressed up for it, taking the children to grandparents and ordering a cab – may struggle with too early a ceremony.
- If children play a big part, a late ceremony may be hard on them and cut short their parents' stay at the reception.
- Once the clocks go back, at the end of October, and it's dark soon after 4.30pm, a candlelit, legal ceremony is possible in England and Wales.

THE NUMBERS GAME

Numbers – and the need to keep them down – are the cause of many a woe. You may want just 50 people, but if your parents plan on inviting 35, you've either got some heavy-duty diplomacy on your hands, or a different kind of wedding to the one you originally envisaged. Whatever the outcome, the clichés are true: it's your wedding and you mustn't feel bad about who you choose to share it with – unless you're being plain old spiteful! (*See* Chapter Sixteen for ways to handle conflict.) Marrying overseas, or in a far corner of the UK, hits most numbers' problems on the head. At the other extreme, a big party can make for a wonderful wedding. If you're undecided about scale, it's worth considering the implications of two crucial wedding calculations:

- **The spend-per-guest formula:** This isn't about being mean, or cutting costs – it's about the opposite. If you have a fixed wedding budget, and a big guest list, you could be about to embark on a long and stressful period of trying to make those funds go way beyond what's good for them. Think what you could do if you spent all that money on just, say, 35 people. You could really go to town! Or have just 16 to the house party of a lifetime. Contrast that with a wedding where the same budget has to stretch to 150 people: if you're happy with a basic buffet, a pay bar, a home-recorded music selection – because having the whole crowd is what matters – that's great. Just think about that choice before you make it. For more on money, *see* Chapter Seven.

- **The minutes-per-guest formula:** If your wedding reception lasts eight hours from start to finish, and you have 150 guests, you'll have about 3.2 minutes to speak to each of them. And that's optimistic. In fact, at least an hour of your day will be given over to speeches and cake-cutting, another hour to dancing or other entertainment, and an hour to photographs (you see how fast it goes). Then you're down to two minutes per guest. Many will have travelled hundreds of miles to come to your wedding, and while they're likely to enjoy the wedding as part of the crowd, *you* may feel cheated.

BEING YOUR GUEST

Your wedding wouldn't be anything without guests, and an invitation is asking a lot of anyone: to give time, effort and money, in the form of gifts, outfits, accommodation, travel and childcare arrangements. The average guest in the UK spends over £400, according to a survey carried out by the Goldfish credit card company: £67 on a present, £72 on accommodation, £42 on travel, £120 on a new outfit, £30 on a hat, plus an extra £87 on stag/hen parties. The obligation is one that people accept happily, but don't think you're doing them a favour ...

Set an ideal number based on your wedding style, budget and location options. Add 10% to allow for people who are unable to come.

Make a series of lists: Call them 'definitely', 'should invite', 'want to invite', 'only if there's room' and 'no chance' and put everyone in one of these lists. Consider every name in your address book, to avoid embarrassing realisations later. If you're having a second batch of arrivals in the evening, dealing with lower priority guests is much easier. Put 'gangs' of friends or relatives together in one category.

When there are other hosts to the wedding (normally parents), the modern approaches are:

- Split the invites three ways: 50% to the couple, 25% to each set of parents. Parents should be responsible for keeping their peers/generation within their quota. Or
- Allocate a batch of invites to each set of parents, dependent on contribution and involvement, financial or otherwise. Or
- Explain to parents that a mixed-generation wedding was not what you'd imagined – and be prepared to surrender any cash. Or
- Work together on choosing guests you'd all like to be there.

When you have distant relatives or old family friends that you'd rather not invite: If there are only one or two, consider giving in. If there are a lot, and you're under pressure, stand your ground. Argue that if they never make contact and didn't even know you had a boyfriend/girlfriend, you can be forgiven for not considering them a part of your life. If they're keen on a family reunion, they can host one, can't they?

When ex-partners are still on the scene: However relaxed *you* may be, ex-partners only have a place at a wedding when *both* parties are keen. If you have children with your ex-partner, and relationships are good (it does happen!), the other parent's presence at the wedding can help the child.

When someone's likely to be loud, drunk or embarrassing: If nothing will make them behave, then leave them off the guest list. A well-meaning chum – or relative – with a tendency to social *faux pas* is a different matter. They'll be on their best behaviour, because they'll know how important it is, and a subtly appointed 'guardian' should be able to keep them in check. In any case, you'll be much too busy to notice exactly who's doing what.

When you have to get numbers down: Bear in mind –

- You don't have to invite a companion for every guest, although it's courteous for people who would otherwise be travelling alone and don't know the rest of the guests.
- It's often easier to cut out whole groups (say, everyone from work), than shave off one or two here or there: heavy politics and hurt feelings are minimised.

Etiquette issue: Inviting the vicar, registrar or celebrant

Two people you should invite to the reception, if yours is a religious wedding, are the minister and his wife. If you know them, and your parents are hosting, this'll be relatively easy. Even if everyone's young (and the vicar's not), you'll be so high you probably won't worry about them anyway. If the occasion isn't very appropriate for them, tactfully let them know the form: they probably won't want to stay long! The modern question is whether this politeness should also extend to inviting a registrar or other celebrant: if they've become quite involved in your plans for your ceremony, it's usually the natural, appreciative and courteous thing to do.

- Are old friends also current friends? A great work mate who's helped mop up your tears and had you breathless with laughter, versus your best friend from school who you see every five years and find even that a bit of an effort? Apply the '12-month' question: Have you been in contact in the last year? If not, don't feel too bad about leaving them out. If you're afraid of tears and tantrums at your decision, ask yourself if that's the kind of friend you want.
- Shift more guests to the 'evening only' list.

When you don't want hundreds of children: You don't have to invite people's children to your wedding, any more than you have to invite them to a dinner party. If the wedding's nearby, later in the day, and relatively short and sweet, it's fine to make it a grown-up affair. Just leave children's names off the invitation. That said, parents attending a wedding without their children have some logistical problems, so be sensitive about what you're asking of people and prepared to be accommodating – or to have some refusals. For more on these politics and childcare, *see* Chapter Sixteen; for entertaining children, *see* pages 165 and 262.

When someone can't make it: It's nice to send an invitation to close friends and family, even if you know they can't come.

Be our guest

'We had seven weddings to attend last summer, which cost us a fortune. We went to most minus our daughter out of choice, felt honoured to be invited, and had a fabulous time. But to the invitation which fell out of the envelope with a John Lewis gift list pamphlet, a map of some remote part of the country, and the sole words "No Children", we could barely be bothered even to let them know we weren't coming.' Guests, 29 and 24.

'Even if I feel hurt at not being invited to a wedding, I wouldn't dream of making a fuss about it. How humiliating would that be? And anyway, I respect their decision.' Guest, 28.

ELOPING, TINY WEDDINGS AND KEEPING IT PRIVATE

If you want to be alone (but for the witnesses), or far from home, that's your call. If you sympathise with parents who want to join you, be ready with alternative hotels so that they don't need to stay in the same one as you. And if you take friends or family to an overseas wedding, but want to be alone for the honeymoon, book a separate resort, or even country, for phase two of the trip.

Money-wise: What to expect

*Spend on each guest (average including venues, food, drink, entertainment):
    about £60*
Being a wedding guest, average spend: £422

Contacts

Weathercall Customer Service: 0870 600 4242
AA traffic and three-hourly weather updates: 09003 444 900
Online Weather: www.onlineweather.com
Goldfish: 08457 609060; www.goldfish.com

chapter
five

the perfect place:
finding and assessing venues

If you've got just the place in mind, count yourself lucky. There are almost 4000 approved premises for civil marriage in this country, churches in every parish, plus other approved religious buildings and register offices in practically every town. For the celebrations afterwards, there are thousands of hotels, restaurants and other locations, together, of course, with our own back gardens, parks and riverbanks. What's more, the options abroad can make ours seem quite paltry (*see* Chapter Six), but *still* many of us struggle to find the perfect place to marry.

Comfort yourself with the knowledge that not even the professionals find it easy. 'It's one of the most frustrating aspects of what we do,' says venue expert Doug Showell of wedding consultancy, Alternative Occasions. 'There are simply so many venues out there, with very little consistency in the way the information is presented, making comparisons of facilities, services and prices very difficult.'

The other problem (logistics, numbers and geography aside) is the fact that wedding venues so often *feel* and *look* like wedding venues. When The

Wedding Industry steps in, beautiful places can be reduced to conveyor belts of romance by decor and marketing. As you trawl from one venue (or brochure) to another, you begin to ask yourself why so many reception venues have hideous and wildly patterned carpets (they don't show the dirt, they're cheap to manufacture and they're quick to replace, in fact), or to wonder if you could ever reduce this most important of days to a choice between the gold, silver or bronze package.

The good news is that there *are* plenty of stylish, beautiful, romantic, fun and exciting places where you can stage a wedding ceremony or reception: you just need to know where to look.

WHAT DO YOU NEED?

You may need two venues: one for the ceremony and one for the celebrations, or you may combine everything into one place. Even if you don't need an approved civil wedding location, it helps to know that a venue which holds a licence is usually geared up to weddings in general.

- **A religious venue?** Church of England, Catholic and Nonconformist churches, synagogues and some other religious buildings are authorised for legal marriage ceremonies. Quaker and Jewish ceremonies can also sometimes take place in a non-approved building, such as your home. You must normally be resident in the parish where you plan to marry, but this may change soon. It may not always be obvious which is your parish church, since there is no systematic listing: the best lines of information are still *Yellow Pages* and personal enquiry.

- **A premises approved for a legal, civil ceremony?** You can either go to the registrar – at any register office in the country – or ask him/her to come to you at an 'approved premises': certain rooms in certain buildings have been given special status as the location for a legal marriage ceremony. Such a place must be a permanent structure, open to the public and appropriate to the solemnity of the occasion. It is not currently possible to apply for approval of a location for your wedding alone, but the law is under review and soon civil ceremonies may be able to

Where they wed

'By the time we found our venue, I'd all but given up hope. And we thought that was going to be the easy bit! Most of these places look nothing like the pictures in the brochures.' Bride, 36.

'It was going to be in a marquee in a field, but then there was the foot and mouth crisis. We had a few panics, and we ended up in a barn. Although it wasn't what we'd planned, we were relieved just to have somewhere by that point - and I don't think it could have been any better.' Bride, 31.

'We surf a lot. Some friends of ours found a little church on an otherwise fairly deserted island off Penzance, and the vicar agreed to let them marry there. They're staying out on the island the night before, but about sixty friends are camping overnight on the Cornish coast, then we're all going out on a boat the morning of the wedding. It might be a bit chaotic!' Guests, 27 and 25.

take place at *any* 'suitable' location, indoor or out, that the registrar agrees.

- **A location suitable for a vow-exchange ceremony or religious blessing?** Because there are no legalities involved, the scope is theoretically unlimited – hotels, gardens, galleries, hillsides, ancient ruins ...
- **A reception or party venue?** Which may be at the same place as a legal or vow-exchange ceremony or religious blessing, or not.

WHERE TO LOOK

The perfect venue obviously won't bear a neon sign proclaiming its whereabouts or virtues, so a little detective work is usually called for. To save yourself wasted trips, first call in brochures or make telephone enquiries for anywhere promising. Staff should be willing to spend a little time answering your questions on the phone, especially if they don't have printed literature.

Home and garden

Start at home. You might be lucky, with acres of space and lush green lawns, but even if it doesn't seem practical at first, lateral thinking might turn your home into the ideal wedding venue. Take a slow walk round your house and garden, with an open mind and the knowledge that marquees and canopies come in just about any shape or size. Hills, trees and corners can all be negotiated, French windows opened out onto a canopied dance floor, speeches made from a balcony or staircase.

The joy of being at home is that you can make it whatever you want. It's the obvious starting point for a low-key, no-fuss wedding reception or private vow-exchange ceremony. If you like to cook and create, you'd be in the perfect position. If you want to relax, you can add caterers, staff and cleaners. An at-home wedding can also be very grand, although a larger space helps, of course. The money you save on a venue will be ample to dress up your house or garden.

The downside to having your wedding at home is that you'll work much harder. Consider the issues outlined below regarding practicalities such as equipment, furniture, heating, space, loos and parking. Have no doubt, too, that lawns will go brown, plants may get trashed, and prize ornaments could be broken. Tell your insurers beforehand to check that you're covered for such an event, and employ a security guard if your house will remain open.

Other practicalities, on the other hand, could work out far simpler: you'll have far fewer packing or transport issues, and any of the personal possessions you might need will be close by. And importantly for parents, your children will probably find it less stressful.

Everyday (or unusual) places you might not have thought of

The answer could be a place you see every day of your life. Is the local school pretty? Does your park have a bandstand? Could you put up a riverside canopy? What about less-than-flash boat or cricket clubs? They often have the space, facilities and potential good looks, but aren't plush enough to target the usual wedding market. The beauty is that they may let you dress them up however you like, and a hundred metres of white muslin and organza ribbon still won't cost half as much as a commercialised wedding venue. If you live in a city, what about photographic studios, warehouses or private art galleries in your area? And if you live in the countryside, could a farmer lend you a field? Or is your village hall in a pretty setting and ripe for a lush, autumnal transformation? An open and creative mind – plus some willing helpers – could be all you need. As with a wedding at home, do consider all the practical implications and hidden costs of this route.

Searching with books, websites and guides

If the perfect venue guidebook existed, it would be a glorious, full-colour volume with plenty of photographs of every approved civil marriage venue, every hotel, stately home, country house, garden, restaurant, gallery, and lots of crazy and imaginative locations, too. It would give prices and capacity, catering details, and feature nearby accommodation, maps and more. It would cost a fortune, however, and be out of date within weeks.

It's possible, though, to find most of that information just by knowing where to look. Some of the references listed below are large, dedicated guides carefully designed to aid your search; others need to be approached in a spirit of detection. The reward for trawling the less obvious resources is discovering an unusual or little-used location – after making a lot of phone calls and reading a lot of bumf. Fortunately, you'll quickly get a feel for what's a waste of time and what's promising. Some organisations such as the National Trust or Country House Wedding Venues will also offer further information over the phone, so it's worth asking.

Wedding-specific venue guides

- **Noble's Wedding Venues Guide** is a book that lists most of the civil wedding venues in the UK. It's revised regularly, contains much of the information you need, but only a few photographs. Available in bookshops; an online version is at www.confetti.co.uk
- **General Register Office List of Approved Premises** is complete with every single licensed venue. It's available from the Office of National Statistics; call 0151 471 4817 for ordering details. It's now online, too, at www.statistics.gov.uk, and updated monthly. Although it lists only the address and contact details, it combines perfectly with other guides

because you can look up any venue you come across to see if it is approved for civil marriages.

- **Wedding Venues and Services:** Quarterly magazine, with thousands of civil ceremony and reception venues. For many, there is plenty of detail, including several pictures, menus, price ranges and accommodation facilities. Available at newsagents, or see venues at their website at www.weddingvenues.co.uk
- **Wedding Directory UK:** A twice-yearly magazine which lists almost all the civil venues, with colour pictures and details about many of these, and reception-only venues too. Out April and October, from W.H. Smith, or call 01296 658652 to order direct or go to www.the weddingdirectory.co.uk
- **London Wedding:** A magazine-format directory of venues and services in London and the South-East. From newsagents.
- **Country House Wedding Venues** runs a database of around 400 private houses, public schools and other locations available for receptions. Many are approved for a civil ceremony or would be suitable for a non-legal vow-exchange ceremony. You don't pay an agent's fee directly, but both the venue and any associated suppliers that you book will then pay a commission which they may pass on to you, so get this clear before you sign. Call 01244 571208 or go to www.wedding-venues.co.uk
- **Alternative Weddings** is a paid-for database of around 450 venues. Either select and pay for details one venue at a time, order a specially compiled book, or a CD ROM complete with all their venue information. Call 00353 91638 085, or go online at www.alternative-weddings.com
- **More venues on the web:** The best is **www.perfectvenue.com**, an excellent free site with a comprehensive interactive venue search facility and thorough rundown of essential details (including any downsides). Other websites with venues' sections worth checking out include:
  - **www.confetti.co.uk:** Venues are sorted simply by region but links to the venues' own sites are useful.
  - **www.getspliced.com:** Sorts a large number of venues by themed categories such as Rock & Roll, Boats & Beaches, Theatre & Literature.

- **www.hitched.co.uk:** Thousands of venues, with basic details and reviews from former customers, and the opportunity to post your own comments.
- **www.placestomarry.com:** Listing similar to that of the General Register Office.

Guides to country houses, hotels and party venues

As well as possibly leading to a gem of a wedding venue (some licensed, some not), these guides may also be useful for checking out guest accommodation.

- **Hudson's Historic Houses & Gardens:** Symbols indicate approval for civil marriages and any accommodation or hospitality available. From bookshops, or via their website, www.hudsons.co.uk, which includes some venue information, too.
- **National Trust** properties often have an approved civil marriage room or wedding party facilities. Call 020 7222 9251 for a free list, or look at the website at www.nationaltrust.org.uk. Some bigger estates have cottages where family and friends can stay, too.
- **Where to Stay in Britain and Ireland** is a CD ROM from the AA. A database of 7000 of their hotels and B&Bs is searchable by civil marriage facility and function room size, and includes pictures of most hotels. Call 0800 389 2795 to order a copy.
- **Noble's Party Venues Guide:** Compiled as a partner to their guide to civil marriage premises, this edition includes restaurants, galleries and private houses with overnight guest accommodation. From bookshops.
- **Noble's Big Holiday Houses:** Guidebook to just that – and a teepee or two – in the UK and Europe. For Noble's contacts *see* above.
- **Johansens** guides, from bookshops, feature hotels, stately homes, historical buildings, museums, galleries, hotels, gardens, inns and castles, all marked with appropriate symbols. Some of the content is published online at www.johansens.co.uk
- Certain **hotel groups** are worth contacting: *see* the list of corporations and guidebooks on page 65.

- **Sawday's** guides include some of the smaller, most charming, country hotels which you could book out in their entirety. Some have a licence for weddings or can accommodate an alternative ceremony – but these aren't specified so you'll need to ring and ask, or check against the General Register Office List of Approved Premises. From bookshops, or via their website at www.sawdays.co.uk
- **Agents for grand, large or unusual holiday properties** are well worth trying for their mansions, castles and historic buildings – which could be just the thing for a private vow-exchange and a week/end with your closest friends. They include Rural Retreats, 01386 701177, www.ruralretreats.co.uk; Vivat Trust, 0845 090 0194, www.vivat.org.uk; Blandings, 01223 293 444, www.blandings.co.uk; and The Landmark Trust, 020 7947 3290, www.landmarktrust.co.uk. Look too at classified ads in publications like *Country Living* magazine and the *Sunday Times*.

Consultants

For a few hundred pounds, a venue consultant could save your sanity. Good ones will know the venues well, drawing up a shortlist of half a dozen or more that will fit your needs. They'll know upfront if you're looking for the impossible (saving you much time and angst) and be able to present an alternative approach you may not have thought of. If they really can't help, they should tell you so before you part with any money. Many will also guide you in the best choice of the venues' affiliated suppliers, too – which in itself could be worth the fee. Wedding consultants – and how to find them – are on pages 239–40.

Celebrity venues

Madonna & Guy Ritchie: Skibo Castle, Scotland

Pierce Brosnan & Keely Shaye Smith: Balintubber Abbey, then Ashford Castle, Ireland

Joan Collins & Percy Gibson: Claridges Hotel, London

Victoria Adams & David Beckham: Luttrellstown Castle, Ireland

Jamie Oliver & Juliet Norton: All Saints Church, Rickling, Essex, then Jamie's parents' house nearby

WHAT TO CONSIDER

The points below relate to all but religious venues. Which ceremony you can have where is covered in Chapter Eight, and answers to some of the reception planning, marquee, catering, costing and logistics' questions are in Chapters Ten, Eleven and Twelve.

Style: Where you marry or celebrate should obviously fit your vision: a cool urban gallery for a hip wedding; a castle for something lavish or historical; a barn to jig and reel. Look at every room you'll use: no amount of Regency façade or Capability Brown landscaping will compensate for a marriage room with wallpaper that hurts your eyes.

Location: Because weddings traditionally mean travelling to the bride's home, an hour or two's journey is usually accepted. The location ideally should be easily accessible by road and public transport, with affordable, good quality accommodation nearby. Finding a venue and organising a wedding a long way from home can be time-consuming and costly, although many people do it successfully.

The ceremony factor: When both ceremony and celebrations are to happen in one place, ensure that the arrangements work. Do your guests have to be shunted outside, whatever the weather, while the marriage room is transformed into a party room? Is there a PA system so you can play music? Can you make an aisle, if you want to? If it's in a garden, is there an awning available to protect from high sun or wet weather? When the ceremony and reception are in different locations, they obviously need to be within easy reach of each other – an hour's journey is generally considered the maximum.

Numbers: Check capacity specifically for the event(s) you require: ceremony and/or reception. Everything can be perfect until you discover that although a brochure claims capacity for 150, they're only talking about the reception. Don't be tempted to squeeze in too many people. If you need to calculate capacity yourself, for a ceremony, simply calculate how many chair-widths will fit, allowing for an aisle and plenty of knee-space between rows; standing only allows higher numbers, but insurance considerations will still limit them. For a reception, allow about $2.5m^2$ per person for standing guests, a little more for a sit-down meal, and if you want both, you'll need about 5m² per person overall. This allows for a buffet table and serving area, but not a stage or dance floor; a stand-up reception area may double as a dance area later. Avoid rooms that are too big (over-large space can drown out atmosphere) and check the venue won't insist on a minimum number you'll struggle to meet.

Cost: Venue prices can range from free (just the promise of a substantial bar spend) to several thousand pounds. One thing's certain: it's wedding boom-time and costs are spiralling. One famous and beautiful venue raised its fee from £850 to £3600 in less than eighteen months. That's a huge hike in profit for the venue, with precious little extra for the consumer. All we can do is shop around, make sure we get our money's worth, and comfort ourselves with the thought that new legislation could mean the bubble bursts soon!

It's vital to establish the real cost when you ask for a quote. Does it include chairs, tables, crockery and linen hire? Is there an additional fee if the ceremony takes place there? Corkage, cover charge, service charge and VAT should be clearly specified. Keep in mind that it could work out cheaper to pay considerably more for the venue if you have freedom to use your own suppliers and bring in your own drink without penalty or corkage charge.

Be cautious, though: freedom and uniqueness can add costs, too. An empty shell may offer a fabulous blank canvas to work with, but if there's no furniture, no PA system, no loos, no heating and crude lighting, you may have an expensive transformation on your hands. You could even need to organise an alcohol and entertainment licence. A marquee, whether at home or a hired venue, can add thousands: *see* page 160 to ensure any quote is comprehensive. For more on money, *see* Chapter Seven.

Freedom and control: A unique and personal wedding calls for lots of both. So if you're told that 'the bride and groom stand here', 'choose from these two pieces of music', then 'have photos here' – at least check that you won't have to. Check too, that yours would be the only wedding there on that day, at least, or better still, that week/end. Freedom comes at a price, though, so weigh it up: whatever-you-want venues tend to offer little in the way of help or guidance.

Catering and suppliers: In an ideal world, the venue should allow you to make your own choices; in fact, many venues allow only their own services and contractors. If this is the case, establish upfront that they are flexible, very good and reasonably priced. If any detail is of particular importance (like the colour of the table linen) check it out from the start. If you plan to cater yourselves, what are the facilities for preparing, cooking and storing food?

Final and important points, when you have a shortlist of venues: Be prepared to visit several places, and try not to set your heart on one before you've seen it and ironed out all the little details (tough as that can be!). Confirm the main points, even if they're in the brochure. Then consider: Do you like the staff, owner or co-ordinator? Do the logistics and settings of the place work? Walk it through, if possible, from guests' arrival, ceremony, drinks, food, speeches, dancing. Is it photogenic? Is there somewhere for guests to put their coats? What are the loos like, and how many? What happens if it rains? There's a 33% chance of rain on your wedding day here in the UK – so take a realistic approach. If relevant, is it child-friendly, and safe? Are there one or two quiet rooms for breastfeeding mothers and sleepy children? Is there somewhere children could watch videos and play? Is it easy for older and less able people to get around, and can they sit down? Is the venue warm/cold, and what are the heating arrangements? Is there somewhere for you both to change or freshen up? Somewhere secure for presents? What time will you have to end the party? What about parking? Confetti? How much scope is there to decorate, and are candles permitted? When can you have access to make such preparations?

From the expert: Keep costs down

Doug Showell at Alternative Occasions:

'Some venues charge a premium rate for wedding receptions, simply because they can get away with it. Try not to tell them you're enquiring about a wedding: ask for a quote for a dinner-dance instead.'

CHECK THE CONTRACT

You should be given time to check over the contract, and ensure that you understand and are happy with *every* detail. Don't be afraid to ask for additional points to be added into the contract. Not only does it protect your interests if things aren't right later on, it also focuses everyone's minds on what was said.

VENUES IN BRIEF

This is by no means an exhaustive list, but may give you some ideas. An asterisk indicates an approved civil marriage premises. (In Scotland, a religious marriage can take place at any suitable venue.)

Weekend house party
Cromlix House Hotel, Scotland: 01786 822125; www.cromlixhouse.com
Lucknam Park Hotel*, Wiltshire: 01225 742777; www.lucknampark.co.uk
Silchester House*, Berkshire: 0118 970 1901; www.yoursexclusively.co.uk

London parks
Pump House Gallery*, Battersea Park: 020 8871 7572;
    www.wandsworth.gov.uk/batterseapark
The Orangery*, Holland Park: 020 7603 1123;
    www.rbkc.gov.uk/Venuesforhire/orangeryhire
Pembroke Lodge*, Richmond Park: 020 8940 8207;
    www.pembrokelodge.co.uk

Castles
Highclere Castle*, Berkshire: 01635 253210; www.highclerecastle.co.uk
Herstmonceux Castle*, East Sussex: 01323 834479;
    www.herstmonceux-castle.com
Bodelwyddan Castle*, Denbighshire: 01745 584060;
    www.bodelwyddan-castle.co.uk

Theatres and galleries

Theatre Royal*, Bath: 01225 448815; www.theatreroyal.org.uk
The Georgian Theatre Royal*, North Yorkshire: 01748 823710;
    www.georgiantheatre.com
Dulwich Picture Gallery, London: 020 8299 8709;
    www.dulwichpicturegallery.org.uk

Contemporary London

Soho House*: 020 7734 5188
20th Century Theatre, Notting Hill: 020 7229 4179

Something different

British Airways London Eye*: 0870 220 2223; www.londoneye.com
Bluebell Railway*, Sussex: 01825 722370; www.bluebell-railway.co.uk
Deep Sea World*, Fife: 01383 411880; www.deepseaworld.co.uk

Ships, boats and islands

HMS *Warrior**, Portsmouth: 023 9277 8604; www.hmswarrior.org
Mersey Ferry, Liverpool: 0151 330 1458; www.merseyferries.co.uk
Temple Island, Henley Royal Regatta*, Oxfordshire: 01491 572153;
    www.hrr.co.uk

Gardens and zoos

The Gazebo at Eastwell Manor*, Kent: 01233 213000;
    www.eastwellmanor.co.uk
London Zoo*: 020 7449 6374; www.londonzoo.com
Birmingham Botanical Gardens*: 0121 456 2244;
    www.bham-bot-gdns.demon.co.uk
Cambridge Cottage, Kew Gardens*, Surrey: 020 8332 5641;
    www.rbgkew.org.uk

Sport and society

Newmarket Racecourse*, Suffolk: 01638 663482;
    www.newmarketracecourses.co.uk

Cheltenham Racecourse*, Gloucestershire: 01242 541570;
www.cheltenham.co.uk
Lancashire County Cricket Club*, Manchester: 0161 282 4020;
www.lccc.co.uk
Silverstone Circuit*, Northamptonshire: 01327 857271;
www.octagonmotorsports.com

Grand and elegant
Cliveden*, Berkshire: 01628 668561; www.clivedenhouse.co.uk
Longleat*, Wiltshire: 01985 844400; www.longleat.co.uk
Stoke Park Club*, Buckinghamshire: 01753 717171;
www.stokeparkclub.com

Money-wise: What to expect
Venue hire, average spend: about £1200
Village hall hire: £100+
Licensed civil marriage premises hire: about £500+
Venue-finding specialist: £200+
Hotel, castle or private country/town house, all-day location fee: £1000–£3000+
Restaurant hire: often free (they should make their money on the food and drink) but some now charge a hire fee

Remember: Many venues charge a full-day rate, regardless of how long you need it for. Many more then take a cut on your food and drink spend, too. If your wedding isn't an all-day affair, look for a venue which charges on an hourly basis, and allows you to use your own drink and caterers without extra fees, such as the Conservatory at Ransome's Dock, Battersea, London: 020 8874 8505; www.theconservatoryvenue.co.uk

chapter

six

weddings abroad:
locations and logistics

There are endless possible reasons to marry overseas: great weather, an outdoor ceremony, something different, or it could simply be the answer if hassle, expense or parents are a problem.

WHAT'S YOUR STYLE?

Beach wedding
Regrettably, their ease can also be their downfall: tales of white tulle queuing along the beach at hotels which schedule a ceremony every thirty minutes have given such wedding packages a sorry reputation. Fortunately, many are more sophisticated and, since a peak several years ago, many of the culpable tour operators have been shamed into being less brazenly commercial. So if you want a sunset, beachside wedding, don't be deterred.

City wedding

Big cities have an energy and excitement to them: if that's your thing, take your pick from romantic cities like Salzburg and Rome; glitzy ones like New York and Sydney; or pleasure-palaces like Disneyland or Las Vegas.

Country, mountains or wildlife wedding

Anyone who's ever spent a skiing holiday in an idyllic snow-covered alpine village, seen Jean de Florette's Provence, or taken an African safari trip, might be tempted to make it the setting for their wedding.

PLANNING YOUR OVERSEAS WEDDING

First, consider the following:

- Overseas weddings are a great way to avoid wedding stress – especially if you have to go out early to fulfil a residency requirement. All you can do is relax – and wait!
- You're unlikely to see the location before the day.
- The weather is more reliable, but it's still not guaranteed.
- Do you have the right personality to cope with uncertainties, and be happy with the outcome if it's not what you imagined?
- Do freedom and privacy compensate for the fact that family and friends will miss the biggest day of your life?
- European locations are generally a better choice if you want family and friends to come too.
- Language issues may mean you won't understand the ceremony well: ensure it's in English if possible, or organise a translator.

Then, consider how you'll organise your wedding: There are three options: a specialised consultant, doing it yourself, or a travel agent; with all of them, nothing is more important than making sure you have the right paperwork and the necessary residency qualifications. Legalities are covered in Chapter Eight.

Specialised overseas wedding planners

If you have no idea where to start, but you want something relatively ambitious, you may need this kind of help. Some countries make the paperwork notoriously difficult to negotiate, making a specialist invaluable, and if you're planning a large, traditional wedding overseas, a dedicated wedding planner could be essential. They can take on the hard work and anxiety, without restricting you to a package, and should know the locations very well, have a good number of venues for you to choose from, and local staff to organise everything from that end. Some are small one-to-one consultants (best for a full-blown wedding and reception), while others are larger organisations of wedding travel specialists. To find an overseas wedding consultant:

- Personal recommendation, as always, is best.
- Scour wedding magazines for real-life overseas wedding stories. If a wedding planner or specialised consultant is involved, their details will usually be at the end of the article. Look in classified ads at the back of the magazine, too.
- The Internet is also a good starting point. Look at wedding sites for listings (see Chapter Eighteen).
- Check out a planner's credentials, as you would any other supplier, before trusting them with your wedding – and be sure that you like them.
- Make sure that any travel bookings are with ABTA approved companies.
- See the list starting on page 64 of this chapter.

DIY

Caution first: Creating the whole thing yourselves is possible, but to be approached with great caution, and only if you have plenty of time, together with a knack for organisation and detail. Liaising with the authorities can be problematic, so if you have doubts, consult a travel agent or specialist. A DIY approach is easier if your chosen location has at least two of the following in its favour:

- It's near enough for a reconnaissance trip.
- It's English-speaking, or you can speak the language well.
- You know the place very well already.

- You have friends or family who live there and can help you with local arrangements.
- Legalities are simple and quick to fix, so that you can spend the first week of your trip finalising arrangements, and get married in the second.

Still determined? Enough of the high-level warnings. Many couples have done it before you, and fixing your own wedding in a familiar or favourite place in the world can reap wonderful rewards. A quick and private wedding in Vegas or the Caribbean can be relatively simple to negotiate, as long as you do a little homework first. If you want a 'proper' wedding, with guests, full reception and all, it's more challenging, but possible to manage without professional help. The plan of action below is based on the experiences and suggestions of couples who have successfully organised their own European weddings.

1 Choose the location where you'd like to marry. It might be a country you're in love with, or a particular town, region, building, hotel.

2 Check that it's legally possible for you to marry in that country: contact the UK embassy of your chosen country, or the British Consulate overseas (*see* Chapter Eight). If it isn't, consider marrying in the UK first, then having a blessing or vow-exchange ceremony abroad instead. You're likely to require a civil ceremony before any religious ceremony in many European countries, in any case.

3 Then *either*:

   a Choose a hotel that you'd like to stay at and use as a base for your wedding. Hotel guides are listed later in the chapter. You need a friendly, efficient hotel, because you're going to need their help with your wedding. When you phone to enquire about a booking at the hotel, explain that you're hoping to get married while you stay with them. (Many Europeans quickly become very enthusiastic and helpful!) Ask them where you might marry near the hotel, if they can suggest an English-speaking church, or let you have the number of the town hall or mayor's office (where most Continental civil marriages take place). The local tourist office and British Consulate should also help you find the necessary information.

or:

b   If you don't want to stay at a hotel, decide on other accommodation that suits you: there are plenty of villas, houses and chateaux where you can base a house party (*see* **Contacts** below). Unless the owner or contact is very helpful, you'll need to rely on the tourist office for information about local churches, town hall or mayor's office, as well as any reception venue.

4   Ring the civil official or church minister to discuss the options for a marriage or blessing. If all's well, let him know you plan to visit shortly.

5   Start to process any paperwork via the appropriate embassy or consulate.

6   If you're planning to have a wedding reception of any kind, discuss the possibilities with your hotel, or ask them – or the tourist office – to suggest suitable restaurants or other venues.

7   When you think you have the skeleton of a wedding, it's time to make a trip there, if you can. Amazingly, many couples seem to cram one big planning session into a long weekend. Before you go, make appointments with the church minister, mayor or official and let the hotel know that you're coming. Take all necessary legal paperwork with you, and get it checked. Arrange to stay at your wedding accommodation if you can – especially if you are planning to party there. Otherwise, make appointments to see three or four other candidate venues.

8   Once there, things should hopefully fall into place. Visit the minister/ church/town hall/hotel/restaurants you've got on your list, decide whether you're happy with the options and make your choices. Book a provisional date – and time – for the wedding ceremony and discuss details such as music and readings. Check with your celebration venue or hotel, discussing details like timing, menus, drinks. Make hotel reservations for everyone who'll be staying with you, and check out other hotels in the area for guests on different budgets. Get e-mail addresses and fax numbers for all your contacts to make communication as simple as possible once you're home again. Your hotel will probably be able to suggest florists, hairdressers, or anything else you need.

9   Once home, you should be able to sort out the rest of the details by phone, e-mail or fax, and finalise all the legalities before you go. Invite

your friends and family, if you want to, and get them to confirm their hotel reservations asap!

Self-planned weddings

Venice

'I'd always wanted a wedding like the one in The Godfather *– and then found a husband-to-be with an Italian history! We started to investigate a hotel and church in Venice, and it all fell into place so easily, we decided to go ahead in a couple of months' time. We had a civil marriage here, then 40 friends joined us for an Anglican wedding ceremony over there. We took a gondola to our reception, where we had Bellinis and a six-course dinner on the terrace of the Hotel Gritti Palace, overlooking the canal.' Bride, 28.*

Greek Islands

'Because we have family over there, we organised the whole thing ourselves. It was on a tiny island – and we had some hairy moments! The hotel where everyone was due to stay – about 70 guests – fell down, and the mayor told us at the last minute that he wasn't going to do the ceremony after all ... The restaurant seemed to think vegetarian food was an impossibility (lots of us were vegetarian) and the videographer broke his thumb. The decorations on the (white) cake came off (after my mother had made and transported it all the way from England) and the restaurant took it upon themselves to fix it with bright green icing. Still, the mayor relented, and the wedding was wonderful: I wore a fabulous white trouser suit, we had horse-drawn carriages and Greek dancing, and we wouldn't have done it any other way!' Bride, 28.

Las Vegas

'After two big family weddings in as many years, we decided on Vegas – Elvis and all. We didn't tell a soul – just took a flight, turned up, booked it, went off to find some saloon-style gear, and were married the next day. Out there, no-one seemed to know much about Elvis weddings, so we felt quite adventurous! Elvis was very busy: he swept the chapel steps, chauffeured our limo, witnessed the marriage and sang some rousing ballads, too!' Bride, 27.

Tour operators and general travel agents

You could simply book your wedding from a holiday brochure. As well as beach weddings (or 'weddingmoons' as the brochures sometimes call them), many tour operators (*see* the end of this chapter) offer a number of city and 'location' weddings, such as at the The Ice Chapel at The Ice Hotel in Sweden, or in the rainforest of Queensland, Australia. As with holidays, booking through a travel agent doesn't always mean a fixed package. Austravel, for instance, start with your requests and build a trip around them. If you choose a package, or popular beach resort, you can help avoid the conveyor-belt wedding by asking the following questions:

- How many weddings take place each day at the hotel/location?
- Can you choose the time of day?
- What is the actual location of the service? Don't just assume it's a lovely part of the beach or beautiful hotel terrace.
- Will other hotel guests be looking on? Can you be somewhere private?

BOOKING THE WEDDING

Check exactly what's included in a wedding package, as the typical one is fairly basic, with extras quickly adding to the cost. Some offer the wedding 'free' as part of the holiday, but others have a sliding scale of charges.

As well as travel and accommodation, a wedding package typically includes:

- Organisation of legal procedures (although it is entirely *your* responsibility to check and produce the correct paperwork and certificates as required).
- Services of the officiant and the ceremony itself (sometimes offering a choice between civil and religious – or even a choice of religions).
- On-site wedding co-ordinators will usually help with any specific or personal requests, sometimes at additional cost.

Extra costs:

- Flowers, cake and a glass or two of champagne may or may not be included.
- Hairdresser, music, photographs, dinner plus local traditional features, such as local dancers will usually be additional costs.
- Any special transport.

Surprise!

'We decided to run away to get married in Mexico – and made the mistake of telling my parents. The day before we left, they told us they were coming too!'
Groom, 29.

Surprise! Surprise!

'After our secret Vegas wedding, we sent cards and photos to everyone to tell them about it. When we came home, the surprise was on us: a close friend had got hold of my address book while we were away and organised a surprise party in a restaurant for all our friends and family!' Bride, 27.

☺☹ *'There was no doubt that her parents would completely take over, and it scared me. So we went to Key West. It was a really happy wedding – and holiday – but we were sorry our friends weren't there to share it with us. We tried to plan a big party for all our friends when we came home, but the in-laws hijacked that instead, and invited all their friends from the golf club. I wish we'd handled it better.' Groom, 29.*

INOCULATIONS

Not all jabs are last minute: discuss with your GP, or call British Airways Travel Clinics to find out what you need a few months ahead (*see* **Contacts**).

THE SEARCH IS ON: CONTACTS AND SOURCES

Specialised overseas wedding planners

Australian Dream Weddings: 00 61 2 9662 3933;
    www.australianwedding.com

Italia Romantica: 020 8830 2090; www.italiaromantica.com
New Zealand Wedding Services: 00 64 3 359 3993;
    www.nzweddingservices.co.nz
Perfect Weddings: 01292 611892; www.perfectweddings.uk.com
Prague Weddings: 00 420 777 218480; www.pragueweddings.com
Weddings Abroad: 400 locations worldwide; 0161 969 1122;
    www.weddings-abroad.com
Weddings Made In Italy: 020 7520 0470; www.weddingsmadeinitaly.co.uk
See Chapter Fifteen for general wedding planners, many of whom will
    organise weddings overseas

DIY wedding planning

Whilst some hotels, guides and locations may be able to provide information
on weddings, many others will leave you entirely to your own devices.

SPECIAL OR LUXURY HOTEL GROUPS OR REPRESENTATIVES
Four Seasons Hotels & Resorts: 00800 648 86488; www.fourseasons.com
Macdonald Hotels: 0870 400 8855; www.macdonaldhotels.co.uk
Hilton: 0800 856 8000; www.hilton.com
Hyatt Hotels & Resorts: 020 8334 8098; www.hyatt.com
Leading Hotels of the World: 020 7290 1000; www.lhw.com
Mandarin Oriental Hotels: 00800 282 83838; www.mandarin-oriental.com
Mason Rose: 020 7235 3245; www.masonrose.com
Relais & Chateaux: 00800 2000 0002; www.relaischateaux.com
Ritz-Carlton Hotels: 0800 234000; www.ritzcarlton.com
Small Luxury Hotels of the World: 01372 375116; www.slh.com

THE BEST HOTEL AND TRAVEL GUIDES
Condé Nast *Traveller* magazine: The ultimate upmarket world travel glossy
    magazine, also at www.cntraveller.co.uk. Browse for great location
    ideas, including special hotels, chateaux and villas.
Charming Small Hotel Guides: Various editions cover France, Greece, New
    England & New York City, Switzerland, Tuscany & Umbria, Italy. Some
    also cover restaurants.

Hip Hotels by Herbert Ypma (Thames & Hudson) are a collection of beautifully photographed guides to funky or elegant hotels. Includes Italy, France, Escape, City and Budget.

Johansens guides feature beautiful hotels and symbols to help assess facilities. The website, www.johansens.co.uk, includes hotels worldwide.

Special Places To Stay, from Alastair Sawday, includes guides to Italy, France, Portugal, Ireland and Spain. More info at www.sawdays.co.uk

All the above from bookshops or newsagents.

SPECIAL PLACES

Accommodation or wedding venues to inspire you …

Confetti's website carries information on specific overseas venues at www.confetti.co.uk

Caribbean villas: privately owned, stylishly furnished and hired via The Owners' Syndicate, who will organise your wedding and celebrations to include anything from paperwork to a gospel choir: 020 7801 9801; www.ownerssyndicate.com

'Chapel in the Forest' wedding at Hunter's Country House in South Africa. Book via Elegant Resorts: 01244 897 888; www.elegantresorts.co.uk

French Connections: Chateaux and country houses in France at www.frenchconnnections.co.uk

Hotel Gritti Palace, Venice: 00 39 041 794 611

Hotel Tugu in Bali: Stylish hotel and Indonesian culture; hotel will organise; 0062 361 731 701; www.tuguhotels.com

---

Celebrity venues worldwide

Dave Stewart & Anoushka Fisz: *Private villa at Juan les Pins on the French Riviera*

Michael Douglas & Catherine Zeta-Jones: *Plaza Hotel, New York*

Chris Evans & Billie Piper: *Little Church of the West wedding chapel, Las Vegas*

Jamie Redknapp & Louise Nurding: *Yacht on the coast of Bermuda*

Hotel Vatulele: Fijian boutique hotel with just 18 rooms – take it over! Book holiday and wedding via Holiday Options: 0870 013 0450; www.holidayoptions.co.uk

Mirabel Palace, Salzburg, Austria: Royalty wed there. Book via Weddings Abroad: 0161 969 1122; www.weddings-abroad.com

Noble's *Big Country Holiday Houses*: guide book

Something Special: Houses, villas and chateaux in France, the Mediterranean and Florida; 08700 270 508; www.somethingspecial.co.uk

Stopover Connections: French chateaux and country houses; 0114 2669301; www.stopoverconnections.com

The Ice Hotel, Sweden: Made every year, entirely from ice, complete with Ice Chapel for weddings; 00 46 980 66800; www.icehotel.com

Tour operators

SPECIAL INTEREST OR AREA SPECIFIC

Africa Travel Centre: 020 7387 1211; www.africatravel.co.uk

African Pride: Includes game lodges and locations by the Zambezi river; 01904 541000; www.african-pride.co.uk

American Round-Up: Specialise in ranch locations in US and Canada; 01404 881777; www.americanroundup.com

Arctic Experience: Weddings on ice, Northern Lights, and other dramatic Arctic experiences; 01737 218800; www.arctic-discover.co.uk

Argo Holidays: Greek islands, including the tiny St Nicholas at Kefalos, Kos; 020 7331 7095; www.argo-holidays.com

Austravel: Build an Australian holiday – and wedding – around your self-styled itinerary of city, beach, or natural wonders, with stopovers on the way; 0870 055 0223; www.austravel.com

Cyplon: Church and civil weddings in Cyprus; 020 8340 7612; www.cyplon.co.uk

Crystal Holidays: Sea, lakes and mountains, Austria and Slovenia; 020 8939 5439; www.crystalholidays.co.uk

Discover the Bahamas: 01737 218803; www.discover-the-bahamas.co.uk

Kirker Holidays: Specialise in travel to Prague, can help guide you in locations, leaving you to organise the wedding itself; 020 7231 3333; www.kirkerholidays.com

Moswin Tours: German weddings in fairy-tale settings like the real Sleeping Beauty castle; 0116 271 9922; www.moswin.com

Norvista: Weddings in Finland; 0870 744 7315; www.norvista.co.uk

Scantours: Nordic/Scandinavian lakes, mountains, snow, countryside and cities; 020 7839 2927; www.scantours.co.uk

WORLDWIDE WEDDINGS

Airtours: Canada, Cyprus and Italy with wide choice of locations and optional extras; 08702 412568; www.mytravel.com

British Airways: Worldwide, includes Caribbean, Far East, Hawaii, Las Vegas and Disney; 0870 442 3847; www.britishairways.com

Carrier: Stylish, luxuriously priced locations in Africa (safari as well as beach), Caribbean, Indian Ocean; 01625 547030; www.carrier.co.uk

Elegant Resorts: Upmarket (and not cheap) resort weddings in the Caribbean, Bermuda, Florida, Maldives and other beach locations, plus Hunter's Country House in South Africa; 01244 897 888; www.elegantresorts.co.uk

First Choice: Includes Africa, South America, Europe and Canada; 0161 742 2262

Hayes & Jarvis: 0870 333 0068; www.hayesandjarvis.co.uk

Kuoni: Worldwide beaches, plus Sydney, New York and San Francisco; 01306 747007; www.kuoni.co.uk

Somak: Worldwide beaches and African game parks; 020 8423 3000; www.somak.co.uk

Tropical Places: Long haul only; 01342 330777; www.tropicalplaces.co.uk

Money-wise: What to expect
Specialised overseas wedding planner: £1000+
Wedding ceremony as part of a holiday package: £300–£1000+
(plus, of course, the cost of the trip itself)

Contacts
British Airways Travel Clinics: 020 7439 9584/020 7606 2977;
www.britishairways.com

chapter seven

money matters:
getting married without going broke

There's no 'ideal' budget, and no right or wrong way to finance a wedding. Experts and guides are quick with clichés about cutting our coats according to our cloth, while telling us we'll 'get what we pay for', and 'only do it once'. Unless it sends you into the kind of scary debt that you'll be cursing long after your photo album has been confined to the loft, you've got to do what feels right – and seems (kind of) possible. The only rule is to keep your head: however important the wedding seems now, heavy debt is invariably regretted.

HOW MUCH?

You can only start with what you've got, not what everyone else spends. Early on, there's a tendency to think that the figures you hear quoted for the cost of a wedding are not relevant to you ... they're way too high. Other people may spend £10,000, £20,000, £30,000 on a wedding, but they've got to be rolling in it … haven't they? And a simple wedding dress in a magazine may cost £2000, but that's just magazines … isn't it?

Once you start to make decisions and bookings, however, the cold reality will dawn. Those figures aren't high at all; in fact they're quite conservative. Weddings cost a small fortune. For the record, the average spend is around £14,500, but that's about as helpful as quoting the average shoe size when you get round to buying your very own glass slippers. There are bankable facts, however:

- However much you expect to spend, it will be considerably more.
- The best weddings are not necessarily the most expensive ones.
- You've got to be a lot sharper, and work a lot harder, to organise a wedding on a small budget.

We know that there's virtually no upper limit on the cost of a wedding: it's barely remarkable that Hollywood stars can spend a million dollars on a wedding with more staff than guests. On the flip side, the minimum cost (here) is about £100. That's the lower end price of a register office ceremony; it would be about £200 if you went for a basic church wedding. Seems crazy then that another £14,300 (on average) gets spent on the accompanying paraphernalia.

Hidden costs

And then there's the bit you don't always notice. Besides the considerable expenses that fall to your guests (over £400 to each, on average), fuelling the wedding industry but at least not your overdraft, you may find yourselves much worse off in ways no one warns you about:

- First, what you discover you need to pay after you thought you'd covered everything. Like the cost of trips to meetings with suppliers at your long-distance venue and dry-cleaning and boxing up your dress after the wedding (not cheap).
- Second, what you spent because of the wedding, rather than on it. This is chain-reaction spending. Like you've shrunk with the stress of it all, so you decide to enjoy it with some new clothes. Or you have a bust-up with your mum, so you send her some flowers. Not money you mind spending, of course, but spent nonetheless.

● Finally, what you didn't earn because of the wedding. Overheads that only become apparent months after the wedding: your overtime pay is much lower than last year, or your bonus was down (and you're not altogether surprised) or, if you're self-employed, your tax return is worryingly modest this year.

WHO'S PAYING?

How much you plan to spend is intrinsically tied up with who's paying. Tempting though it may be to go first to the bride's parents to ask for a budget, it's wise to work out a basic wedding structure first, with an idea of total cost – and establish whether the bliss of having your wedding paid for would have long strings attached.

In fact, the primary burden has shifted from the bride's parents to the couple themselves: according to *You & Your Wedding* magazine, over a third of modern couples pay for their own wedding, only about 20% have the bride's parents pay the entire bill, and half share the costs with one or both sets of parents. If this is second time around for either of you, and especially the bride, you'll probably pay for the whole thing yourselves. Whatever the division, the system remains largely the same: those who pay the most, say the most. A lucky few have parents who hand over tens of thousands and tell the couple to do whatever they want, but that's rare; other parents are unable, or unwilling, to contribute at all; most fall somewhere in the middle. You may decide not to accept any help even if it's offered, but some brides' fathers feel that paying for the wedding is a point of honour, and turning them down can be complicated and even hurtful *(see* Chapter Sixteen).

Financial contributions may be more easily managed when they're 'tagged': the giver pays the bill for the flowers, or the drink, or the photographer, or several such items, rather than handing over hard money. It simply limits the control that the money buys: the giver of champagne can add plenty of advice on which one to choose; the giver of unallocated funds might feel entitled to an opinion on everything.

Try to settle who's paying for what early on. Vague offers of 'help' are

Who paid?

'My parents didn't pay anything (they're divorced), but my mother believed that she should be in charge, with her name at the top of the invitations. She even insisted on making a speech.' Bride, 25.

'My parents gave us a cheque for £250.' Bride, 31.

'We paid for the wedding; my husband's parents gave us £10,000 for a deposit on our house.' Bride, 28.

'My husband paid 90% – my mother and stepfather paid the rest.' Bride, 27.

'Both sets of parents paid a third; I wished more than once we'd just gone to Vegas.' Groom, 30.

'My father paid all £30,000. He's not wealthy but he'd been saving all his life. My mother and I planned the whole wedding together with barely a hitch. I do know how lucky we all were!' Bride, 35.

kind but confusing; be ready for such conversations with a tentative but positive response on what would be appreciated.

Who pays for what – and where does it go?

Many families find themselves struggling with the 'modern' approach of sharing out the costs. In fact, tradition does it very nicely for us. The common assumption is that the bride's family pays for everything, and an offer of – or request for – help from, say, the groom's family, is rather '21st century'. It isn't. If costs were divided according to strictest tradition, things would be fairer: the traditional financial responsibilities on the groom's side amount to at least a quarter of the overall budget; that goes up to a whacking 39% if you count in the honeymoon!

Traditional financial responsibility	Average cost*
Bride's side	**£**
Stationery	225
Bride's clothes, accessories, etc	1500
Cars for bride and family	170
Reception venue	1200

Drinks	1000
Food	2250
Photographs/video	1100
Flowers for church and reception	275
Cake	230
Total	**7950**

Groom's side	£
Rings	1560
All other cars	170
Ceremony and legal costs	300
Groom's clothing	300
Bouquets and buttonholes	200
Honeymoon	2750
Total	**5280**

* Approximated figures based on average national spends from the *You & Your Wedding* reader survey, 2001.

Modern financial responsibility

Ability to pay is probably the most reliable modern guide, but a fairer approach, which nods to tradition but still keeps the bride and groom as major shareholders, might be:

- **Bride and groom:** Their own outfits, rings, hotels, honeymoon, stationery, flowers, decorations and attendants' clothes.

Etiquette issue: Can you ask for the money instead?

No. If you decide to run away, or have a tiny wedding, when you know there's a hefty wedding fund put by for you, it might be tempting to try to get your hands on it anyway. But if your parents know your situation, and like the idea of giving you the money instead, the thought will occur to them. Drop the most subtle hints if you absolutely must. And, while asking guests for money in lieu of gifts might be standard in some cultures, it's not usually a good idea in ours.

- **Bride's family:** Reception venue, food and wedding cake.
- **Groom's family:** Ceremony costs, wedding cars, drink, music and entertainment, photography.

PLANNING YOUR BUDGET

Budgeting is a continual process during the months of wedding planning; it's one area where being a control freak literally pays off.

1 First, what have you got? Include all the money you could get your hands on between now and the wedding date (move it to a later date while you can, if that helps).

2 Then decide how much of it you feel comfortable spending: if you've never liked debt, you're not going to enjoy it now; if you've been saving for a new kitchen, how are you going to feel when you get back from honeymoon to the same old tatty cupboards?

3 Now think about what you'd like to do. Have a completely open mind, but stick to your principles.

4 Now reign in your ideal to fit your budget.

5 Divvy up your funds to each aspect of the wedding: venue, catering, dress, etc. Allow extra for things that are important and be pessimistic: things always cost more than you think.

6 Once you have a plan you can afford, put a rough budget breakdown on paper – or on your PC. Allow at least 10% contingency: this is annoying, and you'll be sorely tempted to miss it out, but you *will* need it. There's a budget planner on page 76, or look on wedding websites such as Confetti, or *Brides* magazine.

7 Start getting quotes from suppliers. Give them your budget upfront, and see what they can do with it. Get shot of people who make you feel foolish about it as fast as you can: there's no finer way to get ripped off. *See* Chapter Eleven for getting the best out of suppliers.

8 As quotes come in (at least three of each) you'll undoubtedly need to adjust some of your fund allocation, but don't be tempted to up your overall budget. Be *absolutely* certain that everything is included in their price.

Money management ...

'We decided it had to be done properly. For me to look like a princess and everyone to drink nothing but champagne. So we limited numbers and kept it short.' Bride, 29.

And mismanagement ...

'We're not great with money, either of us, and there were two things we should have done: first, agreed upfront who was in charge of money, and how we were going to manage it, because it caused a few arguments at the beginning; second, been more honest with ourselves about what the final cost was likely to be. We came back from honeymoon with a massive overdraft: we'd just been burying our heads in the sand.' Groom, 28.

'Our wedding officially cost £18,000. If I add all the extras to that, and think about the real cost, my stomach turns over: every single one of our guests stayed overnight in a hotel or B&B, and of course had fabulous outfits and gave us lovely presents; my parents hired a second car for the week and put their dogs in kennels for five days; all our sisters and brothers came down the night before to help, and stayed in our hotel with us. I'm self-employed, but turned down loads of work because I felt completely overloaded in the months before the wedding. And I bought seven different foundations before the wedding, trying to get exactly the right one!' Bride, 32.

9   If parents or other benefactors are paying for specific items, get them to approve the estimate and arrange for them to be billed direct.

10 Open a bank account for wedding funds and expenditure.

11 Go back to your budget breakdown every few weeks, setting actual costs and payments made against your estimate and quotes. Keep a tally of how much has been spent or allocated, and how much money you're left with.

12 Do a final tally a few days before the wedding. You may be able to make cuts if things are getting out of hand, or at least be prepared with back-up arrangements when the bills come in!

REAL WORLD BUDGET PLANNER

Item	Who's paying	Budget	Estimate/ quote £	Deposit paid £	Final cost £	Date balance paid
Engagement ring						
Announcements						
Engagement party						
Legal/registrar/church fees						
Venue/marquee						
Catering/equipment hire						
Drinks						
Cake						
Wedding dress						
Bride's accessories						
Skincare, make-up, hair						
Groom's clothes						
Groom's accessories						
Attendants' clothes						
Going-away outfit						
Bouquets/posies						
Buttonholes/corsages						
Flowers church/reception						
Decor and details						
Wedding cars						
Invitations/stationery/postage						
Music						
PA system						
Other entertainment						
Photographs						
Video						
First night hotel						
Honeymoon or overseas wedding travel						
Thank-you presents						
Favours						
Professional planning fees						
Tips						
10% contingency						
Totals						

Other possible expenses:

- Travel costs for planning meetings – childcare – power supply/electrician/cables – transport for guests (minibus/bus) – loos – lighting – furniture hire – guest book – stamps – wedding consultant – stag and hen parties – pre-wedding dinner – planning book/stationery/CD ROM – post-wedding brunch.
- If you're doing anything yourselves, don't forget to cost in equipment or overheads: cooking utensils – cake tins/boards – transportation containers – floristry accessories/tools/vases – CDs – furniture hire – glass/cutlery/crockery – sewing equipment – van hire if you have large amounts of food, drink or equipment to transport – licences for music or bar.

LOOK AT IT ANOTHER WAY: LOW-COST, HIGH-STYLE ALTERNATIVES

Weddings simply don't have to cost a fortune. There's so much hype around the 'perfect venue', and the 'most important day of your lives', we can all get sucked into believing venues, menus and dresses that cost several thousand each are the only civilised option. Which is when it all starts to become One Big Rip Off. The fact is that many couples have created lovely – even exceptional – weddings for a fraction of the 'average'. And there is always the option of taking off abroad: a fortnight at the most gorgeous hotel can cost less than an hour or two's unremarkable dining for a 150 people!

The key is to negotiate well, shop around, and do things yourself. What are your talents, and who else's can you draw on? If you have time on your side to DIY without panic, you can save a lot of money. Whether you want to marry on a sixpence or just shave a few hundred pounds off your bill, the following may help:

General
- Ask, ask, ask. If you have an idea for a bargain, follow it up. People can only say no, after all.
- Radically re-appraise your idea of what a wedding *is*. It's the big vanilla

white weddings that cost a fortune; *see* The Numbers Game in Chapter Four and look for wedding alternatives in Chapter Three.

- Timing is important. Starting early does give you the choice you need, and helps to avert expensive panic buying. The downside is that the longer you plan your wedding, the more you'll find to spend money on. A short engagement could actually lead to a more modest wedding.
- Get loads of quotes. Three is a minimum; bargain hunters go for seven or eight.
- To avoid unjustified wedding premiums when enquiring about prices, don't say 'wedding'; say party, or dinner-dance.
- Keep a very open mind: setting your heart on something in particular might be costly.
- Spend time shopping around. You need *just one* perfect-but-bargain dress, caterer, venue: it doesn't matter that the rest are overpriced, as long as you keep looking for the one that isn't.
- Cut down your guest list and keep the reception short to instantly reduce your food, drinks', furniture, crockery, and flowers' bill.
- Choose a time and date that's as off-peak as possible. The whole world wants a Saturday afternoon in the summer, leaving you to pick up the cheapest slots with venues and suppliers.
- Don't bother with a honeymoon. Stick around to enjoy the post-wedding fun – and go away in a few months' time.

Venue

- Forget 'wedding venues' altogether: think pubs, village halls, local cricket, rowing or rugby clubs.
- Look at local outdoor space in quite another way, be it a park, riverbank, school field. Could you hire it? Could you put up a canopy or marquee? Approach the local authority and be persistent.
- Schmooze friends with big gardens: you don't have to have a riot. If the house can be locked up while still leaving access to a kitchen and loos, a garden party can stay safely in the garden.

Ceremony

- A register office or church is usually cheaper than a licensed venue.
- A humanist or vow-exchange ceremony can take place anywhere – and that includes wild, free land.

Flowers and decoration

- Use fruit, candles, bunches of wheat – anything, in fact, that isn't expensive flora. Put sequins, petals, confetti on tables, windowsills and other surfaces.
- Ask friends if you can raid their gardens for hydrangeas, lavender, wild flowers and foliage.
- Use single, bright flowers such as gerberas instead of elaborate decorations.
- One or two large displays look more impressive than lots of little ones.
- Use the plainest of pots and vases: take trips to Ikea, Homebase, Woolworths and consider drinking glasses and food storage jars for flowers as well as vases. Jam jars and aluminium cans, simply decorated, cost next to nothing.
- Forget favours, or give only to the female guests. Make them cheaply yourself: wrap sweets or sugared almonds in tulle and tie with ribbon.
- Buy plain white cake boxes, and pretty ribbon, so you can give slices of cake instead of favours.
- Move decorations from ceremony to reception, or from day reception to party room, rather than duplicating.
- Make confetti over the coming months. Raid all your friends' gardens and dry flowers in the airing cupboard. Avoid pale petals which can go brown.
- Carry a single long-stemmed rose, instead of a bouquet. Very understated, very stylish.
- If another couple is using the same church or venue on the same or previous day, you might be able to double up and share the cost of some of your flowers.

See Chapter Ten for more on DIY decorating ideas; page 147 for stockists.

Food

- If you're using a caterer, give them a budget, however low, and ask what they can do with it.
- Brunch and afternoon tea can be done with maximum elegance at minimum cost.
- Simple to serve and inexpensive everyday food always goes down well: sausage and mash, fish and chips, chilli and jacket potatoes. Easy to do yourself, too.
- Have canapés *or* a starter, not both.
- Even if you want a sit-down meal, choose a serve-yourself buffet to save on staff costs.
- A table laden with delicious-looking bread, salads, salami, whole cheeses and fruit is impressive, easy and needs no professional input.
- Ask your caterer to do cheap, child-friendly food for the kids, like sausages or pasta. They'll much prefer it anyway.
- Ask your guests to help: they could bring a picnic or a buffet dish.

See Chapter Eleven for alternative eats, Chapter Twelve for more on doing your own catering on the cheap.

Drink

- Champagne is for the rich. Good sparkling wine is virtually identical, unless you're a real connoisseur. Or welcome guests with punch, cocktails, Pimm's, or mulled wine.
- Go to France to get your drink, and do it off season when channel crossings are cheap. Shop around: crossing prices vary massively for no apparent reason.

See Chapter Eleven for more on alternative drinks and corkage charging; Chapter Twelve for DIY.

Stationery

- How's your handwriting? Pretty – or funky – paper with handwritten lettering looks great for invitations, menus or order of service sheets. Takes ages though!
- Don't bother: text-message (or phone) your invites, use the church's

hymn books and order of service sheets, write on leaves or pebbles with a metallic pen for place cards.

● Get busy with your PC. Bulk-buy simple A5 light card, a couple of colour ink cartridges and be creative with layout and typeface.

See Chapter Ten for more DIY stationery ideas and material suppliers.

Rings and jewellery

● Antique rings can be a fraction of the price of new ones.
● A family heirloom makes a perfect engagement ring/necklace/bracelet.
● High street stores – anything from Argos to Zales – sell simple wedding bands for next to nothing.
● Go to cheap and cheerful accessories' shops like Accessorize, for a tiara, wedding jewellery and bridesmaids' accessories.

Clothes

● Wedding dress shops have sales in January, just like the rest of the world. Check their stock before Christmas and ask what's likely to be in the sale.
● Chain store wedding dresses can be gorgeous: look at Monsoon, Bhs, and Debenhams. Even Asda and Littlewoods are getting in on the evening-and-bridalwear act: worth a look. The plainest can be customised with your own details.
● Shop in the party season, or just after: evening dresses make great wedding dresses, and come November and December the high street is groaning with silk, sequins and slinky little numbers.
● If you can sew, and have *plenty* of time, there's no doubt that it could save you a fortune. Just don't bite off more than you can chew.
● You don't have to buy new: wedding dress bargains can be had at The Wedding Warehouse Sale. Hired wedding dresses are better than they were, second-hand dresses are only once-worn, and shop samples often sold off at the end of a single season. Try Modern Bride and Déjà Vu for ex-samples; *see* **Almost new** on page 198 for once-worn.
● Theatrical costumes can be hired; *see* stockists on page 199, **Contacts** on page 224.

- Wear a bridesmaid's dress, even if you're the bride. Manufacturers like Watters & Watters and Lazaro do altered-to-fit, well-made dresses in lots of colours, including white. And they're way cheaper than a wedding dress.
- Cheap accessories are everywhere: try Hennes, Topshop, Accessorize and Monsoon Girl (for children).
- Sell your dress immediately after the wedding: approach the second-hand outlets mentioned on page 198.
- Choose adult bridesmaids' outfits off the peg in the high street: as well as being much cheaper, a clever buy from Mango, Topshop or Oasis looks much more contemporary.
- Mini bridesmaids can wear fairy costumes from department stores and toy shops, party and summer dresses from chain stores. The Vertbaudet children's catalogue does a range of French celebration clothes for boys and girls which are amazingly good value.

Earning it back

If you can sell exclusive rights for your wedding pictures to Hello! *or* OK! *magazines, you could be richer after the wedding than before it. Press reports claimed that:*

Victoria Adams & David Beckham *spent around £500,000 on the wedding – and earned back a fee of £1m for* OK!*'s coverage of the event*

Earl & Countess Spencer *were among the first to enjoy* Hello!*'s money for wedding picture rights, earning an estimated £350,000 for the coverage over ten years ago.*

Catherine Zeta-Jones & Michael Douglas *hit the big one: £1m for* OK!*'s exclusive (but were still apparently out of pocket with a wedding spend of £1.5m). The* OK! *fee – together with guests' wedding donations (in lieu of gifts) were all paid into a charitable trust in son Dylan's name.*

Claudia Schiffer & Matthew Vaughn *signed a £450,000 deal with* Hello! *for exclusive coverage of their Suffolk wedding.*

But two of Britain's best, **Kate Winslet** *and* **Zoe Ball**, *had the style to turn them all down. And so, to be fair, did* **Brad Pitt & Jennifer Aniston**.

More dressing ideas, plus contacts and stockists, are in Chapters Fourteen and Fifteen.

Travel
* Ask a friend with some glamorous wheels to chauffeur you; don't forget to thank them with a pre-wedding car wash (!), a full tank of petrol and a gift afterwards.
* Give the biggest and newest family car a polish and tie big tulle bows on the windscreen wipers.
* Go for the ordinary: walk, take a river ferry, or a London cab.

More transport ideas on page 146.

Music
* Ask musical friends to perform.
* Make a few CDs of the coolest background music and best-ever dance tracks. Spend your money on a hiring a good PA system and the sound will be anything but cheap.

More music ideas on pages 163–5.

☺☹ *'I felt continuously vulnerable about money: as the wedding drew near, little charges emerged, or things weren't as agreed. But what could we do? If we pulled out, we'd never find another venue or caterer in time. The fact is, suppliers have too much power. It must be so easy to rip people off. Is there a solution? I wish we'd agreed at the quoting stage that 10% of the payment would be held back till after the wedding. And those wedding websites ought to have notice boards where you can post anonymous complaints and warnings about suppliers.'*

INSURANCE?

This is a personal decision, but for under a hundred pounds, it could be one 'what the hell' expense you're glad you made, if only for peace of mind. People sometimes say that insurance is just another rip-off, but I've never

Money-wise: Where did it go?

'We spent £7000 on the full white wedding. Mum did lots of the food, her friend made the cake, and a local farmer lent us his field where we had a marquee and spit-roast barbecue.' Bride, 29.

'We married at the local church, and had a party in my parents' garden. My sister did most of the food, and various friends brought puddings, nibbles and champagne. I bought my dress at Monsoon. We spent £1,800.' Bride, 27.

'We went to St Lucia a few years ago. I think it cost £2,200 for two weeks, including the wedding.' Groom, 29.

'We budgeted £10,000, did lots ourselves, and spent £20,000! We got the drink from France, made the cake, and my mother-in-law made the bridesmaids' dresses. We don't know how it got so out of hand, because we thought we were being careful!' Couple, 33 and 34.

'We spent £35,000 – and we weren't even especially extravagant!' Bride, 38.

'We went to Greece – with 70 friends in tow – and the whole thing cost £4000.' Couple, 27 and 28.

liked to tempt fate. Our two small children have given us many a terrified flight to casualty (as they do) and it seemed perfectly possible they'd choose our wedding day for another. If your wedding situation makes you feel vulnerable, why not get insured? The small print often sails just the right side of legal, so it's *imperative* to read it with the greatest of cynicism before deciding.

If suppliers fail you, however, you will have to claim against them: wedding insurance will only provide cover for the supplier going out of business. Bear this in mind if anything goes wrong – you'll need to make the supplier aware of the problem at the time, and keep some record of it, in order to make a claim against them.

Contacts

Confetti: www.confetti.co.uk
Brides magazine: www.bridesuk.net

section
three

it's *your* ceremony

*Deciding what's right for you ... the legalities, here and abroad ...
making every moment meaningful and personal*

chapter eight

legal requirements
and ceremony choices

WEDDINGS IN THE UK

As our culture diversifies here in the UK, so do the ways that we marry. Some take care of the legal and spiritual in one:

- **A church or religious wedding** follows a set of rituals from which the classic wedding 'vision' has arisen: a procession, aisle, hymns, prayer, gowns and spiritual vows. Some, like the Church of England ceremony, are fixed in style and content, while the most liberal, such as the Unitarian Church, give more control to the couple. Any recognised religion may conduct legal marriages on approved religious premises.
- **A civil wedding** can be simple and official or, if you prefer, more ceremonial, incorporating personal and traditional features, such as an aisle, giving away of the bride, special vows, readings and music. It must be entirely secular.

These options may not be right for you. They may not fit with your beliefs or may be too set in format. You may be restricted by divorce or differing faiths; or you may want to marry at night, or at home, when the law does not currently permit it.

Two in one

'Everyone should get married twice! Our register office ceremony was so private, we were able to really focus on what was happening, and take it all in. Then we had two 'stolen' days to enjoy being newly married and look forward to celebrating with a blessing and reception for all our friends and family. I never felt the come-down so many people describe afterwards – and I think it's because we had time to adjust and savour it all.' Bride, 29.

- **A 'two-stage' approach** might suit you better: standard practice in much of Europe (*see* Chapter Three), such weddings deal first with civil legalities, and then, separately, with the spiritual. That spiritual stage can be:
  - A traditional religious blessing, which follows a set format like a wedding ceremony, enabling those with strong religious convictions to celebrate their marriage in their faith. It usually takes place in a religious building.
  - A personal, 'custom-made' ceremony: religious, secular or a combination of the two – but without the traditionally associated constraints. This could be a personal 'vow-exchange', a humanist ceremony, or a religious ceremony built around beliefs or circumstances that don't necessarily conform to the church 'rules'. Every bit as dignified as a legal ceremony, you may have the tradition of a celebrant, aisle, readings, music and 'marriage' vows (and most people do), or choose something quite different.
  - This part of the wedding is under no legal restraints: place and time are without restriction, and in some, so are words and procedure. *See* page 102 for different types.

THE RULES OF LAW

In England and Wales, for your wedding to be legally recognised, there are requirements that relate both to you, and to the wedding ceremony itself.

About you

The law says you must:

- Both be free to marry, and fully consenting.
- Be one man, one woman.
- Both have lived in a registration district of England or Wales for seven days immediately prior to giving notice of your intended marriage.
- Be unrelated. The law and churches specify which familial connections prevent a couple from being married, but generally forbid all close blood ties, as well as many by adoption and marriage.
- Both be over eighteen, or over sixteen with parental consent.

The religious bodies say you must:

- Meet specific additional criteria for a religious wedding. This is where issues such as faith, church attendance, divorce and mixed faith may be relevant.

About the wedding

It must be conducted:

- By a registrar at a civil ceremony in a register office or approved civil premises, *or*
- By a Church of England or Church of Wales minister, in the local parish church, *or*
- By another religious celebrant of any other recognised religion, at the appropriate religious location approved for the solemnisation of marriage. Any such religion can apply for such approval; otherwise, a civil registrar's attendance is required to legalise the marriage.

Whether civil or religious:

- The marriage must take place between 8am and 6pm.
- The venue must be open to the public. It must also be a structure which is fixed, permanent and has a roof.
- The ceremony must be witnessed by two people.
- There is a minimum waiting period of fifteen days between notification and the marriage itself.

There are a very few exceptions to these rules:

- Jewish and Religious Society of Friends (Quaker) weddings: place and

time of marriage are a matter for negotiation between celebrant and couple, within certain restrictions. Marriages may not necessarily have to take place in religious buildings or between 8am and 6pm.
- Housebound, terminally ill, or detained people: on a case-by-case basis, location and waiting period for the marriage may be varied under an additional set of rules.

Which means ...

There is much confusion about where and when you may wed in England and Wales. Exceptions aside, for the vast majority:

- Church of England weddings must take place in the parish church local to one of you, and may not usually take place in a church elsewhere in the country. Exceptions have been made to this rule.
- Nonconformist churches, which for the most part are governed by civil legislation, can marry couples from any registration district.
- The Catholic Church will only marry a divorcee under certain circumstances; the Church of England will not officially marry any divorcee, but this is less strictly adhered to. *See* **Types of ceremony** on page 95.
- All civil wedding locations are available to everyone, wherever they live.
- Neither religious nor civil weddings may take place at your home.
- Weddings may not take place in the open air.
- Weddings may not take place at night.
- Weddings may not take place in a marquee.
- A premises can not be approved only for your own wedding.
- You cannot marry in a ship at sea, but you can in one which is permanently moored.

Variations around the UK

IN SCOTLAND
- You can marry from the age of 16.
- You can be now be married by a civil registrar at an approved premises as well as at a register office, and over the next few years a wide choice of venues are likely to gain such approval.

- In theory, time of day is unrestricted, but will be limited by the registrar's working hours.
- You can be married by a minister of a recognised religion, either at a religious location or another place agreed between the parties concerned. This could be outdoors, or at night, but restrictions do apply. You are not confined to your own parish.

IN NORTHERN IRELAND

- Some churches have the power to marry couples in premises other than churches; most are restricted to the local parish or diocese.
- Civil ceremonies must take place in the register office of the district where at least one party lives.
- The law is extremely complicated, and currently under review (*see* below).

The changing laws, nationwide

At the time of going to press, much of the legislation relating to marriages is under review. For England and Wales, that means that a greater choice of location, time, wording and celebrant are all likely, and in a year or two we may be free to marry in the evening, at home, by the river or anywhere else suitable. The Anglican Church, too, is considering permitting couples to marry in any church to which they can show a significant connection, and not just that of their own parish. It is also considering a change in policy

Getting to know the minister

'We were slightly taken aback when we realised that our personal life had become the vicar's business. But it is – that's the nature of this kind of marriage. I was dreading any questions about sex – like if we'd already done it – but he kept clear of that! Despite our initial reservations, we were really glad in the end that we'd had a chance to get to know him properly before our wedding. It made the ceremony much more profound and personal – for us and our guests. It seems odd that before this, we would have been quite happy to have been married by a stranger.' Couple, 36 and 35.

Register office weddings: Three of a kind

'It was just us and our two best friends at the local register office. It felt a bit naughty and exciting!' Couple, 26 and 32.

'The registrar allowed loads of us to cram into the room for the wedding of two great friends. There was no music, just a highly charged atmosphere! Even though it was the quickest, it was one of the happiest, romantic weddings I've ever been to.' Guest, 26.

'It was just the right mix of traditional and modern: I walked in with my father, my sister read a sweet poem called "Valentine" by Wendy Cope, and I threw my bouquet to the girls as we left.' Bride, 28.

towards divorcees. In Northern Ireland, an entirely new system could be in operation as early as 2003; it's intended to be very similar to the Scottish model outlined above.

Documents you'll need

Dependent on the circumstances, ensure that you have what you need at any meeting. The main ones are:

- Birth certificates/adoption certificates.
- Passports (since 1999, you are required to declare nationality when giving notice of marriage).
- Death certificate of a former spouse, if relevant.
- Decrees absolute of any former marriage ending in divorce.
- Proof of residency (normally water rate and council tax notices).
- Certificate of Baptism (not normally required for a Church of England wedding).
- Certificate of Confirmation for a Roman Catholic wedding.
- Certain churches, circumstances or countries may require additional statements or licences, some of which are detailed in this chapter. Check what applies in your case with the celebrant or registrar.

STANDING ON CEREMONY

Words that wed

DECLARATORY AND CONTRACTUAL STATEMENTS

For a marriage to be legal in this country, there are some words that must be spoken, whatever the ceremony, circumstances or religion. First a 'statement' from the celebrant tells the couple and witnesses about the nature of marriage, that it is legally binding, and entered into for life to the exclusion of all others. This is followed by the couple's 'declaration', stating who they are, and that they are free to marry. Then each must say that they take the other as husband/wife, and finally the celebrant must pronounce them husband and wife.

THE BARE MINIMUM

If you want to pare civil legalities to an absolute minimum for any reason, the ceremony can be only minutes long, with just a 'core' set of words (the shortest of a choice of three) that each must say in a civil marriage ceremony. After the registrar's statement, she/he simply says: 'Are you free lawfully to marry (name)?' to which you reply 'I am.' Each of you says in turn to the other, 'I (name) take you (name) to be my wedded wife/husband.' The registrar can then pronounce you husband and wife. You need no guests – just two witnesses – and, of course, you can wear everyday clothes.

Special circumstances

MIXED FAITH

The options depend on your religion. The Church of England will marry anyone who is a British national, regardless of whether they are a member of the Anglican Church. The Catholic Church will conduct a wedding ceremony as long as one of you is a member of the church. A non-Muslim man must convert before he can marry into the faith, and non-Jews must convert before a Jewish wedding can take place (*see* **Types of ceremony** on page 99 for details).

If your churches are open to it, it may be possible for a minister from another church to take part in the ceremony, or to have a wedding in one faith and then a blessing in the other. Alternatively, consider a 'liberal' blessing: a non-denominational celebrant, like Bishop Jonathan Blake, is free to create a blessing based on any faith, or incorporates two or more religions. He will use the words of a full 'wedding' ceremony, if you wish. Rabbi Guy Hall will perform a blessing where only one of you is Jewish, and is willing to co-officiate over a ceremony with a priest from another faith.

SECOND MARRIAGES

Approximately four out of ten weddings are second marriages for one of the partners, and the majority of those people are divorced. Civil marriage is of course possible, but many couples would have a religious wedding if they could. The policy on re-marriage of divorcees is under welcome review in some religious institutions, while others already take a more accepting approach.

The Church of England do not 'officially' perform marriages of divorcees, but there is evidence of flexibility; the Catholic Church has strict rulings against divorce, but since it does not recognise some marriages, or may declare some 'annulled', there *are* second Catholic weddings; Church of Scotland and the Nonconformist churches will usually give favourable consideration to the marriage of divorcees; and divorce which is recognised under Jewish law can be followed by a second Jewish marriage. *See* **Types of ceremony** below for details. The natural alternative for many couples is to follow a civil marriage with a traditional or liberal religious blessing.

SAME-SEX PARTNERSHIPS

The government has announced that it is looking into the issues around civil partnership registration and the attached rights and responsibilities, which could include some recognition of same-sex relationships. Right now, while the state does not yet recognise same-sex marriage, many other organisations do, and they will enable you to publicly celebrate your commitment – and enjoy a full 'wedding' if you want to.

Almost all of the non-denominational blessings and non-legal ceremonies below are open to gay couples – it's just a question of finding the one that suits you. The Lesbian and Gay Christian Movement will help you to organise a religious blessing, and The Gay and Lesbian Humanists'

Association will help provide a secular ceremony. Independent ministers such as Bishop Jonathan Blake will also celebrate a same-sex 'marriage'.

It is also possible to give your partner some of the legal protection of marriage, such as in making out a will, and giving power of attorney under specific circumstances.

WHEN YOU HAVE CHILDREN OF YOUR OWN

Whether they are gaining a stepparent, or just seeing their own mum and dad marry each other, the number of children attending a parent's wedding is growing. Such parents will have their children foremost in their minds, so need no reminding of the importance of helping them understand, take part in, and enjoy what's happening. In addition, matters such as the children's names, inheritance and guardianship may need to be addressed.

The majority of institutions conducting marriage ceremonies have no prejudice whatsoever against children born out of wedlock – but neither do they have any procedures designed to *involve* them. If you have children or stepchildren, and you want to involve them (and they want to be involved), discuss it with the minister or registrar. Less orthodox and non-conventional

A family affair
Your own children are now the essential wedding ingredient, if these celebrity nuptials are anything to go by:

Madonna & Guy Ritchie *shared their wedding day with their son Rocco and her daughter Lourdes.*

Victoria Adams & David Beckham *brought son Brooklyn in on the mix'n'-match purple combos.*

Catherine Zeta-Jones & Michael Douglas *married with their baby Dylan close by, and the groom's son Cameron as best man.*

Keely Shaye Smith & Pierce Brosnan *celebrated with a total of five children between them, including their baby son, Paris.*

J.K. Rowling*'s daughter Jessica was bridesmaid at her mother's wedding to Dr Neil Murray.*

celebrants – such as humanists – may be the most helpful if you want to make your children an integral part of your ceremony. For the psychologists' views on children at their parents' weddings, *see* Chapter Sixteen.

Types of ceremony

These are just an outline: entire books could be written about each one of these wedding ceremonies. Further information can be obtained via the **Contacts** list at the end of this chapter.

CIVIL CEREMONY (ENGLAND AND WALES)

Legally recognised? Yes.

Conditions: Legal documentation and requirements as set out above.

Venue: Register office or approved civil marriage venue.

Preliminaries: Both of you must notify your local superintendent registrar in person at least 16 days and no more than a year before you plan to marry; if you live in separate districts, each of you needs to notify the registrar in your own district. You must have lived in your district for at least seven days immediately prior to registration. Notice of your intended marriage will be posted on a notice board at the register office, so that anyone who objects can do so. It's the civil equivalent to banns' reading. For marriage at an approved premises in a different registration district to the one where you live, you'll need first to notify your local registrar, *and* book the registrar for the approved premises. Your local registrar will later give you a certificate to pass on to the one who conducts your ceremony.

The wedding: Conducted by the superintendent registrar with the registrar present. You must bring with you two people to witness the marriage. The only requirement is to state the minimal legal wording, although many registrars have additional material that they add. If you do not want it, ask that it be left out. You must sign the register immediately afterwards.

Making it personal: Music, readings and additional personal vows, chosen by the couple, are allowed by law. They must be suitable, solemn, secular and agreed in advance by the registrar. Many registrars encourage or even contribute to your efforts to personalise the ceremony, and the room may be laid out with an aisle. The length of time allowed may be limited, particularly in a register office.

CHURCH OF ENGLAND AND CHURCH OF WALES

Legally recognised? Yes. The Churches of England and Wales are self-governing for the legal registration of marriage.

Conditions: Legal documentation and requirements as above. You do not have to be a baptised member of the church. Neither party may be divorced, under usual circumstances, but the parish priest has final discretion. If marriage is not possible, a service of blessing usually is (*see* below).

Venue: The church in the parish local to one of you *or* your place of usual worship. Occasionally, other *significant* connections (such as that it is the parish of your family home and the church is their usual place of worship, or you have temporary residence) may enable a minister to marry you in his/her church outside your parish. The Faculty Office governs such special permissions, in consultation with your minister; *see* **Contacts**.

Preliminaries: At the initial meeting with the minister, papers are completed to provide your personal details, and the wedding ceremony is explained in some detail. Banns will be read on three consecutive Sundays in your parish (or parishes of both parties if necessary) prior to the marriage, unless a Special Licence (if the church is outside your parish) or a Common Licence (for other special circumstances relating to nationality or residency) are necessary – your minister will advise you as to the best approach. You will usually be offered 'marriage preparation', which is not compulsory and designed to be helpful, and a wedding rehearsal.

The wedding: Taken only by an ordained Church of England minister. After the traditional entrance of the bride, on her father's right arm, and procession of choir, minister and wedding party, the ceremony begins with an introduction by the minister. As well as hymns, prayers, readings or Psalms, a sermon is usually given, together with the marriage itself and blessing of the rings. The couple goes to the vestry to sign the register, and finally exit in the bridal procession. The full wedding ceremony text and procedure is available from Church House Bookshop.

Making it personal: The wording of the ceremony is clearly prescribed, with only small variations permitted, such as the omission of the word 'obey'. Readings and hymns are ultimately the decision of the minister, who will always take the couple's wishes into account.

TRADITIONAL CHURCH BLESSING

Legally recognised? No. Must follow a civil ceremony.

Conditions: Where the church does not allow marriage, or you wish to renew your marriage vows, it may offer a blessing. Where you wish to marry in a special place outside of your parish, a blessing may provide the solution. There are no legal requirements.

Venue: Not restricted by law.

Preliminaries: Spiritual only.

The blessing: A traditional blessing, by the Church of England or Catholic Church, for instance, follows a set format and words. It includes vows, readings, hymns and can appear very similar to a wedding ceremony.

Making it personal: For most churches or celebrants, a blessing ceremony is as constrained (or unconstrained) by protocol as their wedding ceremony. Some sections may be included, or not, or a choice of wording given, depending on the couple's preferences.

ROMAN CATHOLIC CHURCH

Legally recognised? Yes. However, a registrar may need to attend the ceremony to validate it, depending on the church in question.

Conditions: As well as legal requirements, one of you must be baptised and confirmed in the Roman Catholic Church. The regulations regarding divorcees can be complicated, and depend on the form the first marriage took (religious or civil), and whether it would be recognised by the Catholic Church in the first place. If your first marriage is annulled by the Pope, a second Catholic wedding may take place.

Venue: Catholic church, normally in the parish of the bride if she is the Catholic, but can be outside the parish.

Preliminaries: Six months' notice must be given to the priest. Arrangements will be discussed, dispensation must be applied for if one of you is not

Catholic, and you will be invited to take part in some marriage preparation. Notice must be also given at a register office at least 16 days prior to the wedding.

The wedding: A Catholic priest or deacon conducts the ceremony according to the Rite of Marriage. It may be a Nuptial Mass, or a marriage ceremony without Mass and Holy Communion.

Making it personal: There is much set ritual and tradition. However, couples may be invited to express preferences as to whether there is to be Mass and Communion, how they enter the church, whether they face the congregation or the altar, and in the choice of readings, music and prayers.

NONCONFORMIST CHURCHES: METHODIST, RELIGIOUS SOCIETY OF FRIENDS (QUAKER), EPISCOPAL, BAPTIST, UNITED REFORMED, UNITED FREE AND UNITARIAN

Legally recognised? Yes. The minister may be authorised to register the marriage, and the building registered for the solemnisation of marriage. If they are not, the district registrar will need to attend the wedding itself.

Conditions: Amongst these churches are the more flexible, open ministers. Legal requirements obviously remain, but divorce is met with greater tolerance. Many welcome non-worshipping couples; others prefer church members.

Venue: Church anywhere in the county. Religious Society of Friends (Quaker), weddings may take place at the meeting house, or another chosen location.

Preliminaries: As well as a meeting with the minister to discuss preliminaries, you will be required to give formal notice of your marriage to the superintendent registrar of the district where you live, and follow the same procedures as for a civil ceremony/approved marriage premises.

The wedding: Usually a traditional church ceremony, with hymns, Psalms, vows, ring exchange and prayers, but often with a lesser degree of structure and formality. Quaker weddings are very informal, and the couple lead the ceremony themselves.

Making it personal: As long as the legal requirements are met, the couple is frequently encouraged to add personal words and prayers to the ceremony. The Unitarian Church, in particular, holds particular respect for a person's own understanding of religion. As such, it gives the couple great freedom to create a ceremony around their own beliefs.

JEWISH

Legally recognised? Yes.

Conditions: Standard legal requirements. Both parties must be Jewish. A liberal rabbi may bless a mixed faith couple after a civil ceremony. Marriage is allowed after divorce, but if the first marriage was under Jewish law, then the divorce must be granted under the same auspices.

Venue: The *chuppah* (wedding canopy) can go anywhere, but normally will be in a synagogue or, less usually, a hotel or private house.

Preliminaries: Legally you are required to give notice to the registrar's office in your district at least 16 days beforehand. Arrangements must be made with your own rabbi, and you must apply three or four months in advance to the Office of the Chief Rabbi to arrange an appointment to obtain authorisation for your marriage. Proof of your Jewish status and eligibility to marry must be provided. There are traditional preliminaries; marriage preparation and teaching is also given.

The wedding: A number of rituals make Jewish ceremonies particularly remarkable, of which these are just some: immediately before the ceremony, the groom may visit the bride for the *bedeken* or unveiling, when he checks to make sure he's marrying the right woman; the wedding ceremony itself takes place under the *chuppah*, a cloth canopy; first the bride, and sometimes the groom, 'circles' the *chuppah* three or seven times, followed by a series of customs, blessings and recitations, the groom's giving of a ring, and his 'smashing of the glass'. The register is then signed. Immediately after the ceremony is the *yichud*: ten minutes or so for the bride and groom to be alone.

Making it personal: Jewish law and custom must be respected, but personal choices may be accommodated.

ASIAN CEREMONIES (MUSLIM AND OTHERS SUCH AS HINDU)

Legally recognised? Sometimes recognised here, as long as the celebrant is authorised to register the marriage, and the wedding takes place in an authorised religious building. If not, the district registrar will need to attend the wedding itself, or a separate civil ceremony may be necessary.

Conditions: Normal civil legal requirements, plus the stipulations of the faith.

A Muslim man can marry a non-Muslim woman of certain other faiths, including Christianity, but a non-Muslim man must convert before a Muslim woman can marry him. An interfaith 'blessing' is usually only possible where the man is Muslim.

Venue: Muslim mosque or, for Hindus, a *mandap* (a wooden canopy, brightly decorated), or other location.

Preliminaries: As well as making preparations with the celebrant, you must follow formalities to notify the district registrar as for a civil marriage above. Many Asian weddings are preceded by betrothal ceremonies.

The wedding: The ceremony itself may be relatively short, but there can be three days or more of associated rituals and rites. As well as joining man and wife, the process bonds the two families together.

Making it personal: Not all celebrations include all the traditions. Abbreviated ceremonies have been developed.

Variations in Scotland and Northern Ireland

CIVIL

Legally recognised? Yes.

Conditions: Basic legal documentation and requirements as above.

Venue: Register office, and additional approved civil premises that are now operating in Scotland, and are anticipated in Northern Ireland soon. Currently, though, in Northern Ireland, you may only marry in the register office of your own district.

Preliminaries: In Scotland: both parties must submit marriage notice forms, fees and documentation to the registrar in the area where they plan to marry, at least 16 days and no more than three months before the wedding date. This can be done by post – you do not have to live in Scotland – but you will need to visit the registrar in person a few days before the wedding.

In Northern Ireland: currently, both parties must give notice in person in the district where they have been resident for the preceding seven days (for a certificate) or for the preceding 15 days (for a licence). Either the certificate is issued after a further 21 days, or the licence after seven more days; both are valid for three months. This system is likely to match the Scottish one soon.

The wedding: Conducted by a registrar. You must bring with you two people to witness the marriage. The only requirement is to state the minimal legal wording.

Making it personal: Music, readings and additional personal vows, chosen by the couple, are allowed. They must be suitable, solemn, secular and agreed in advance by the registrar. Many registrars encourage or even contribute to your efforts to personalise the ceremony. Check on restrictions as to length of ceremony, however.

CHURCH OF SCOTLAND AND OTHER CHURCHES IN SCOTLAND

Legally recognised? Yes.

Conditions: Standard legal documentation and requirements. Ministers are not obliged to marry divorcees, but they are free to do so if they wish.

Venue: Anywhere that the minister agrees to marry you, within certain limitations.

Preliminaries: Both parties must submit marriage notice forms, fees and documentation to the registrar in the area where they plan to marry at least 15 days and no more than three months before the wedding date. This can be done by post, and you do not have to live in Scotland, but a marriage schedule will be issued only in person up to seven days before the marriage ceremony, to which it must be taken.

The wedding: A traditional church ceremony. Although the Church of Scotland has a similar role to the Church of England, the style of worship is more akin to the Nonconformist churches. The Marriage Schedule must be signed by the couple, minister and witnesses, then returned to the registrar within three days.

Making it personal: As in England and Wales, some encourage input from the couple more than others, but the Scottish churches tend to be among those most open to personal words and vows.

CHURCHES IN NORTHERN IRELAND

Legally recognised? Yes.

Conditions: Legal restrictions and documentation as above. Additional rules and procedures are varied and complicated, but the system should be simplified and become similar to the Scottish system following new legislation plans.

Venue: Currently, some churches have a limited freedom to conduct marriages in venues other than a church. The ceremony may be required to take place in the parish or diocese where at least one party is resident.

Preliminaries: Place and time of notice depends on the church; discuss with the minister.

The wedding: Dependent upon the religion.

Making it personal: As in England and Wales, some encourage input from the couple more than others.

Alternative, personal or other non-legal ceremonies

BUDDHIST

Legally recognised? Only very occasionally. Otherwise must follow a civil ceremony.

Conditions: None. Buddhists generally regard weddings as secular affairs, so there is no formal wedding procedure. The Buddhist part of the ceremony is usually one of blessing and open to the many Western people who practice Buddhism.

Venue: To be legal, it must take place at a temple licensed for marriages such as the London Buddhist Vihara (*see* **Contacts**). A blessing may take place anywhere suitable.

Preliminaries: Traditionally, a marriage broker would introduce the two families. Civil preliminaries are required for a legal marriage.

The blessing: Bride and groom separately ask for the blessings of Buddha earlier on the wedding day, and the ceremony follows later with chanting, recitations, candles, incense and the offering of flowers to Buddha. Rings can be exchanged and vows spoken.

Making it personal: Each ceremony can be a different assembly of varied rituals, and the couple are not bound by specific rules, only a respect for Buddhist beliefs.

HUMANIST

Legally recognised? No. It's usual to follow a register office civil ceremony. Alternatively, you may be able to arrange for the humanist ceremony to take place at an approved marriage premises, immediately following the civil part of the ceremony. In this way, the richness of a personal ceremony can be combined seamlessly with the significance of the legal commitment, before all your guests. Your celebrant will guide you in liaising with the registrar.

Conditions: None. Humanism is a set of non-religious beliefs, ideals and values, to which most of us instinctively subscribe. You do not have to be a member of the Humanist Association to have a humanist ceremony, and can celebrate your commitment to someone in this way whatever your circumstances or gender.

Venue: Any that's appropriate, barring practical limitations. Evenings, outdoors, the riverside, and your home are all possible.

Preliminaries: Preparation of the structure and content over a period of weeks or months, guided by an experienced humanist celebrant.

The ceremony: The ceremony is serious and sincere, but warm and informal, and entirely flexible. Many involve traditional elements, such as an aisle, a procession, music, vows and reading, and are led, with a degree of structure and formality, by the celebrant. You may sign a wedding book in lieu of a register. However, since each couple starts with a blank sheet of paper, some ceremonies are quite different! Full information is given in the book *Sharing the Future* by Jane Wynne Willson, from The British Humanist Association.

Making it personal: There are no restrictions. So if you have any original ideas, from where your guests sit and who takes part, to the words you say or a 'ritual' you might have in mind, then your celebrant will help you make them a success. The content should be secular, but the rules against religious influences are less strict than for a civil marriage ceremony.

HANDFASTING

Legally recognised: No. Civil ceremony also required.
Conditions: None.
Venue: Anywhere, anytime. Outdoor locations are often chosen.
Preliminaries: To prepare the ceremony itself.

The ceremony: Conducted by a lay person, priest or priestess, the 'wedding' is not standardised. Adapted from pagan marriages throughout history and now adopted for modern use by a New Age following, it's simply an ancient form of marriage or betrothal ceremony that may include the exchange of rings, vows, prayers and handfasting itself: the hands are tied together with gold, silver and green cords, to symbolise the union, then untied to show that they remain together of their own free will. 'Jumping the broomstick' is also an ancient symbol of commitment.

Making it personal: The traditions are entirely open to personal interpretation.

VOW-EXCHANGE

Legally recognised? No. Civil ceremony would be required. *See* Humanist above.

Conditions: None whatsoever. This ceremony is only about you and your understanding of marriage. There are no principles or beliefs from outside parties involved.

Venue: Anywhere, anytime.

Preliminaries: To prepare your own personal ceremony with the help and guidance of an experienced celebrant.

The ceremony: With traditional structure and a blend of whichever elements, secular or otherwise, you feel is right for you. Celebrants can lead for you, or show you how to lead the ceremony as a couple.

Making it personal: No restrictions. You can mix personal, secular and religious elements.

NON-DENOMINATIONAL/INDEPENDENT RELIGIOUS CEREMONY

Legally recognised? Usually not, unless special arrangements are made for a ceremony in some churches. More commonly follows a civil ceremony: *see* Humanist above.

Conditions: None, besides a basic harmony on the ideals and principles at stake.

Venue: Anywhere, anytime.

Preliminaries: To prepare a religious-based ceremony with the independent minister, outside of any denominational or established procedure or expectation.

The ceremony: Normally structured loosely around the tradition of aisle, vows, prayers and readings, but incorporating as little or as much of the formal marriage ceremony as you wish. The ceremony may combine two or more faiths, involve same-sex couples, can be shared between two ministers, and be rich with rite and ritual. At the other end of the scale, there may be no mention of God by name at all, with spirituality introduced through other language, and it may be quite unlike other weddings.

Making it personal: As you wish.

Wacky weddings

Bungee jumping, the Internet, underwater, skydiving – we've all heard about such 'weddings', when in this country, they are in fact only vow-exchanges. If you want one, you just need to find a willing celebrant: many of the contacts listed below for non-conventional ceremonies are open to new requests.

Overseas, it's quite different: in countries where the power to marry is vested solely in the minister (and not the location), a legal marriage can be anywhere that she/he is prepared to go.

Photos, flowers, confetti and videos

Ask your minister or celebrant for guidelines and any restrictions – and let them know about any unusual dress code, too, such as black tie or theatrical dress.

CAN WE ELOPE?

Not here, at least not in the true sense of the word – not even to Gretna Green. Locations like Las Vegas, with its 24-hour marriage office and no pre-marriage waiting laws, are the place to go for right here, right now weddings.

MAKING IT LEGAL, WORLDWIDE

Most countries welcome couples for weddings, but others make a legal ceremony almost impossible for 'tourists'. Long residency qualifications, or systems of bureaucracy which might defeat even the most determined, can make a blessing a better bet. Despite being our geographical and economic partner, Europe can be the worst for this: countries like France and Spain require at least one of you to have been living there for many weeks to qualify, making it virtually impossible for most.

There are, however, European countries that are more embracing of their romantic guests: places like Italy, Finland and Greece have manageably short residency qualifications – and wonderfully romantic settings. The easiest places to negotiate may be further afield, and include the myriad beach locations in places like the Caribbean or Mauritius.

As in the UK, a variety of ceremonies may be possible at your overseas destination, but if you're having a religious ceremony it's doubly important to check that the marriage can take place: restrictions are complicated.

Paperwork and residency qualifications

If you're planning to marry overseas, there is absolutely no substitute for getting (and double-checking) the most up-to-date legal and residency stipulations directly from your wedding consultant, travel agency or appropriate government office (either from the British Consul in your chosen place of marriage, or from that country's embassy in the UK). Bear in mind that some countries have regulations that apply to the whole country, while others – like Greece and the USA – have local or regional laws. The golden rule is to check, check and check again. Do it before you plan your wedding, and again well before you leave this country to get married.

Will our marriage count once we get back home?

Yes, as long as you precisely follow the regulations of the country where you marry. If the marriage is legal where it took place, then it's valid at home, too.

The marriage that wasn't

*Mick Jagger seemed a bit smug when his Bali wedding to **Jerry Hall** turned out to be legally invalid. They simply hadn't got the paperwork sorted properly. Happily, she still managed to take good care of herself in the 'divorce'.*

You cannot subsequently register the marriage in the UK, but you can lodge the original marriage certificate with the General Registrar here, so that certified copies can be issued as needed.

Documents for an overseas wedding

Basic documentation usually required for any wedding:
- Birth certificates.
- Adoption certificates, if relevant.
- Ten-year passports valid for six months beyond your return date.
- Death certificate of a former spouse, if relevant.
- Decrees absolute of any former marriage ending in divorce.
- Certificate of Baptism for a church wedding.
- Certificate of Confirmation for a Roman Catholic wedding.
- Deed poll for any name change, including brides who have reverted back to their maiden name after a first marriage.
- Proof of address.

You may well also need:
- Return tickets to your home country.
- Single status affidavit or certificate of non-impediment.
- Signed witnessed passport photographs (check how these should be: Bali, for instance, wants 10, with both bride and groom in the same picture, and the groom on the right-hand side of the bride as you look at the picture!).
- Consent of parents or guardians if you are under 25.
- Evidence of your state of health, immunisations or other medical requirements.
- Certificate of former marriage, to show in conjunction with death certificate or decree absolute.
- For a religious wedding, statements from your parish priest to confirm, for instance: that you have undergone marriage preparation; that he/she requests the overseas celebrant to officiate over the wedding; that you are both of the same denomination.
- Documents which detail the names, dates of birth, addresses and occupations of your parents.

Paperwork

'I got really very stressed about the paperwork for our wedding in Greece. I was liaising directly with the mayor's office there, and every time I did a final check, they'd say "Oh, and you need this, too." There seemed to be every chance they'd think of something else when it was too late, and the wedding wouldn't happen. But it was fine on the day, of course!' Bride, 28.

Also note that:
- Many countries require notarised translations of documentation, certified by the appropriate authorities.
- In most cases, you can – and should – submit paperwork by post or in person to the appropriate authority well in advance of your trip (but not too early, *see* below). Three months is usually about right.
- Documents which have been prepared specially (such as a certificate of non-impediment) should be less than three months old.
- Final preparations and paperwork will also be required upon arrival.
- Some countries require both parties to be 21.
- Any inconsistencies within your documents could cause problems: check that all spellings, names, dates, etc are identical.

Country by country

It's impossible to create an up-to-date and exhaustive list; the following chart should serve as an indication *only*. Residency stipulations, local notification and waiting requirements, or just the time it takes to deal with basic practicalities, may dictate how long you will have to be in a country in order to marry there – even if you've organised everything you can from home beforehand. It goes without saying that giving a relative's address to try to pass yourself off as a resident won't work. You may be able to speed things up, but err on the side of caution. 'Further complications' means additional documentation or procedures can be involved – some might be enough to drive you crazy! Check them out, get professional assistance if in doubt, and consider a blessing or vow-exchange instead if the obstacles seem insurmountable.

Country	How long will we need to be there to get married?	Any further possible complications?
Antigua/Barbuda	Four working days	Possibly: allow plenty of time for arrangements.
Australia	Three working days	
Austria	Two working days	
Bahamas	Two working days	A 15-day residency requirement can be waived by completing an application on arrival.
Bali	Seven working days	You must visit the British Consulate on arrival before the wedding ceremony; considerable paperwork. Men must be 23; women 21. Specialist/travel agent help is advisable.
Barbados	Two working days	
Bermuda	Four working days	
British Virgin Islands	Four working days	You must both be 21.
Canada	Two working days	
Cuba	Three working days	
Cyprus	Six working days	
Czech Republic	Six working days	
Dubai	Four working days	
Dominican Republic	Six working days	
Eire	Up to four weeks	
Fiji	Five working days	You must both be 21.
Finland/Lapland	Two working days	Complete papers from the Helsinki Registry Office before your wedding.
Florida	Three working days	
France	Six weeks	
Germany	Two to three weeks	
Greece	Up to eight working days; varies between islands	Yes, procedures can be more complicated. Specialist advice is advisable.
Hawaii	Two working days	
Iceland	Two working days	

Country	How long?	Any further possible complications?
India	One month	It can be a complicated process.
Italy	Seven working days	Allow time for local translations and procedures.
Jamaica	Four working days	
Kenya	Four working days	
Las Vegas	One working day	
Malaysia/Penang	Eight working days	Possibly, if you are under 21.
Malta	Two working days	Yes: allow time for local procedures.
Mauritius	Three working days	A religious wedding may require over two weeks' residency. Recently divorced women need a local certificate of non-pregnancy.
Mexico	Six working days	Local blood test required.
Netherlands	Six months	Only citizens can marry there.
New Zealand	Three working days	
Seychelles	Four working days	
Ship at port	As for the country of port	
South Africa	One working day	
Spain	Three weeks	
Sri Lanka	Six working days	You must both be 21.
St Kitts	Four working days	
St Lucia	Four working days	
Sweden	Two working days	Paperwork can be tricky.
Switzerland	Up to five weeks	
Tanzania	One working day	
Thailand	Six working days	Certificate of non-pregnancy required for recently divorced women; legalities at the British Embassy and District Registrar's office must precede the wedding. Professional advice is advisable. Must both be 21.
Turkey	Two working days	
US	Up to six working days	Some states require blood tests.
Zanzibar	Five working days	Must both be 21.

Money-wise: What to expect

IN THE UK

Civil ceremony: from £100, up to about £200+ at an approved premises

Church of England ceremony: about £15 for banns' reading in each parish, £142 for the marriage service, and additional costs for the organist, choir and other 'extras'

Church of England Special Licence: £120

Church of England Common Licence: £55

Other churches: about £200 excluding music and extras

Humanist ceremony: about £150

OVERSEAS

Package ceremony: £0 to £1000+

Contacts

CIVIL REGISTRATION AND TRADITIONAL RELIGIOUS CONTACTS

Baptist Union of Great Britain: 01235 517700; www.baptist.org.uk

Catholic Marriage Care and Advisory Council: 0207 371 1341; www.marriagecare.org.uk

Church House Bookshop: 020 7898 1300; www.chbookshop.co.uk

Church of England Faculty Office: 020 7222 5381; www.facultyoffice.org.uk

Church of Scotland: 0131 225 5722; www.churchofscotland.org.uk

Episcopal Church of Scotland: 0131 225 6357; www.scottishepiscopal.com

General Assembly of Unitarian and Free Christian Churches: 020 7240 2384; www.unitarian.org.uk

General Register Office for Northern Ireland: 02890 252036; www.groni.gov.uk

General Register Office for Scotland: 0131 334 0380; www.gro-scotland.gov.uk

General Synod of The Church of England: 020 7898 1000; www.cofe.anglican.org

Hindu Society: 0208 534 8879; www.hindunet.org; www.hinduweb.org

Jewish Marriage Council: 0208 203 6311; www.jmc-uk.org

Methodist Church Headquarters: 0207 486 5502; www.methodist.org.uk

Muslim Information Centre: 020 7272 5170
Muslim Law (Shariah) Council: 020 8992 6636
Office of the Chief Rabbi: 020 8343 6314; www.chiefrabbi.org
Religious Society of Friends: 020 7663 1000; www.quaker.org.uk
Registrar General for England & Wales: 0151 471 4803;
    www.statistics.gov.uk
United Reformed Church: 020 7916 2020; www.urc.org.uk

LIBERAL, VOW-EXCHANGE OR ALTERNATIVE CONTACTS
Alternative Occasions Personalised Ceremonies: 01932 872115;
    www.alternative-occasions.co.uk
Bishop Jonathan Blake: 020 8303 0461; www.bishopjonathanblake.com
British Humanist Association: 020 7430 0908; www.humanism.org.uk
Buddhist Society: 020 7834 5858; www.thebuddhistsociety.org.uk
Gay and Lesbian Humanist Association: 01926 858450; www.galha.org
Lesbian & Gay Christian Movement: 020 7739 1249; www.lgcm.org.uk
London Buddhist Vihara: 020 8995 9493; www.londonbuddhistvihara.co.uk
Pagan Federation: BM Box 7097, London WC1N 3XX;
    www.paganfed.demon.co.uk
Rabbi Guy Hall: 020 8343 0069

chapter
nine

from the heart:
readings, music, vows

Everyone loves a good cry – and no more so than at a wedding. Besides all the emotional tension that's built up over the months of preparation, they're a wonderful, happy way to focus on the things that really matter in love and life. Music, readings and personally worded vows really make the most of that.

THE RULES AND LIMITATIONS

For a civil ceremony, everything must be secular. Even music without words must have no religious connotation; no mention of the divine or heavenly is allowed, and even words like 'spirit' or 'soul' will be scrutinised. Certain contractual and declaratory words must be said, (*see* Chapter Eight), but you may also make promises and have readings of your own, as long as they're solemn, appropriate and dignified, and agreed well in advance with the registrar. Some will limit you to their list of personal or 'ring exchange' vows and readings. While you are not restricted to such a list by national legislation, the final veto is with the registrar, so a diplomatic approach is most likely to get the desired result if you want something 'off menu'. The duration of the ceremony may be limited.

For a traditional religious ceremony, religious words and music are most commonly used. The marriage ceremony and vows in the Catholic Church or Church of England are almost entirely fixed, with minor variations permitted. Even a non-legal blessing follows a set path. More open are Methodists, Baptists, Quakers and other Nonconformist ceremonies: while (as for a civil ceremony) certain legal words must be said, some encourage you to prepare additional personal words, especially the Unitarian Church. Some ministers may permit a contemporary reading or poem.

Once more with feeling

'It helped that I'd been planning my wedding for, well, most of my life! Every book and poem I'd ever read, every film I'd seen, every ceremony I'd ever been to, I'd been clocking the real tear-jerkers and stashing them away till I needed them.' Bride, 34.

Church blessing

'Our church blessing was full of tradition and very moving. The reading we wanted turned out to be Hindu, so we couldn't have it, but the alternative, "Footprints in the Sand", was very special.' Bride, 28.

Humanist wedding

'We choose a leafy dell for our ceremony, which was to combine our wedding with the naming of our four-month-old baby. The three of us went down the hill together, followed by a jazz band, to the clearing in the trees where all our friends and family were waiting. We'd planned that people would sit down, but everyone instinctively gathered round us in a group as the wedding began. We'd spent weeks writing the words and vows for ourselves and for our baby boy (with the help of the celebrant), but it was worth it. As we said them, it all felt exactly right.' Bride, 24.

From the expert: Combining civil and spiritual ceremonies
Bishop Jonathan Blake

'There's nothing in the law that says that a civil ceremony in a licensed premises cannot occasionally be followed by a spiritual, or even religious celebration. Once the registrar has left the building, the strictly secular rule no longer applies. There may be some resistance, but it is not actually forbidden.'

For a non-legal ceremony, such as a vow-exchange, 'alternative' religious ceremony or humanist celebration, you are free to compose the ceremony virtually from scratch. Classic wedding structure and ritual can provide a good 'framework' on which to build, but ultimately the choices are all yours to make: whether to have an aisle, whether you enter the room together or the bride is 'given away', definition of marriage, vows, hymns, music, and more. There will be no legal vetting, and you'll have all the time you want.

Overseas, there is generally some scope for creating a legal wedding with your own content. The US, in particular, makes much of vow-writing. Check with the registrar, minister or travel agent.

Copyright should not usually be an issue, but if you photocopy sheet music, print lyrics or prose in a service sheet, or rearrange a piece of music, it's best to seek permission from the Music Publishers Association or MCPS/PRS Alliance (*see* **Contacts** on page 128).

MUSIC

What you may need

- **Prelude:** Music to play as guests arrive
- **Processional:** Music for the arrival of the bride or couple
- **Hymns:** Three, usually, during a church service
- **Music for signing of the register**
- **Recessional:** Music for the exit of the bridal party

Where to find inspiration

Classical and religious music are the norm for a traditional wedding, but they're not obligatory, and a civil wedding often calls for something more contemporary. Live music is best but a good PA system will suffice.

- How about a gospel choir? They're both fun and stirring, the perfect combination.
- If you'd like to be a little more *au fait* with classical music before you choose, turn your dial to Classic FM or Radio 3 for a couple of weeks. Operas and arias are often stirring. Invest in a couple of compilation albums.
- Jazz and swing also make great wedding music, especially for an exit: think Louis Armstrong, Frank Sinatra and Harry Connick Jr.
- Invest in a specially compiled CD, to save legwork while you choose. There are many to choose from:
  - WMC Records' three CDs of inspiring wedding music: *Love Divine*, for church weddings, *The Power and The Glory*, a guide to organ music, and *Music for a Civil Wedding*. The basics – like 'Arrival of the Queen of Sheba' and 'Ave Maria' – are covered, but offbeat tracks stretch as far as the Monty Python theme tune! From WMC Records.
  - *The Ultimate Guide to Wedding Music* is a compilation of 70 music snippets, together with a helpful booklet. From Cherry Street Productions.
  - *How to Choose Your Wedding Music* from New World Music.
- Film scores can be a great source of wedding-friendly music, as they're deliberately written to rouse the soul (and the audience) and heighten big moments.
- Don't forget the Internet and MP3 for hearing or downloading tracks: MP3.com and Amazon.com are just two of many sources.
- Kitsch classics are great for a fun entrance: Elvis Presley's 'Can't Help Falling In Love' or Abba's 'I Do I Do I Do I Do' will set the tone instantly.
- Exits of equal wit include The Beatles' 'When I'm Sixty-Four' and 'Bring Me Sunshine', the legendary Morecambe and Wise Show theme song.
- Handle the pop song with care; it can be corny!

Contacts are at the end of the chapter. For live music contacts, *see* Chapter Eleven.

From the experts: Choosing music
Andrew Truslove, WMC Records

'Music is such a vital part of the ceremony, it's madness to leave it till last. Once you have a shortlist, take a portable stereo to the venue and play each candidate piece in situ. And, since the walk down the aisle is far shorter than most pieces of music, let it play for a few minutes before you go in, so you reach the top of the aisle as the music finishes. It makes for a better entrance.'

The wedding classics
You know them when you hear them; with the name and composer you can ask for them instead of humming! Processional and recessional classics often serve well for either. Websites like WMC Records/CDs For Life, Wedding Guide UK and Wedding Globe sample online. If the popular ones below give you the wrong kind of shivers down your spine, they're the ones to avoid!

PROCESSIONAL

'Wedding March'	Wagner (as in, 'Here Comes the Bride')
'Wedding March'	Mozart (from *The Marriage of Figaro*)
'Grand March'	Verdi (from *Aida*)

SIGNING THE REGISTER

'Ave Maria'	Schubert
'Jesu, Joy of Man's Desiring'	Bach

RECESSIONAL

'Trumpet Vountary'	Jeremiah Clarke
'Wedding March'	Mendelssohn (from *A Midsummer Night's Dream*)
'Arrival of the Queen of Sheba'	Handel

Hymns we love

There's nothing like a good rousing hymn: it's the ones you all remember from school that get everyone singing with gusto!

'Love Divine, All Loves Excelling'
'Praise My Soul the King of Heaven'
'Guide Me, O Thou Great Redeemer'
'O Jesus I Have Promised'
'All Things Bright and Beautiful'
'Bread of Heaven'
'We Plough the Fields and Scatter'
'Lead Us Heavenly Father Lead Us'
'Give Me Joy in My Heart'
'Lord of All Hopefulness'
'Morning Has Broken'

Choir, organist and bell-ringers

These don't necessarily come as part of the church package. Make arrangements and discuss with the minister in good time, organising outside musicians if necessary.

21st-century dilemma: Giving the bride away

A special moment with your dad, or downright insulting? The tradition of handing over a woman from one man's ownership to another's was undoubtedly sexist, but so were the times. Now, it's a gesture of love and support, so if it's what you want, don't worry too much about times past. Alternatively, the bride could enter with both parents, or with anyone else special or important, and begin the ceremony without being 'given away', if she prefers. Some brides walk in with their mother, or hold the hands of their own children. Most contemporary is for the bride and groom to arrive together, or for the (confident!) bride to walk up the aisle alone.

A different kind of entrance
Lisa Kudrow walked down the aisle on the arms of both her mother and her father, without a bouquet. When they reached the top, all of her close friends each brought her a single flower. Her parents bound them into a bouquet and then handed them back to her, ready for the ceremony to begin.

WRITING WORDS AND VOWS

If you distil it down to its core, the vows *are* the wedding. And after the wedding, the vows *are* the marriage. In fact the word 'wed' is simply Anglo-Saxon for 'vow'. So much is from the heart, most couples (even the ones who struggle with words) find writing their vows surprisingly easy. Once they think about what they want to say, the words almost write themselves:

- The 'classic' wedding vows have a wonderful pattern and rhythm. Don't copy all the words, but be inspired by the lyricism and repetition: 'To have and to hold, from this day forward; for better, for worse, for richer, for poorer, in sickness and in health; to love and to cherish, till death us do part ...'
- Use pretty language and emotive words: these are personal promises, not an official document.
- Don't feel obliged to make promises you don't believe in. You may feel a vow to love until death is not yours to make, because you do not have that much control over the future. Promise action rather than feeling.
- Only include the parts that you want: keep everything short and to the point – it'll be much more powerful.
- If you have children of your own, you may wish to refer to them, the part they play in your lives, include them in your promises or ask them to speak if they want to.
- Even if you decide to speak without prompting, have your words written down on cards, and give a copy to the celebrant.
- If you prefer not to do too much of the talking, but have much that you want to say, the celebrant can turn all your words into a question, 'Will you promise to ...' to which all you need say is: 'I will.'

- Remember that there's a fine line between cheesy and romantic! Keep really private or schmaltzy stuff for when you're alone.
- If the ceremony is a legal one, ensure that you're staying within regulations.

Once you have the general content, structure what you want to say into the following sections:

- **What marriage means:** A natural start to the ceremony, after welcoming all the guests, is to express your feelings on why you're there. This is often done by the celebrant, but can be shared with the couple, or done by them alone. In a legal ceremony, the formal definition of marriage will have to be put, but you may be free to add your own thoughts, such as: What is marriage to you? Why are you getting married? What do you want from it?
- **Promises to each other:** As well as the promise each makes to take the other as their husband/wife, this could be about your intentions for your marriage. What aspects of your relationship make it good, and are worth continuing? What will each of you do to keep your marriage strong? Honour, share, trust, value, respect, love, support, adore, amuse, laugh, cherish, be honest, kind, faithful, considerate? Instead of repeating the word 'promise', you could 'vow', 'seek', 'pledge', 'try', 'swear'.
- **Ring exchange:** If you choose to exchange rings, what do they symbolise to you? Permanence, commitment, eternity, oneness, a public statement, the hope for children? An alternative to exchanging rings is to light candles for each other.
- **Declaration:** Normally done by the celebrant, this is the announcement that you are now husband and wife.

Shocking!

*The traditional route can be most provocative of all: press reports reveal that the **Hon. Jaqueline Hamilton-Smith**, celebrity make-up artist, chose to 'obey' actor **Sean Pertwee** in front of all their rock- and film-world guests, because, 'Everyone was so shocked when I mentioned it!' Her ushers, in a scant version of classic grey morning dress, were **Kate Moss** and **Sadie Frost**.*

READINGS

Two or three is the norm; keep them short if you have more. It's customary for a close friend or relation to direct them at the whole congregation, but some couples are choosing to do readings themselves – and to direct them at each other. Shakespeare (mostly with Sonnet 116, 'Let me not to the marriage of true minds …' or Sonnet 18, 'Shall I compare thee to a summer's day? …') and the Bible have a bit of a monopoly on weddings (and deservedly so). But beyond there are many other wonderful works of poetry, song and prose …

Start searching

WHERE SOMEONE ELSE HAS DONE THE WORK:

- Wedding Guide UK: A great online source of poetry and prose, especially under 'Love poems, readings and quotations'.
- Confetti: Their book, *Wedding Readings*, is published by Conran Octopus, and there's a good online source, too.
- *Sharing the Future*: The British Humanist Association has rounded up some of the best in this book. (Buy direct, *see* page 112.)
- Service sheets from other weddings. Ask friends to help in rounding them up: readings (as well as music and prayers) might even be printed in full if you're lucky.

THE SATISFACTION OF FINDING YOUR OWN:

- Dictionaries of quotations: Key words like 'love' or 'wed' should lead you in the right direction.
- Quotation Central: Although paid for, this is a fresh source of online quotations if you've exhausted all the dictionaries.
- Presence in Poetry: Yvonne Marie Wright will write a poem especially for the occasion, based on personal information.
- Modern prose: Novels, autobiographies, even newspapers can deliver some gems. The search can be long (the readings below will save you time), but the tone should be particularly relevant and contemporary.
- *The Nation's Favourite Love Poems*, edited by Daisy Goodwin (BBC Consumer Publishing), will get you in the mood as well as delivering the goods.

- Song words, whether from modern or traditional songs, can be especially meaningful – or quite funny. Again, beware the pop song: used wisely, it can be wonderful; used badly, everyone will cringe.
- The Bible holds all the religious classics, such as the *First Epistle to the Corinthians*, Chapter 13: 'Love is patient, love is kind. It does not envy, it does not boast … And now these three remain: faith, hope and love. But the greatest of these is love.' Bible Gateway is an online Bible which makes searching much easier.
- Look for religious poems and passages in books and on the Internet, where you'll find such gems as Margaret Fishback Powers' 'Footprints in the Sand', which ends: '… I love you and I would never leave you. During your times of trial and suffering, when you see only one set of footprints, it was then that I carried you.'

Or choose one of these …

CONTEMPORARY NOVELS:

- From *Captain Corelli's Mandolin* by Louis de Bernières: 'Love is a temporary madness, it erupts like volcanoes and then subsides. And when it subsides you have to make a decision. You have to work out whether your roots have so entwined together that it is inconceivable that you should ever part. Because this is what love is. Love is not breathlessness, it is not excitement, it is not the promulgation of promises of eternal passion … That is just being "in love", which any fool can do. Love itself is what is left over when being in love has burned away, and this is both an art and a fortunate accident. Your mother and I had it, we had roots that grew towards each other underground, and when all the pretty blossom had fallen from our branches we found that we were one tree and not two.'
- From *Like Water for Chocolate* by Laura Esquivel: 'Let me tell you something I've never told a soul. My grandmother had a very interesting theory; she said each of us is born with a box of matches inside us but we can't strike them all by ourselves … we need oxygen and a candle to help … In this case, the oxygen … would come from the breath of the person you love; the candle could be any kind of food, music, caress,

word or sound that engenders the explosion that lights one of the matches. For a moment we are dazzled by an intense emotion. A pleasant warmth grows within us, fading slowly as time goes by, until a new explosion comes along to revive it. Each person has to discover [who] will set off those explosions in order to live, since the combustion that occurs when one of them is ignited is what nourishes the soul. If one doesn't find out [who] will set off these explosions, the box of matches dampens, and not a single match will ever be lit.'

- From *On Green Dolphin Street* by Sebastian Faulks: 'What does it mean to love …? It means that at some point you give up the idea of yourself as a person capable of infinite expansion. It means that if an impossible choice is to be made between his life and yours, you choose his. And it means that you cannot repine for this hard moment, because he is grafted on to you; that what you do for him you do also for yourself and for some separate entity that is greater than the sum of both, because the dangerous enterprise of your joined life is more dramatic, more arresting and more exciting than any alternative could ever be.'

ROMANTIC POEMS:
- 'Love's Philosophy' by Percy Bysshe Shelley
  The fountains mingle with the river
  And the rivers with the Ocean,
  The winds of Heaven mix for ever
  With a sweet emotion;
  Nothing in the world is single;
  All things, by a law divine
  In one spirit meet and mingle.
  Why not I with thine?—

  See the mountains kiss high Heaven
  And the waves clasp one another;
  No sister-flower would be forgiven
  If it disdained its brother;

And the sunlight clasps the earth
And the moonbeams kiss the sea:
What is all this sweet work worth
If thou kiss not me?

● 'Sonnet from the Portuguese XLIII' by Elizabeth Barrett Browning
How do I love thee? Let me count the ways.
I love thee to the depth and breadth and height
My soul can reach, when feeling out of sight
For the ends of Being and ideal Grace
I love thee to the level of every day's
Most quiet need, by sun and candlelight.
I love thee freely, as men strive for Right;
I love thee purely, as they turn from Praise.
I love thee with the passion put to use
In my old griefs, and with my childhood's faith.
I love thee with a love I seemed to lose
With my lost saints—I love thee with the breath,
Smiles, tears, of all my life!—and, if God choose,
I shall but love thee better after death.

OFFBEAT:

● From *The Way of the World* by William Congreve: (This made a charming and humorous 'retort' at the wedding of a close friend who was marrying a reformed commitment-phobic after sixteen years of courtship! For my friends, it was a funny acknowledgement that the proposal had been a long time coming ...)

'I'll never marry, unless I am first made sure of my will and pleasure ... My dear liberty, shall I leave thee? My faithful solitude, my darling contemplation, must I bid you then adieu?... I can't do't, 'tis more than impossible ... I won't be called names after I'm married ... Ay, as wife, spouse, my dear, joy, jewel, love, sweetheart and the rest of that nauseous cant in which men and their wives are so fulsomely familiar—I shall never bear that ... don't let us be familiar or fond, nor kiss before folks ... Let us be as strange as if we had been married a great while, and as well-bred as if we were not married at all ... more conditions ... liberty to pay and receive visits to and from whom I please ... without interrogatories or wry faces on your part. To wear what I please ... Come to dinner when I please, dine in my dressing-room when I'm out of humour, without giving a reason ... to be sole empress of my tea-table, which you must never presume to approach without first asking leave. And lastly, wherever I am, you shall always knock at the door before you come in. These articles subscribed, if I continue to endure you a little longer, I may by degrees [agree to be your] wife.'

PUT IT ALL TOGETHER: SERVICE SHEETS

Service sheets aren't vital if you're on a budget, but they help to involve guests and provide a worthwhile keepsake. The format for an order of service sheet will depend on the ceremony you will have, so discuss it with the celebrant, but an outline will be:

Religious ceremony

(Cover)

The marriage of
Clare Mary Bride and Adam Groom
Venue
Date

(Inside)

The arrival of the bride
(music title and composer)

Introduction and welcome

(name of minister)

Hymn (name, composer and words)

The Marriage

The Anthem
(name of choir)

Blessing of the rings

Hymn (name, composer and words)

Reading
(title of text/first line of extract and name of reader)

Reading
(title of text/first line of extract and name of reader)

The Address

Hymn (name, composer and words)

The Prayers

The Lord's Prayer

The signing of the register
(music, composer, performer)

The Blessing

Recessional
(music title and composer)

Non-religious ceremony

(Cover)

The marriage of
Clare Mary Bride and Adam Groom
Venue
Date

(Inside)

The arrival of the bride
(music title and composer)

Introduction and welcome
(name of celebrant)

Reading
(title of text/first line of extract and name of reader)

The Ceremony

Reading
(title of text/first line of extract and name of reader)

The exchange of rings

The signing of the register
(music, composer, performer)

Recessional
(music title and composer)

Order of the day

For a less traditional wedding, you could extend the order of service to another page to include details of the entire day or weekend. Specify times for a drinks' reception, a photocall for all guests, the speeches, dancing, cabs or buses home, and perhaps a time and venue for brunch or lunch the next day. As weddings become more complicated and unpredictable, people really appreciate knowing where they are and what to expect.

Contacts

PERSONALISED CEREMONIES AND VOW-WRITING
See **Contacts** *on page 112.*

OTHER
Amazon.com: www.amazon.com
Bible Gateway: www.biblegateway.com
Cherry Street Productions: 01926 497078
Confetti: www.confetti.co.uk
MCPS/PRS Alliance: 020 7580 5544; www.mcps-prs-alliance.co.uk
MP3.com: www.mp3.com
Music Publishers Association: 020 7839 7779; www.mpaonline.org.uk
New World Music: 01986 781682; www.newworldmusic.com
Presence in Poetry: 020 8402 1374; www.presence-in-poetry.co.uk
Quotation Central: www.quotations.com
Wedding Globe: www.weddingglobe.com
Wedding Guide UK: www.weddingguide.co.uk
WMC Records: 020 8314 1273; www.cdsforlife.co.uk

section
four
it's *your* party

Style, food, drink and entertainment
for the best party you'll ever throw

chapter ten

the wedding look

Until not so long ago, The Dress (and possibly the bride in it) routinely took centre stage at any wedding. Today, I'm happy to say, the dress is sharing the spotlight with the wedding itself. A fabulous setting, personal and imaginative details, idyllic scenes, fresh, fragrant flowers – all capture the eye and heart of guests as much as any gown.

Colour schemes have long had a place at weddings – but we've come a long way since matching your napkins to your chrysanthemums did the job nicely. 'Colour is still essential, both for flowers and for decorative details,' explains wedding stylist Clare Nolan, 'but now it's about creating a mood and tone for the day itself, whether that's wintry and cosy, fresh and summery, or utterly simple.' Think way beyond flowers: a whole array of lights, candles or lanterns, details in tulle or muslin, different ribbons, cord or sequins, all can help create a magical spectacle. Your stationery, car, even the food, might all add to a single vision.

Whether you decide (bravely, madly even!) to do all the decorating yourself, or to entrust all (or some) of it to a professional, this can be one of the most enjoyable and rewarding ways for you to make your wedding your own.

WHAT'S *YOUR* LOOK?

'A theme often begins with a one thing – like the groom's yearning for a 60s E-Type Jaguar, the bride's decision to wear her mother's wedding dress, or a distinctive location,' says Clare Nolan. 'Travel is also a great influence on party decor now,' she adds, 'and films seem to follow and interpret the trends, as *Monsoon Wedding* did with the Bollywood look.' Historical dramas, children's stories, an old movie, even a single flower or colour, may provide a theme, and interiors' books, flower shows or markets, home design shops – and wedding magazines, of course – can be rich with inspiration, too. 'Invariably, though,' she explains, 'a couple instinctively knows what look is 'them' – most girls have been thinking about this all their lives – and there's really no point in trying to do 50s retro if you feel all country bride!'

'However,' Clare warns, 'there's a danger of overwhelming the real theme of the day – which is, of course, your wedding. Once you've decided on a look, express it with a few well-chosen details and touches, instead of matching up everything you possibly can. And be sure to let the food talk – you've dedicated time and money to it – so don't drown it out with too many decorations or scented candles.'

Wedding looks: Ten of the best

- **Funky:** Perspex invite, knee-length dress, edgy suit, single fresh or paper flowers in hot shades and a retro car.
- **Subtle modern:** Low-key contemporary invitation, column dress, impeccable tailoring and sculpted flowers.
- **Vanilla white:** Heavy white card stationery, classic wedding gown, veil, morning dress, church and tradition.
- **Country:** Out of town, outdoors (in summer) or in a barn (in winter), bundles of flowers and fruit, a stroll instead of cars, and a home-made cake.
- **Fairy tale:** Sleeping Beauty, Snow White or Cinderella? Castle, laced bodice, fairy princess bridesmaids and a five-tiered cake.
- **Oriental:** Mix deep pink, black and white; shocking-pink invitations with Japanese-inspired lettering/a tight satin cheongsam dress/Thai and Japanese food/Chinese lanterns/architectural flowers.

Decor stress

'If one more person had told me not to worry so much about the crockery and the table linen, because the important thing was that I was marrying the man I loved, I'd have completely lost it!' Bride, 25.

- **Colonial:** Nostalgic canopy from the Raj Tent Club, Edwardian dress (think Kate Winslet in *Titanic*), peacocks on the lawn and a decadent afternoon tea.
- **Shakespearean:** Corseted dress (he doesn't have to wear doublet and hose!), sonnet and song, strolling minstrels, Elizabethan banquet.
- **Alice in Wonderland:** Invitation to step 'through the looking glass', mad hats for everyone, picnic on the lawn, waiters in White Rabbit, Mad Hatter, Tweedledum and Tweedledee costumes, croquet and favours marked 'Eat me'/'Drink me'.
- **Asian:** Red dress, hennaed hands, Nehru-collared suit, spicy cuisine, garlands and Bollywood decor.

Making it happen

Find professionals who can achieve your vision – or start planning how you're going to achieve it yourself. There's a lot that will have to be done at the last minute (far too much for you to take on alone), so start early and recruit *plenty* of help. If you're not naturally creative, but would like to be, craft superstores like Hobbycraft (*see* **Contacts**) can make things seem a *lot* more possible; and up-market design shops like Cox & Cox will help to inspire! And if money's tight, look too at the short cuts in Chapter Seven.

What's in a look?

STATIONERY

Reveal your wedding style upfront, with well-chosen invitations. Make sure you allow enough time; for logistics, wording and timing, *see* Chapter

Eighteen. As well as the invitations, you may also choose to have service sheets (*see* Chapter Nine), menus, place cards and thank-you cards printed at the same time. When buying stationery, ask to see a proper sample, not a photograph, so you can properly judge the look, weight and quality. The options are: a specialist company for customised design; pre-designed stationery from stationery stores and departments, printed specially with your wording; pre-printed, ready-to-write stationery to buy in packs off the shelf; and the print shop, who can design and print simple cards to order.

The DIY option

Home-made stationery can be beautiful – or fun – and look surprisingly polished! Use your PC (invest in some stationery software if necessary) or create by hand:

- Take inspiration from design that's all around you: menus in restaurants, birthday cards, magazines, art galleries.
- Create a pretty collage: start with an A5 sheet of handmade paper, leave space for the wording, and play around with buttons, feathers, Love Heart sweets, pressed flowers, ribbon, beads and sequins until you have a prototype you're happy with. Write or print the wording onto a smaller sheet, and stick it in place. Keep it simple and use a strong, clear-drying PVA glue. Stylish flowers and leaves are available from Cox & Cox; sequins and beads from Ells & Farrier; feathers from Confetti.
- Make it high-tech: cut an A5 sheet of heavy acetate (from office stationers), add foil or plastic details, such as sequins, and write with a metallic pen.
- Plain and simple: use plain heavy white card, print on your PC and tie like a parcel with organza ribbon.
- Tracing paper flatters a simple invitation. Overlay a sheet on flat card, cut to exactly the same size, and secure with ribbon tied through a hole in both layers. For a folded card, cut the tracing paper to the full width, fold and put the two layers together like a book; tie a ribbon round the spine to hold them together.
- In the envelope containing the invitation, put loose dried-flower petals, Love Heart sweets, a foil-wrapped chocolate heart, sequins or confetti, which will tumble out when it's opened.

Special guests

'Our friends and family were what the wedding was all about, so our invitation design was simple: the name of every single guest printed on the front, with our own names amongst them, brought out in a larger typeface.' Bride, 27.

● Print plain service sheets or menus on a simple A4 page. To make them look special, roll up, tie with ribbon and put in a big basket for guests to pick up at the entrance to the church or dining room.

For materials and stockists, *see* **Contacts**.

FLOWERS

What will you need?

Most venues welcome flowers, but do establish what the rules are first. Where are flowers allowed? Must you use a designated florist? Are you expected to remove flowers afterwards? Register offices typically allow personal flowers, but not room decoration. Depending on the scale and originality of your wedding, your requirements could include:

PERSONAL FLOWERS FOR THE BRIDAL PARTY

Remember that there's no rule that says you *must* carry flowers, if it doesn't feel right. If you'd like them, though, you could have:

● A bride's bouquet and flowers for her hair.
● The same for bridesmaids; posies or other flowers for younger girls.
● Buttonholes for the groom, best man, ushers, fathers.
● Corsages for mothers and any other women in the bridal party.

Bouquet options include:

● A large teardrop, which trails over and down in front of the bride.
● A formal posy, tightly packed and a neatly rounded shape.
● A hand-tied or informal bouquet, which is looser, taller and less regular in shape.

- A bride can carry a single, long-stemmed flower.
- Arrive empty-handed, collecting individual flowers from friends or bridesmaids at the top of the aisle, like Lisa Kudrow on page 119.
- Instead of a posy, a child can hold a flower-decorated bag, basket or fairy wand. Young children won't hold anything for long; if it's uncomfortable they may refuse altogether.
- Flowers should naturally flatter, not dominate.

Buttonholes:
- Traditionally, a carnation or single rose.
- Nowadays, herbs, grasses and sculptural lilies are just a few of the many original options.

FLOWERS FOR A CHURCH OR OTHER CEREMONY

Wherever you put your decorations, make sure they're high (or low) enough not to obscure a view, but prominent enough to be visible even when the place is full of people. Don't forget candles and other props, too. (*See* Design and Detail on page 141.)

Good spots might include:
- The entrance, doorways and arches.
- Pew or row ends.
- Windowsills and tables, where small arrangements in vases can double as table decorations later.
- Centre stage: pedestals or tall vases can be placed at the front of the room, beside the altar or by the registrar's table.

RECEPTION FLOWERS

Depending on the venue, and their rules, keep the following in mind:
- Table decorations should be very low, or well above eye-level.
- As well as the usual table centres and flower displays, you might put loose flowers or petals on tables, windowsills, fireplaces, the cake, and on the ground.
- Decorate outside as well as in:
  - Tuck flowers into trees and bushes.

- Decorate garden sculptures, statues, fences and stonework.
- Use outdoor lighting, candles and decorations to illuminate your work.

Choosing a florist

- Go by recommendation if possible, either from friends or your other wedding suppliers. For a list of retail members of the Flowers & Plants Association, *see* **Contacts** at the end of this chapter.
- Scour wedding magazines for florists' work you like.
- Visit florists and ask to see portfolios of their work.
- At your first meeting, decide whether you're comfortable with the florist. Do you like what's on display in the shop or workroom, photographs of their work, and the florist's initial comments on your wedding?
- Even if they're recommended, follow up references.
- Once you've chosen, give your florist plenty of information: dress-style and a fabric swatch, colours, textures, theme, music, entertainment. They should suggest visiting the venue(s), unless they know it already.
- Have a final meeting, around two weeks before the wedding, to see the flowers and combinations you've agreed on and confirm delivery and set-up arrangements.
- If you're working to a tight budget, give the florist a colour scheme and a budget, and simply ask them to choose what's cheapest on the day.

Doing your own flowers

Wonderfully satisfying – or complete madness? It's a big job, without doubt, so be confident of what you're taking on. If you're really committed to the idea, the most sensible strategy could be to appoint yourself as assistant to

---

We missed it ...

'I missed half of the most lavish wedding we've ever been to because we couldn't see through the flowers. They obscured the couple completely at the church, and then created a "wall" in the middle of the table so we could hardly talk to anyone at the meal.' Guests, 29 and 36.

Celebrity flowers

*Barbra Streisand married **James Brolin** amongst 200 lilies, 500 gardenias, 2500 stephanotis blossoms, and 4000 roses. Fifty pink water lilies and 100 candles floated in the swimming pool.*

***Keely Shaye Smith & Pierce Brosnan** re-created an entire secret garden, complete with trees, thousands of peonies, roses and tulips, and an over-grown courtyard for a dance floor – all inside a marquee.*

a talented, keen and experienced friend. Calculate how many additional helpers you'll need, and get their agreement upfront.

FAST-TRACK FLORISTRY

The advice from experts like the Flowers & Plants Association is:

- Keep everything very, very simple.
- Wholesale markets don't generally encourage non-trade customers. Look like you know what you're doing!
- Market hours are from about 3am to 9am. The earlier you get there, the more likely you are to find what you want.
- You'll have to buy in wholesale quantities, such as a box of 20 roses.
- Make a planning visit a few weeks before. Find out about prices, what's currently available, cheap or plentiful. Remember to include foliage, and find out if you need to order in advance.
- Then have a trial run: how many flowers does one decoration use, and how long does it take to do? Multiply by the number of decorations you'll need.
- List exactly what – and how much - you need, with contingency plans.
- Allow time and facilities to treat stock: flowers and foliage have to be conditioned for use, leaves need to be removed, stems need to be cut properly to take up water, and correct temperatures maintained.
- You'll also need to buy vases, flower foam, ribbon, which can be costly. See Floral Short Cuts and Pretty Ideas, and **Contacts** for solutions.
- Logistics and timing may be tricky: you're going to have to buy and prepare

at certain times, have transport and space in which to work at the venue, and lots of help.

* Wired bouquets, headdresses and buttonholes are especially fiddly; consider leaving them to a professional.

For more guidance and inspiration:

* *See* the Flowers & Plants Association's website, a rich source of cut-flower information.
* Invest in a good book, such as *Living Colour* by Paula Pryke (Jacqui Small); *Jane Packer's Flowers* by Jane Packer (Conran Octopus); *Grow Your Own Cut Flowers* by Sarah Raven (BBC Consumer Publishing); or *Cut Flowers* by Trisha Guild (Quadrille).
* Courses run at most adult education centres: look in the *Floodlight* guide or phone your local authority. Leading florists such as Paula Pryke and Kenneth Turner run courses in wedding floristry, but they're more of an investment.

FLORAL SHORT CUTS AND PRETTY IDEAS

* Assess the room before you decorate, and imagine it full of people: what are the focal points?
* To save on last-minute preparations, choose potted marguerites, herbs, lavender or flowering bulbs that will stay in bloom for a few days. Paint and decorate pots with ribbons, and simply keep them watered.
* Use jars, aluminium cans, or clay pots (a plastic cup inside makes it waterproof) to avoid the high cost of vases. Clustered together in groups, everyday objects look more country-chic than kitchen-shelf. Try Ikea, Woolworths, Bhs, Homebase for cheap jars and glasses, and think laterally. If it'll hold water, it'll serve as a vase! Paint; add a handwritten label and/or a ribbon, then invite guests to take an arrangement and container home.
* Cut out the need for containers altogether by laying flowers and fruit directly onto surfaces. A single rose, tied with a label, makes a charming place card-cum-favour.
* Clare Nolan always arranges pots and vases in threes or fives for impact.

● Don't forget vegetables and fruit: artichokes, ornamental cabbages, tied bunches of asparagus, as well as limes and berries, are the new 'flowers' – and often a cheaper route.

Flowers by season

You want something amethyst in the autumn ... something white in winter ... you can get them all year round now, but choosing what's in (or close to) season can save you a fortune.

BLUE

Spring: Bluebell, forget-me-not, hyacinth, anemone, cornflower, muscari (blue grape hyacinth)

Summer: Agapanthus, cornflower, delphinium, iris, lavender, foxglove, hydrangea

Autumn: Anemone, hydrangea, iris, lavender, delphinium, passion flower, violet

Winter: Anemone, iris, violet, hyacinth, viburnum berries, muscari

YELLOW

Spring: Daffodil, gerbera, iris, lily, rose, forsythia, tulip, narcissi, ranunculus

Summer: Dahlia, lily, freesia, gerbera, chrysanthemum, gladioli, iris, lupin, rose, sunflower

Autumn: Carnation, chrysanthemum, dahlia, frangipani, freesia, gerbera, iris, lily, orchid, rose, sunflower

Winter: Carnation, daffodil, euphorbia, ranunculus, gerbera, lily, mimosa, pansy, tulip, rose

PINK

Spring: Rose, anemone, hyacinth, orchid, stock, tulip

Summer: Allium, bouvardia, delphinium, freesia, orchid, pink, rose, stock, rhododendron, sweet pea, sweet william, peony

Autumn: Amarylllis, anemone, chrysanthemum, freesia, gladioli, orchid, pink, rose

Winter: Amaryllis, anemone, camellia, carnation, chrysanthemum, heather, orchid, rose, tulip, ranunculus

WHITE

Spring: Freesia, rose, apple blossom, clematis, lily of the valley, orchid, lilac, ranunculus

Summer: Delphinium, freesia, gardenia, iris, lily of the valley, orchid, rose, jasmine, marguerite, lilac

Autumn: Amaryllis, carnation, clematis, gerbera, freesia, hydrangea, iris, lily, orchid, rose

Winter: Amaryllis, camellia, carnation, daffodil, freesia, iris, lily of the valley, orchid, pansy, rose, snowdrop

LILAC/PURPLE

Spring: Anemone, foxglove, lilac, pansy, rose, stock

Summer: Allium, aster, delphinium, foxglove, freesia, lavender, orchid, stock

Autumn: Agapanthus, anemone, gladioli, heather, lavender, orchid, rose, delphinium

Winter: Anemone, freesia, heather, orchid, pansy

ORANGE

Spring: Ranunculus, gerbera, tulip

Summer: Poppy, gerbera, lily, freesia, calla lily

Autumn: Calla lily, euphorbia, freesia, gerbera

Winter: Euphorbia, ranunculus, freesia, gerbera

RED

Spring: Tulip, rose, ranunculus

Summer: Gerbera, carnation, bouvardia

Autumn: Rose, carnation, anemone, bouvardia, euphorbia

Winter: Holly, euphorbia, anemone, bouvardia, ranunculus

CHOCOLATE, BLACK-RED AND MAROON

Spring: Tulip, Black Baccara rose, anemone, calla lily

Summer: Calla lily, chocolate cosmos, anemone

Autumn: Black Baccara rose, pyracantha, anemone

Winter: Black Baccara rose, pyracantha berries

DESIGN AND DETAIL

Ideas, makes and short cuts for your wedding look. For phone numbers and websites throughout, *see* **Contacts** at the end of this chapter.

Dress up a room

If you're working with a shabby hall or barn, and have full permission (written, ideally), change can be dramatic. Ask a team of friends to help.

- Invest in a staple gun, hire a good ladder, and buy lots of cheap fabric, such as net, muslin or calico. Simply cut floor-to-ceiling drops and secure at the top with a staple gun all the way round the room. If you prefer, you can make pleats as you go.
- Switch off harsh lighting, and use pretty alternatives (*see* **Lighting and candles** below).
- If the room has beams or rafters, drape panels of gauzy fabric from them at even, symmetrical points, or suspend fishing wire, and attach little bows or flowers.
- Find a props' house for columns and other theatrical features, such as Theme Traders or the Good Decorating Company.
- An ice-sculpture or vodka luge makes a great centrepiece (could even replace a cake). Try Iceworld, Duncan Hamilton or Ice Creations.

Lighting and candles

A venue can be transformed with lighting. If the professional variety isn't within budget, candles, tea-lights and fairy lights can work wonders on a less than pristine location.

- Make a fireplace into a focal point, whatever the season. Cover the hearth and mantelpiece with tea-lights in holders.
- Put candles in glasses to line steps and windowsills.
- Clare Nolan's party piece is to buy small paper carrier bags (from Bag'n'Box Man), fill the bottoms with sand, and place a tea-light inside each. Use to mark out an outdoor pathway.
- Fill galvanised steel buckets with sand, then push in lots of thin taper candles.

- Float candles and petals in glass bowls of water for gorgeous, low-cost centrepieces.
- Candle sand is literally just that, supplied with wicks. Make little piles in sheltered spots in the garden, or fill jars. From Viva Home.
- Use scooped-out apples, artichokes or limes as candleholders. Cut the bottoms off to give a flat base.
- Buy candles (preferably in bulk) from Prices Candles, the Candle Shop, Candles on the Web, or Wax Workshop: go for slow-burning ones.
- Bulk-buy glasses and tea-light holders on the cheap at Ikea or Woolworths.
- If you have lots of candles to light, invest in a couple of butane gas flame lighters from John Lewis.
- Fairy lights now come in all shapes and sizes: icicle strings, curtains, outdoor lanterns. Shopping at Christmas gives you the greatest choice. Try Ryness, McCord, Habitat, Presents Direct, Lakeland, as well as the usual garden and home centres.
- Use fairy lights and tea-lights on windowsills, twisted into ivy on banisters, or entwined in twigs.
- Florist's lights (or Deco Lights) are battery-powered stems of tea-lights; use them to boost the impact of flowers at an evening party. From Find Me A Gift and Ryness electrical stores.

Important: Put someone in charge of extinguishing candles at the end of the evening; never leave a flame unattended.

Confetti

If paper confetti is out of favour with the vicar and/or venue, organise ushers or bridesmaids to hand out one of the following:

- Paper cones filled with fresh petals: place in a basket at the entrance so guests can help themselves. Make the cones with sheet music of the day, from music shops; contact the Music Publishers Association for help tracking down something unusual, or go online to Music Scores. See the note on page 115 regarding copyright.
- Dried-flower petals. Check that they're colour-fast in the rain, or you

could ruin your dress. From Trousseau, or the Real Flower Petal Confetti Company.

- Edible confetti, from Pat-A-Cake Pat-A-Cake.
- Bubbles: look very pretty in sunlight, and children love them, from www.confetti.co.uk.
- Feather-fetti, from The Very Nice Company.

Table settings and place cards

Alternatives to plain cards and seating plans:

- A 'washing line': write the name of each guest on a folded place card, and write their table number inside. Use wooden clothes pegs to attach them (in alphabetical order) to a line suspended between trees or under a canopy so guests can pick them off on their way to their tables.
- The Table Planner create imaginative table plans to suit your theme, such as a racing page (each table a race and each guest a jockey); or a tube map (each table a line and each guest a station).
- Make your own place cards: write on pebbles or fruit, use luggage labels, or make 'flags' with a cocktail stick and sticky label, then stand each of them in a chocolate.
- Heart-shaped biscuits, iced with a guest's name, can be presented in a tiny cellophane bag and tied with a ribbon to double as a favour. Ask your local baker or patisserie to make them if you're not a natural.
- Buy trade-size reels of ribbon and tie around cutlery, napkins, candle-holders, pots and flower arrangements. Use it to tie flowers or labels to chair backs, too. Personalised ribbon, with your names or the date, can be made by the National Weaving Company. Other ribbon suppliers include V. V. Rouleaux and Barnett Lawson (trade shop open to the public).
- Use sequins and beads (from Ells & Farrier) or flowers and leaves (from Cox & Cox) to decorate surfaces.

Favours

The traditional Italian custom of presenting bonbonnières to each guest (five sugared almonds to represent health, wealth, prosperity, fertility and long life) has caught on here, as have American favours, which can be anything useful, edible or just pleasing to the eye. Specialist suppliers include: Clare Nolan at Scarlet, The Very Nice Company, The White House, Bombay Duck, Confetti, Bonbonnière by Natalie, and Purple Planet. Some also provide materials with which to make your own; but creating them from scratch is more personal and could save money. Sheer numbers can make it hard work, so start well in advance and keep it simple. Tie on a tiny strung label, from Ryman the Stationer, to include a personal message.

- Visit luxury Belgian chocolatiers for inspiration; buy the simplest mini-wrapped squares and put in a pretty personalised envelope or tie with ribbon. For the organic variety, get individually wrapped miniatures from Green & Black.
- Fill containers with ordinary sweets: mini cardboard boxes, clear plastic boxes or mini bags, from Scent-sations or the Bag'n'Box Man.
- Small glassine photographic envelopes can also be filled with sweets or seeds. The envelopes are semi-transparent and cost just a few pence each from Process Supplies.
- Lottery tickets are popular. Put in a pretty envelope with the guest's name to double as a place card. Or do the same with sparklers.
- Make scented sachets from cotton, linen or organza, tied in a pouch or a cracker, or sewn into a mini bag. Fill with dried herbs or lavender. Mini envelopes make a quick alternative: fill, seal and use a hole-puncher to make two holes close together at the top. Thread ribbon through and tie in a bow at the front.
- Stack ribbon-tied plain white boxes of cake in lieu of a traditional cake, then hand to guests as they leave. Boxes from John Lewis or Scent-sations.
- Make tiny seed gardens: buy mini terracotta pots from the Classic Pot Emporium. Cut a 5cm square of lightweight fabric, fray the edges, and place a few seeds in the middle. Gather up the sides into a bundle and tie with a ribbon. Put in the pot with the frayed edges pointing up over the top. Leave the identity of the seed a mystery, or add a tiny label for a message, the guest's name, the name of the seed, or the date.
- Put a note on each table inviting guests to take a little bundle of flowers

home with them. Supply small clear plastic bags, or cellophane sheets from Ryman the Stationer, together with pipe cleaners to secure.

- A booklet of Love Cheques from The Bank of Eros promises the bearer 'breakfast in bed', 'a romantic meal', and more. From W. H. Smith.
- Miniatures of spirits have come up in the world: vodka or tequila with a snazzy label can be ordered from RTL.
- Fill bowls with Hershey's Chocolate Kisses (foil-wrapped chocolate drops in big bags) for guests to share – without or without the usual innuendo! From luxury food departments or Cybercandy.
- Special wedding Love Heart sweets are available in mini tubes, from Swizzles Matlow.

Clever colour

Coordinate all your design and details with colour:

- Use a single colour – anything looks fabulous with white or black.
- For more variety, use all the shades from a single colour group, such as lilacs and purples, yellow and orange, coffee and nut-brown.
- Or team up two very different colours, such as purple and red, chocolate-brown and pale blue, shocking pink and acid-green.
- Use a single flower, such as a sunflower, daisy or gerbera to guide colour and theme throughout. Use as a motif on stationery, seeds as favours, to decorate the cake ...
- For sugar pastels:
  - Fill large glass bowls with sugared almonds, Liquorice Allsorts, marshmallows, or paper-wrapped amaretti biscuits, and use in place of flower arrangements.
  - Fill a collection of glasses or votive-holders with sweets – one colour for each – then group together on a table.
  - Fill tiny semi-transparent bags (from Process Supplies) with jelly-beans or dolly mixture, then arrange neatly on a table.
  - Buy fruit-shaped sugar lollies, then wrap three or four with tissue paper and tie with ribbon for table decorations that make sugar-sweet favours.

- For autumn golds and oranges:
  - Use pumpkins and squashes as 'vases': fill with flowers and leaves. Alternatively, use as candleholders: where you'd normally do a Hallowe'en face, cut out heart-shapes for the light to shine through.
  - Pin autumnal-coloured fruits like golden pears and russet apples with gold labels as name cards.
  - Decorate tables, fireplaces and windowsills with fir cones, conkers, dried orange slices on a thread, and sticks of cinnamon.

Wedding stylists

As weddings here have become more about style, vision and personal touches, and less about tradition and procedure, creative, theatrical and magazine stylists like Clare Nolan have turned their hands to weddings. 'I look at the whole day from every angle, and aim to give customers the confidence to go for a look they want. Instead of simply adding floral decorations at the last minute, I think of the wedding as a whole, linking everything visual – or sensual – from start to finish. Besides flowers, that can include invitations, service sheets, decorations, working with the caterer on food presentation, as well as gifts or favours and a memory book. We also can save the customer time, finding that perfect something, as a personal shopper does,' she adds, 'and cut costs through use of detail, focal points and inexpensive raw materials.' Find Clare Nolan's details in **Contacts**, or search for stylists in magazines, via personal recommendation, or through a wedding specialist (*see* page 239).

Transport

The traditional vintage Rolls-Royce might not be your thing, so consider:
- A self-drive sports car, from Bespokes Classic.
- A VW Beetle stretch convertible: from Classic Rent-A-Bug.
- A boat. If you're marrying close to a river crossing, discuss your plans with the ferryman: he may be willing to help, and even let you decorate the craft with ribbons and flowers.
- A fleet of four-wheel drives: fun, and security against severe weather conditions, too.

- A London-style rickshaw, from Bugbugs, for an Eastern-inspired event.
- A retro Italian scooter; hire locally.
- A white cab from White London Taxis; for a cheaper, spontaneous option in central London, just jump in a cab – or order in advance if it's a busy time!
- A horse-drawn carriage from Haydn Webb Carriages, the London Horse Carriage Company, or find a service at Carriage Driving Global.
- A pastel-coloured Cadillac, the new wedding classic, from American Dreams.
- A Harley Davidson: if you don't want to ride it yourself, urban outlaw style, American Dreams' presidential wedding-car package includes a Harley outrider.
- A limousine: available nationally; check *Yellow Pages*.
- Buses for your guests – and why not ride along with them? Vintage red classics can be hired from Memory Lane.
- Horses, if you're confident riders; or bicycles, if your clothes allow.

Get times, terms and details in writing: *see* supplier tips on page 150.

Money-wise: What to expect
Table centrepiece: £20–£75+
Bouquet: about £50–£150 each
Buttonholes: about £3–£15 each
Car hire: about £300+
Red bus: about £400
Carriage and horses: about £450+

Contacts
American Dreams: 01206 213110; www.americandreams.co.uk
Bag'n'Box Man: 01295 788522; www.bagnboxman.co.uk
Barnett Lawson: 0207 636 8591; www.bltrimmings.com
Bespokes Classic: 01462 791100; www.bespokes.co.uk
Bombay Duck: 020 8749 8001; www.bombayduck.co.uk
Bonbonnière by Natalie: 020 7636 1120
Bugbugs: 020 7620 0500; www.bugbugs.com

Candles on the Web: www.candlesontheweb.co.uk
Candle Shop: 020 7736 0740
Carriage Driving Global: www.carriage-driving.com
Clare Nolan at Scarlet: 07957 307613
Classic Pot Emporium: 01206 271946; www.classicpot.co.uk
Classic Rent-A-Bug: 01761 232369; www.vwautobodies.co.uk
Confetti: 0870 840 6060; www.confetti.co.uk
Cox & Cox: 0870 442 4787; www.coxandcox.co.uk
Cybercandy: 0208 808 5177; www.cybercandy.co.uk
Find Me A Gift: 01926 887777; www.findmeagift.com
Duncan Hamilton: 020 8944 9787; www.icesculpture.co.uk
Ells & Farrier: 020 7629 9964; mail order: 01494 778818;
    www.creativebeadcraft.co.uk
Floodlight: 0208 986 4854; www.floodlight.co.uk
Flowers & Plants Association: 020 7738 8044; www.flowers.org.uk
Good Decorating Company: 020 8545 0668; www.gdcprops.co.uk
Green & Black: www.greenandblacks.com
Haydn Webb Carriages: 0118 988 3334
Hobbycraft (craft superstores): 01202 596100; www.hobbycraft.co.uk
Ice Creations: 01580 892977; www.icecreations.tv
Iceworld: 020 7801 0606; www.icesculptures.co.uk
John Lewis: 020 7629 7711; www.johnlewis.com
Kenneth Turner Flower School: 020 7409 2560;
    www.kenturnerflowerschool.com
London Horse Carriage Company: 020 7435 0216
McCord: 0870 908 7020; www.mccord.uk.com
Memory Lane: 01628 825050; www.memorylane.co.uk
Music Scores: www.music-scores.com
National Weaving Company: 01834 861446; www.nationalweaving.co.uk
Pat-A-Cake Pat-A-Cake: 020 7485 0006
Paula Pryke Flower School: 020 7837 7373; www.paula-pryke-flowers.com
Presents Direct: 020 8246 4355: www.presentsdirect.com
Prices Candles: 01234 264500; www.prices-candles.co.uk
Process Supplies: 020 7837 2179

Purple Planet: 020 8969 4119; www.purpleplanet.co.uk
Raj Tent Club: 020 7376 9066; www.rajtentclub.com
Real Flower Petal Confetti Company: 01386 555045;
    www.confettidirect.co.uk
RTL: 01592 263352
Ryman the Stationer: 0800 801901; www.ryman.co.uk
Ryness: 020 7278 8993; www.ryness.co.uk
Scent-sations: 01256 422408; www.scent-sations.co.uk
Swizzles Matlow: 0800 970 0480; www.forgetflowers.com
Table Planner: 01737 226 597; www.thetableplanner.com
Theme Traders: 020 8452 8518; www.themetraders.com
V. V. Rouleaux: 020 7224 5179; www.vvrouleaux.com
Very Nice Company: 01884 232 152; 01884 251 551
Viva Home: 020 8878 0768; www.vivahome.com
Wax Workshop: www.waxworkshop.co.uk
White House: 01905 381149; www.the-whitehouse.uk.com
White London Taxis: 020 8958 7928

chapter
eleven

planning to celebrate

A wedding reception is anything you want it to be. There's an assumption that because you've just got married, you have to celebrate in a certain way, when all you really need to do is plan the kind of party you'd love to go to.

You may simply want to stock up on delicious food and wine, then let everyone turn up and get on with it, or you may want a structured day of special entertainment, ritual and formalities. The choice is obviously yours, but the advice from the experts is that the further you go from tradition, the more important it is to let everyone know what to expect – unless you're sure they'll enjoy a surprise!

GETTING THE BEST SUPPLIERS

Reception planning (like much else in weddings) is largely about combining great ideas with the right supplier. Bear in mind:

● Recommendation and word of mouth are the best starting points. Follow up all references and ask for phone numbers if presented with written testimonials.

- Meet at least three potentials in person, more if you have a tight budget.
- Work only with people who are sympathetic to your ideas, have some of their own, and who you like.
- See, taste or hear what's on offer, if you possibly can.
- Resolve basic details, from tableware to a sample playlist, *before* you sign or pay a deposit. Get everything in writing, specifying that the cost shown is the *final* cost.
- Don't pay in full until you're *completely* happy with everything. If suppliers insist on payment upfront, agree a small retention to be paid after the event.
- Collect up a file of clippings, notes and photographs so that you can present your ideas clearly.
- Ask if they have insurance and what happens if someone crucial is ill on the day.
- Tell them anything specific that you hate: whether it's Celine Dion, carnations or fussily folded napkins. They won't know otherwise.
- Provide any supplier who might need it with food and soft drinks. If the wedding menu is expensive, ask the caterer to do something simpler, but substantial.
- Ask who clears up the next day.

Essential ingredients

FOOD AND DRINK

Working with caterers
In addition to the rules above:
- Set yourself a budget per head, and ask to see menus in that price range.
- As always, ask about extra costs: tableware, preparation equipment and staff costs should all be included. Check whether the price quoted is based on a minimum number of guests.

Checking out suppliers

'I wish we'd followed up more than one reference. Only after the wedding did we find out that while some previous clients were pleased with our caterer, others weren't so happy with the service. We would probably have still used the same caterer, but could have said in advance how we wanted things done. As it was, the food was fantastic, but the meal was very rushed – and it needn't have been.' Groom, 28.

- Iron out details in good time: as well as a menu, think about crockery and cutlery, table linen, glasses, furniture. Ask to see samples.
- Is service included, or is there an 'optional gratuity' which you'll inevitably feel obliged to pay? Is there an overtime charge?
- Have a tasting session of the final menu choices. This should be served by staff, in the correct dress, at a table set up as it will be for the wedding.
- The caterer is central to the smooth running of the day itself:
  - Establish exactly what the extent of their role will be: some simply provide food and drink, others act as an administrator.
  - Ask them to set up as early as possible to allow time for decorations, and a chance for speakers to familiarise themselves with the room.
  - Keep them informed about timings for the day, numbers, and arrangements with other contractors.
  - If you wish, ask the headwaiter to make announcements and keep everyone to schedule.

What's your cuisine?

One of the tests of a good caterer is whether they're imaginative and creative, so devising a refreshing or off-beat menu should be a team effort. We've all had poached salmon and coronation chicken at weddings: they're delicious, but if you'd like something less predictable, discuss alternative kinds of meal, as well as original menus.

Contemporary cuisine

Choose a theme:

- Nursery food, like sausage and mash, steak and kidney pie, or fish pie
- Modern British, like braised lamb shanks or guinea fowl
- Oriental, like Thai chicken curry, or pork with ginger
- Moroccan, like olive-crusted lamb and couscous salad
- Indian, prepared using traditional methods, will look incredibly impressive and be a treat for curry-lovers

Breakfast/brunch

Offer lots of choice:

- Scrambled eggs and smoked salmon
- Honey roast ham, eggs and hash browns
- Kedgeree
- Eggs Benedict
- Pastries, patisserie and muffins
- Yoghurt, honey, strawberries and blueberries
- Bloody Marys, Buck's Fizz and a choice of really good coffees

Canapés

How about:

- Mini Cornish pasties
- Basil, mozzarella and cherry tomatoes on sticks
- Mini sausage and mash
- Blinis with caviar, crème fraîche and red onion
- Sushi
- Mini fruit tarts

Picnic

Baskets filled with:

- Antipasti picnic bread (scooped-out loaf filled with marinated vegetables)
- Mini home-made chicken pies
- Cherry tomato and basil salad
- Mini wooden boxes filled with chunks of ripe cheeses

- Cupcakes, prettily iced
- Berry fruit salads and mini tubs of clotted cream

Buffet

A central idea works well, try:

- Mediterranean, such as grilled figs, Parma ham and mozzarella salad, grilled asparagus, bruschetta and roasted vegetable salad
- Oriental, such as Thai spring rolls, fishcakes, noodle salad and Thai curry
- Indian, such as samosas, tikka kebabs, naan breads, curries

Pudding

- People love a pudding buffet table: include cakes and candy as well as desserts; keep to two or three colours, and dress it up with lollies tied with ribbons and glass bowls of iced biscuits
- His and Hers puddings are fun too: girls can go to chocolate heaven while the boys tuck into apple pie and custard

Afternoon tea

Modern tea parties could include:

- Goat's cheese and roasted courgette sandwiches
- Beef, rocket and Parmesan sandwiches
- Home-made biscuits and shortcakes
- Petits fours
- Lemon and lime cakes, home-made and drizzled with runny icing

Etiquette issue: Modern food manners

You must, of course, consider all dietary requirements and make sure that kosher guests, vegetarians, pregnant women, children and everyone else has good food. If in doubt, consult guests directly on their choice of menu, rather than trying to anticipate what they might feel able to eat. Remember, too, that lots of people have their reasons for avoiding alcohol (not least if they're driving), so don't make it difficult for them.

Let's do tea

Tea is the new lunch, as it were. The Power Tea Set includes **Sadie Frost**, **Sara Cox**, **Meg Matthews** *and* **Kate Moss**, *with chic urban hotels as the venues of choice, all sipping at their Darjeeling and nibbling at dainty cakes. What better excuse to indulge!*

- Strawberries dipped in chocolate
- Earl Grey, lapsang souchong and iced teas

Barbecue/food stalls

With on-site chefs, they're great for atmosphere. Choose one or more:

- Hog spit-roast
- Sausage stall (label them so people can choose)
- Seafood table
- Fish and chip stall
- Thai fast food (noodles, satay, stir-fries)
- Sushi chef
- Ice cream stand

DRINKS

The traditional reception drink at weddings is champagne, or sparkling wine, but alternatives are a great way to make your personal mark. Include something plain to please (almost) everyone and plenty of non-alcoholic drinks and water. Wine is still the best bet with food but, for a reception or party, match your food theme or wedding style with:

Summer drinks, cocktails & coolers

- Pimm's
- Sea Breeze (vodka, grapefruit and cranberry)
- Buck's Fizz (champagne and orange juice)

- Cosmopolitans (vodka, Cointreau, lime and cranberry)
- Bellinis (champagne and fresh peach juice)
- White wine punch (wine, brandy and vodka on ice)
- Planter's Punch (rum, pineapple, passion fruit and lime juices)
- Margaritas (tequila, triple sec/Cointreau and lime juice)
- Long Island Iced Tea (the five white spirits and Coke)
- Black Velvet (Guinness and champagne)

Warming winter drinks
- Mulled wine
- Mulled cider

Beer & cider
- Chilled country cider from flagons
- Bottled traditional ales
- Thai or Japanese beer for an Eastern theme

Shots & ices
- Alcoholic ice lollies
- Vodka shots
- An ice luge
- A tequila bar, serving slammers the traditional way: lick of salt, a shot, then lime

Non-alcoholic
- Elderflower cordial
- Home-made lemonade
- Iced tea
- Fruit smoothies

After the meal
As well as coffee:
- Choice of teas
- Liqueurs

Their wedding

'We're football-mad, so we built a Seventies champagne cascade, in true George Best style!' Couple, 27 and 28.

- Sambuca
- Hot chocolate!

Planning tactics

- Caterers can take care of drinks as well as food, but if your plans are ambitious, ask them about dedicated bartenders or cocktail waiters.
- Buying the drink through your caterer or venue will obviously be more expensive than buying from a wine merchant. They should earn their mark-up by giving you guidance and tastings. If you don't know much about wine, take along someone who does. The advantage is that you don't have to worry about quantities, or running out.
- There will always be guests who don't like champagne or wine, or who would prefer to be drinking beer. Even if you don't want a full bar, a stock of two or three spirits and mixers is good insurance.
- Avoid getting your guests too drunk. Cocktails and coolers can be deceptively drinkable, so keep them weak, and don't serve drink for long without food. Always have non-alcoholic options on offer; don't make people ask for them.
- If you provide the drink yourself, you'll almost certainly have to pay corkage. This can hike up the cost significantly, but may still be cheaper, especially if you want expensive wines. It will also give you more scope, as you won't be restricted to the caterer's or venue's wine list.
- For more on the logistics of organising your own drink, quantities and recipe book suggestions, *see* Chapter Twelve.

THE CAKE

'When you choose your wedding cake,' says Sugarcraft author Tombi Peck, 'you're commissioning a piece of art.' It can tie tidily – or imaginatively – into a theme, or stand alone in all its traditional white-tiered glory.

The classic is, of course, the rich fruitcake in three, five (or more!) tiers:

- Contemporary versions are very simple, stacked on themselves (rather than on pillars) and with minimal decoration.
- Add a twist to the classic cake: decorate with just about anything from Love Heart sweets to flowers, fabric, simple bands of wide ribbon, wire-work and beads or feathers.
- Instead of fruit, have chocolate cake, carrot cake, sponge cake, or one tier of each.
- Icing can be white or dark chocolate, as well as soft paste or classic royal icing in any colour.

Cake-makers have created sculptures in many forms:

- Turreted fairy-tale castles, people, desert islands, windmills, a church, an elaborate Georgian mansion – all are possibilities.
- For modern simplicity, go for a simple shape like a tall cone or pyramid.

Alternatively:

- Choose a *croquembouche* – the classic French tower of profiteroles covered in spun sugar.
- Instead of one big cake, have lots of cupcakes, boxed cake slices or fon-dant-iced squares. Either lay them out flat (each could bear a letter so

Not quite a piece of cake

'An old family friend made our cake, and came the night before to set it up on a table in the marquee that had been put up at a local farm. Just after she left, the farmer's dog bound in, took a huge bite out of the bottom tier, and bound out again. Thankfully, she had made a spare tier, but it was the wrong size, so she spent the whole night rebuilding the cake!' Bride, 24.

they spell out your names or the date) or pile up on a cake stand as a twist on the tiered wedding cake.

- Ask one of the trendy patisseries, like Valerie or Villandry, to make you up one – or several – of their fabulous chocolate cakes.
- Any non-fruit cake can double as a pudding, served with fresh fruit, crème fraîche or ice cream.
- Konditor & Cook in London make fun, slightly haphazard-looking cones and towers.

Finding a cake-maker

The person you choose will depend on the kind of cake you want:

- A traditional baker or confectioner for the classic three tiers.
- A patisserie for something more luscious, like a *croquembouche* or elaborate chocolate cake.
- A cake-making specialist for something witty, sculpted or stylised.
- The British Sugarcraft Guild will provide a list of members in your area to help you find a cake-maker. This isn't a professional qualification or warrant of quality, so check your cake-maker's credentials as you would any supplier.
- Check bridal magazines. *Wedding Cakes*: A Design Source, is a magazine which showcases cake-makers (from W. H. Smith in January and June each year).

CATERING YOURSELF

For a small wedding, and with plenty of help, this may be possible. *See* Chapter Twelve before you decide!

MARQUEES, CANOPIES AND AWNINGS

At home, or at a hired location, canvas will solve most space and weather problems. The humble hire tent now comes in every imaginable size, shape and style. Some are basic (even a little tired-looking); others are quite glamorous.

Star-hung ceilings, magnificent chandeliers or diaphanous pink linings are all up for grabs, and a fairy grotto, Bridge of Sighs, and Roman amphitheatre have all been done!

- Costs are, quite literally, as long as a piece of string; you'll have to ask for a personal quote. As a very rough guide, a marquee to accommodate 100+ people could start at £2,500, including extras.
- Extras can double the cost: make sure lighting (and access to power supply/provision of generator), flooring, heating/air conditioning, linings, dance floor, catering facilities/service tent and loos are included if needed, as well as tables, chairs, table linen and chair covers, crockery, glassware and cutlery.
- The contractor should make a site visit, and provide you with an opportunity to see the type of tent you're going to have, before you decide.
- The marquee should go up at least 24 hours before the wedding to allow other preparations to be completed. A time for dismantling should also be set.
- Get a contact number (or someone to stay on site) for the duration of the wedding.
- Check that insurance and fire regulations are met.
- For a garden party, cricket club or limited open space, one or several colonial-inspired tents look stylish and are very versatile. The Raj Tent Club has a range of canopies, pavilions and awnings with a Moroccan or Indian feel.
- Free-standing small marquees need no guy ropes, so can be erected on a small lawn or over French windows to extend a room into the patio. From Minimarkee.

CATERING EQUIPMENT

Whether you want everything silver and gold, contemporary, Moroccan, or just pure white, the quality of hired equipment has come a long way:
- The following offer ranges that are upmarket, funky – or just nice and simple: Top Table Hire, Coloured Linen Hire, Just Hire, Jones Catering Equipment Hire.

- To calculate how many tables you'll need:
  - Round tables: a 100cm table holds up to 6 people, a 120cm table holds up to 8 people, and a 150cm table holds up to 10 people.
  - Rectangular tables: a table 80+cm wide and 180cm long can seat 8 guests, including one at each end. Add an extra two people for every additional 60cm in length.
  - Small round tables fit more people into a room than large or rectangular ones.
  - Do not be tempted to put tables too close together: once people are sitting down, you still need 40cm of space for staff to get through.
- At a stand-up reception or partially seated buffet, provide seating for at least 30% of your guests.
- When you ask for a quote, check out delivery and collection arrangements at the same time.
- If you can, get everything you need from one supplier; managing a stream of deliveries does not make for a relaxed wedding.

SEATING PLANS

For that lovely reassuring hum and clatter, laughter and chatter of a successfully seated party of guests, you'll need to put in some work. Just don't do it too soon: you'll only have to change it!

1 Write each name on a small piece of paper.
2 Draw a large, rough plan of the room layout with the correct number and shape of tables.
3 Put any natural groups into separate piles, such as all your friends from work or from school.
4 If there are lots of children, consider a table just for them.
5 On each table, put one socially gifted person or couple, each from a separate group.
6 Now allocate everyone you're worried about (whether they're quiet or don't know anyone) close to one of these people or couples. Create good matches, finding personality complements and something in common.

7 The rest of your friends and family should slot in relatively easily: keep groups of friends together, but don't sit one stranger on a table among a crowd of very close friends.

8 Invariably people prefer to sit with their friends, if at all possible. Mix people up only if you're certain they'll thank you for it.

9 Mixing generations rarely works. If you're confident, go ahead, but don't do it on a whim.

10 Don't forget to put space between awkward relationships, painful memories and people who just can't stand each other.

In addition:

- Name tables instead of numbering to avoid offence.
- If there are just too many awkward relationships, have a stand-up or perch buffet instead.
- You'll probably have to make changes to the seating plan even at the last minute. To keep it flexible, take some spare peel-off labels or put each guest's name on a card attached with a map pin.

ENTERTAINMENT

A little background music goes a long way in creating atmosphere, but if you want something more memorable, there are performers and musicians of every kind. For all entertainment:

- Go and see a performance before you book – especially for music.
- Ensure written contracts specify arrival time, performing time, finishing time, and number and length of breaks. Three hours, each with a fifteen-minute break, is standard for live entertainment.
- Provide maps, directions and a phone number so they can contact someone in charge on the day itself. Get a mobile number from them too.
- Check the facilities, amplification and power supply they'll need and make necessary arrangements.

See **Contacts** at the end of this chapter.

From the experts: What to choose

Rebecca Joseph at the Talentbase

'A tribute performer is great for everyone: Tina Turner lookalikes always go down a storm. But always see the artist perform before your wedding.'

David Guest at the Wedding Music Company

'Jump, jive and swing are always winners – and the Ratpack sound (good for weddings) is enjoying a healthy revival.'

PARTY MUSIC

Whatever your musical taste, there's a band who'll do it for you: just be sure it'll fit the mood of the guests, and the day.

- On offer are:
  - Elvis, Abba, Frank Sinatra, Beatles and many other tributes.
  - Ceilidh bands for Irish and Scottish barn dancing, with a caller.
  - Original live bands and singers.
  - Classical musicians, harpists and opera singers.
  - Jazz bands, Caribbean, salsa, flamenco and other Latin American dance styles.
  - Discos: to insure against the dismal wedding disco, never book one you haven't seen, and provide a list of 'must play' and 'no way' songs. The list over-page may help.
- Look in classified sections of wedding magazines, the Internet – or approach musicians you've seen yourself. Check references as you would any supplier. A reputable agent could organise music for both ceremony and reception, saving time and money. Try the Wedding Music Company; Music Finders; Sternberg Clarke; Function Junction; Barn Dance Weddings.
- Ask for a demo tape or CD, or listen to audio clips on the Internet.
- Once you've chosen, be specific about what parts of their act you like, which you'd prefer them to miss out. Don't expect them to do something outside their normal range; better to look for another band.

Music for a musician

Don Henley's wedding entertainment was the most lavish Hollywood had seen: guests reportedly enjoyed a 77-piece orchestra from the Los Angeles Philharmonic, plus performances from Tony Bennett, Billy Joel, Bruce Springsteen, Sting and Sheryl Crow.

- Arrange to have background music playing during breaks in live music; silence breaks up the party all too swiftly.
- Most musicians will perform a specific song or piece of music on the day if you give them enough time to rehearse.

What's your disco style?

Cheesy or cool? The list below will help you choose your 'must plays'/'no ways' from this round-up of perennial disco tracks. Like them or not, they're all guaranteed floor-fillers.

'Groove is In the Heart'	Deelite
'Sing It Back'	Moloko
'Don't Call Me Baby'	Madison Avenue
'Groovejet'	Spilller
'Praise You'	Fat Boy Slim
'Romeo'	Basement Jaxx
'Can't Get You Out of My Head'	Kylie Minogue
'Starlight'	Superman Lovers
'Take Me Home'	Sophie Ellis Bextor
'Like A Prayer'	Madonna
'I'm Outta Love'	Anastacia
'Fast Love'	George Michael
'Spinning Around'	Kylie Minogue
'Independent Woman'	Destiny's Child
'It's Raining Men'	Weather Girls
'You Sexy Thing'	Hot Chocolate
'Club Tropicana'	Wham

'Wake Me Up Before You Go Go'	Wham
'Back To Life'	Soul II Soul
'Dancing Queen'	Abba
'Young Hearts Run Free'	Kym Mazelle

PURE THEATRE

At weddings, theatrical performers often mingle with guests, amusing and entertaining for a few minutes before moving on:

- The right magician will be more David Blaine than Paul Daniels: contact your local Magic Circle (in the *Yellow Pages* or online) for a qualified magician near you.
- Jugglers and fire-eaters can be found at Sternberg Clarke and the Talentbase. A jester is just right for a medieval or Shakespearean themed event: find via The Magic Circle (*see* magicians above); or contact Dante Ferrara (very sixteenth-century).
- Lookalikes cause a stir, from Ab Fab's Edina to Charlie Chaplin: contact Lookalikes and Event Event.
- Stilt walkers amaze and entertain in a variety of costumes: contact Sternberg Clarke.
- If you're tempted to use birds or animals as part of the show, make sure their welfare is well thought through.
- White doves, released just after the ceremony, can be romantic and dramatic. Call the White Dove Company.
- Human statues are disarmingly convincing, painted in stone, zebra stripes, gold or almost any colour you choose. Contact Mechanical Fracture.
- Caricature or silhouette artists give guests something to take home: they create in minutes and entertain adults and children alike. Contact Charles Burns, the Roving Artist, for silhouettes; The Magic Circle (as for magicians above) for caricatures.
- The Comedy Club can recommend a stand-up comedian in your area.
- For children, face painting, a bouncy crocodile or giant slide (from H.S.S. Event Hire), entertainer, clown, music man or a magician can go down really well (with parents too), all via Talentbase.

- For more on keeping children – and the rest of your guests – happy, *see* Chapter Sixteen.
- If you can't find what you want, try Talentbase: an online interactive database to connect you with a multitude of acts nationwide including comedy, dance, music, contortionists, clowns – you name it; or Sternberg Clarke, who have a similar range. Event Event organises anything from Scalextrics to an illusionist.

INSTANT ATMOSPHERE

- Fireworks can be expensive, but magical (and sometimes are organised as a romantic surprise): the Firework Company and Fantastic Fireworks are nationwide.
- Casino tables are fun for a black-tie event: Cabaret Casino Associates supply the equipment and croupiers, too.
- Hold your wedding at a society race meeting like Newmarket; have runners to place bets on your behalf.

TRANSPORT HOME

Guests obviously need to get home. If you can lay on a minibus, it could save everyone a lot of hassle, but will need some organisation – and cash – on your part. If they're relying on cabs, ensure that cab firms are pre-warned and bookings made early in the evening.

RECEPTION FORMALITIES

None of the formal events below are obligatory: it's up to you to decide which, if any, fit your idea of a good day, and what your family and guests will be comfortable with. For second marriages, you may want to tone them down – or make the most of it! (For a minute-by-minute wedding day timetable, *see* Chapter Eighteen.)

From the expert: The receiving line

Bob Grosse, Secretary of the Guild of Professional Toastmasters

'Get it down to 6 people, family only. Quick handshake and pull them through. If they want to chat, say "I'll see you later." You can get 120 people through in 15 minutes like that!'

Receiving line

Traditionally, a chance for every guest to meet and congratulate the entire bridal party.

- **The tradition:** The bride's mother, groom's father, groom's mother, bride's father, bride, groom, chief bridesmaid and best man stand in that order to greet the guests as they arrive at the reception, as they would if welcoming them at home, and introduce them to the next in line as necessary.
- **Alternatively**: Discomfort at making guests wait in line, the incredible amount of time a receiving line can eat up, or the sheer formality of the procedure, have given rise to other approaches. It's important to remember that as the wedding equivalent of greeting guests at a party, it would be rude not to create some kind of welcome: you could, for instance, stand together (but not lined up) near the drinks' supply, encouraging people to come and say hello, or you could circulate in twos and threes (at least one from each family and generation).
- **In any case, help it flow smoothly:** A 'holding area' near the entrance means everyone can be given a drink before they start queuing. Ask a few friends to informally guide in a few people at a time, rather than allowing a long queue to build up, and keep each greeting to just a few seconds (one minute for each of 120 guests will take two hours!). Keep watch on each other: rescue anyone who's stuck with a guest, or struggles to remember a name.

Top table

- **The tradition:** For grace, the meal and speeches, the wedding party sits on one side of a long table looking on to the guests. The guests' view, from left to right, is in this order: chief bridesmaid/groom's father/bride's mother/groom/bride/bride's father/groom's mother/best man. During speeches, everyone has a good view, and it may also help to avoid diplomatic hitches. The strictest etiquette says that the arrangement stands even where one or both parents have remarried, or a parent is estranged from the rest of the family. Exceptions are made when the stepparent has acted as father/mother for many years: if you have the full complement of stepparents, the usual order, from left to right, is: groom's stepmother/bride's stepfather/chief bridesmaid/groom's father/ bride's mother/bride/groom/bride's father/groom's mother/best man/ bride's stepmother/groom's stepfather.

- **The alternative:** The brutal truth is that many couples don't want to spend this party of a lifetime sitting with their parents, and even if they do, they find the arrangement a bit pompous. For this reason, or where family set-ups are complicated, some decide to abandon the top table altogether, and simply sit the wedding families amongst the guests. Others create a much larger, family and supporters' table and some couples sit at a table for two! It matters less than you'd think, because you'll all be circulating most of the time anyway.
- **Help it flow smoothly:** Take great care not to offend, pre-warn anyone who may feel sensitive, and try to come up with considerate solutions. Ensure that you're all in good sight and sound of guests during speeches.

Speeches and toasts

- **The tradition:** After the meal, the best man, or toastmaster announces speeches. The bride's father speaks, then the groom, and finally the best man, and each makes appropriate toasts, before announcing the cutting of the cake and bringing the formal part of the meal to a close. (Good speaking, correct form, toasts and alternatives are all covered in Chapter Thirteen.)
- **The alternatives:** Nerves can spoil a speaker's enjoyment of the day, so many wedding meals now *begin* with speeches. While speeches are a natural highpoint *after* a meal, re-arranging might be the best compromise. Anyone who doesn't want to speak can appoint someone to

speak on their behalf, and the bride, or bride's mother can have her say if she wishes.

● **Help it flow smoothly** by keeping speeches short and limiting the number of speakers. It's vital that all the guests know when the speeches are due to start, and given plenty of warning if the timing is breaking with tradition. People *hate* missing a good speech!

Cake-cutting

● **The tradition:** After the speeches, the best man or toastmaster announces the cutting of the cake. The bride and groom traditionally cut the cake together. Historically, it's a symbolic moment (linked to fertility) and doing it after the speeches focuses everyone's minds and attention back on to the marriage itself. The top tier is kept for the christening of the couple's first child.

● **The alternatives:** Some couples cut the cake before the meal, while they're still looking fresh for photos. Caterers sometimes encourage that, too, so they can slice it or put it into boxes.

● **Help it flow smoothly** by making sure all the guests have plenty of time to get their cameras ready, and plenty of warning if timing breaks with tradition.

First dance

● **The tradition:** More a modern ritual, the bride and groom take to the floor for a few minutes, then the bride dances with the groom's father, and the groom with the bride's mother.

● **The alternatives:** Some couples find the idea horrifying, and don't do it! Instead, you could have a dance to a special song later in the evening, when the attention is off. Others love the ritual and stretch out the first dance to two or three songs, followed by more pairing off within the wedding party (parents from opposite families, best man and chief bridesmaid) before the floor opens up. If you want the moment, but not a whole dance, enlist a few friends and family to join you a couple of minutes into the song.

● **Help it flow smoothly:** No-one needs telling that the choice of music should not be in any way embarrassing (overly smoochy, corny, too fast

We're not alone

'Our first dance was announced, the music started, and we stepped on to the dance floor, all eyes upon us. After a few moments, an elderly relative (who I think must be deaf) came over to us to chat. She just wouldn't go away. I think she saw us on our own and thought she'd take her chance to catch up on a bit of gossip!' Bride, 29.

or too slow). To check, have a practice in good time. Ensure the right music will play: many songs have been recorded in several versions. One or two dancing lessons may help if you're nervous or want to impress. Tango, Ceroc and waltz teachers are all listed by the International Dance Teachers Association and Sternberg Clarke offers First Dance Classes specially for the bride and groom.

Departure of bride and groom

- **The tradition:** A change of outfit and a grand exit. Guests might make a tunnel and throw rice or confetti, waving them off before departing themselves. A highpoint for everyone, it provides a natural end to the day after which guests can leave, too.
- **The alternatives:** Many couples can't bear the thought of missing their own party, so they stay until dawn. Others follow the going-away ritual, for the fun of it, and to enable guests to leave promptly if they wish – then come back twenty minutes later to enjoy the rest of the night! This is a great solution if children need tucking up in bed.
- **Help it flow smoothly:** Ensure guests know in advance if there will be no send-off, to avoid confusion and waiting. However compelling the dance floor, keep watch for guests wanting to say goodbye.

Throwing the bouquet

- **The tradition:** Just before going away, the bride throws her bouquet into a gathering of all the single women. The one who catches it will be the next to marry.
- **The alternatives:** Some brides want to keep and preserve the bouquet.

More importantly, many single women don't relish the idea of a public brawl that may smack of desperation! Some brides make a gift of the bouquet to a close friend, possibly during her speech; others unbind it and hand a flower to each of her close girlfriends later on.

- **Help it flow smoothly:** A second, replica bouquet on standby means you can follow the tradition but still hang on to your own flowers.

Tradition in other cultures

There are, of course, many other post-wedding rituals from a whole variety of cultures and religions, including the clapping in of a Jewish bride and groom and Greek plate-smashing. Whole chapters could be written on each: the Internet is rich with ideas. For a list of websites, *see* page 308.

Money-wise: What to expect

The guides below are the lower end of the average price. Don't be surprised to be quoted double, but persevere if you want even cheaper: they're out there!

Bands, three hours with breaks: £400+
Cake, average spend: about £250
Catering: allow £15–£50 per head; much more for something exceptional
Drinks, average spend: about £1000
Elaborate cakes: £500+
Fireworks: £1000+
Food, average spend: about £2,250
Magicians and performers, three hours with breaks: £300+
Minibus, three hours with a driver: £150+

Breaking with tradition

'We did away with most of the formalities, and the only one I regret was not having a receiving line. We didn't even say hello to one or two people, and I felt terrible about it.'

Contacts

Barn Dance Weddings: 020 8657 2813; www.barn-dance.co.uk

British Sugarcraft Guild: 020 8859 6943; www.bsguk.org

Cabaret Casino Associates: 01932 867486; www.cabaretcasino.co.uk

Charles Burns, the Roving Artist: 0118 947 6637; www.roving-artist.com

Coloured Linen Hire: 01948 860597; www.colouredlinenhire.co.uk

Comedy Club: 020 7732 3434

Dante Ferrara: 01522 512753; www.danteferrara.co.uk

Event Event: 020 8980 5222; www.eventevent.co.uk

Fantastic Fireworks: 01582 485555; www.5nov.com

Firework Company: 01884 840504; www.thefirework.co.uk

Function Junction: 020 8900 5959; www.functionjunction.co.uk

H.S.S. Event Hire: 0845 722 2000; www.hss.com

International Dance Teachers Association: 01273 685652; www.idta.co.uk

Jones Catering Equipment Hire: 020 8320 0600

Just Hire: 020 8595 8855; www.justhirecatering.com

Lookalikes: 01784 257007; www.lookalikes.tv

Mechanical Fracture: 07989 412448

Minimarkee: 020 7796 4715; www.minimarkee.co.uk

Music Finders: 01273 603633; www.musicfinders.co.uk

Raj Tent Club: 020 7376 9066; www.rajtentclub.com

Sternberg Clarke: 020 8877 1102; www.sternberg-clarke.co.uk

Sussex Magic Circle: www.thesussexmagiccircle.co.uk

Talentbase: 07000 282536; www.thetalentbase.tv

Top Table Hire: 01327 260575; www.toptablehire.com

Wedding Music Company: 020 8293 3392; www.weddingmusic.co.uk

White Dove Company: 020 8508 1414; www.thewhitedovecompany.co.uk

chapter twelve

the cheat's wedding feast

I love the idea of creating a feast of simple, fresh food for your own wedding. And when it comes to drink, buying your own often makes plain good sense. The suggestion here is not that you knock up an elaborate sit-down meal, but that the averagely enthusiastic cook can cheat, short-cut and penny-pinch their way to delicious wedding food and drink.

FOOD

The right scenario

Before you decide to do your own cooking, check that it's feasible:

- Are you sure you both want to? It could add a lot of stress. However simple you make it, it's not a project for the timid, highly strung or faint-hearted!

- Do you both enjoy cooking? Have you done much? It helps particularly if the groom is canny in the kitchen. On the morning of the wedding the bride will be more concerned with her tiara than her tapenade.
- Do you have some experience of managing and presenting food for parties?
- Hygiene issues are paramount: if food isn't properly chilled, stored and handled, there's a risk of food poisoning.
- Do you have plenty of help available from people who know (roughly) what they're doing, and won't be playing a central role at the wedding?
- What's the set-up of the wedding location? Think through the logistics in terms of preparation, storage, presentation and clearing up.
- How much freezer space do you have; can neighbours provide some?
- Will you have the time needed in the weeks before the wedding? Heavy work commitments, or young children, for instance, could make it difficult.
- Weigh up the costs: as well as the food, you'll need to hire furniture, table linen, crockery, cutlery, glassware and possibly staff and transportation, too.
- Do you know where to buy high-quality, good-value fresh food in your area?
  - Farmers' Markets are now in almost all towns, and offer seasonal fruit and vegetables, beautiful breads and cheeses at well below supermarket prices. Check locations on their website.
  - For charcuterie, European cheese and antipasti, Italian delicatessens are best, but the deli counters in major supermarkets are almost as good, and often cheaper.
  - A trip to Calais might pay for itself if you're serving lots of charcuterie and cheese. Go up to a week in advance, as long as you have storage.

Deciding on a menu
- Keep it very, very simple. Jamie Oliver may have cooked a lavish meal on his own wedding day, but so he should! For most, one or two buffet dishes, prepared in advance, served up with lots of bread and salad, is a sensible limit.
- Opt for less elaborate ways to feed your guests: canapés, afternoon tea, a buffet lunch or supper.

- Always look for the low-effort option. Go for:
  - Low-preparation food, like cheese and salad.
  - No-cook food, like cherry tomato and mini mozzarellas on a stick.
  - Supermarket-bought canapés (they're very upmarket these days - *see* below).
  - Dishes which can be made in advance, frozen or kept in the fridge.
- Make accurate calculations of quantities and costs before you decide. You'll need:
  - For a casual buffet: two or three main dishes plus simple side dishes, a choice of two or three salads and different breads and cheeses. Served like this, an average family-size recipe or dish will provide about eight servings, with guests taking a serving spoon of each.
  - For nibbles and canapés: allow about six as a starter, up to twenty if it's the only food, and an additional four sweet canapés if you serve them.
  - For afternoon tea: at least one round of sandwiches per head, more if they're small, two slices of cake, and two each of petits fours or home-made biscuits.
  - Fresh fruit goes at the rate of about two/three whole pieces per person in fruit salad.

Food to impress: Easy ways to show off!

Whatever you decide to cook – or not cook – work out a timetable, which runs from the early planning stages right up to the last minutes of laying out and serving the food. It should incorporate shopping, hire of equipment, food preparation, defrosting, transportation, presentation and last-minute deliveries (such as of fresh bread) – as well as clearing up afterwards.

CANAPES AND NIBBLES

- Many canapés can be made in a trice. Hire large glass platters for stylish presentation.
  - Mozzarella cubes, cherry tomato and basil on a cocktail stick
  - Mini smoked salmon, cucumber and black pepper sandwiches, on a stick
  - Sausages cooked in honey and whole grain mustard

- Half a quail's egg and cherry tomato on a stick
- Mini sausages, cut in half lengthways, and filled with piped mashed potato
- Blinis topped with smoked salmon, sour cream and cod roe
- Shop-bought pastry canapé shells, filled with scrambled egg and a little smoked salmon, or rocket and Parmesan shavings rolled in carpaccio
- Parma ham, wrapped around a piece of melon, on a stick
- Supermarkets sell canapés and party snacks, especially during the Christmas season. Marks & Spencer and Waitrose are particularly good, with Italian, Thai, Indian, sushi, mini tartlets, tiny prawn kebabs and delicious sweet nibbles on offer.
- If you're confident enough to go to the next level and make more elaborate eats, choose recipes you can make in advance and assemble at the last minute.

BUFFET
- Build a table of food around simple, impressive basics that require no cooking at all:
  - Huge baskets, filled with large rustic Italian and French loaves
  - A tray of whole cheeses: Camembert, Cheddar, Stilton or Dolcelatte
  - Another of Parma ham, salamis, figs and mozzarella
  - Big bowls of rocket, baby spinach leaves and Parmesan shavings
  - Plates of fresh fruit and bowls of clotted cream or crème fraîche
  - Baskets of home-made shortbread
- Add two or three simple-to-prepare buffet dishes, such as:
  - Poached salmon
  - New potatoes with pesto
  - Giant rustic pizzas: buy a basic pizza dough mix, kneed into a rough oblong shape (as large as your largest baking sheet), and top with a basic tomato sauce, selection of marinated vegetables, thinly sliced mozzarella and a drizzle of olive oil. Bake as specified for the base.
  - Pasta salad: fusilli, penne or shells, stirred together with toasted pine

kernels, grilled red and yellow peppers, and topped with Parmesan shavings.

- Get a professional to provide one or two key dishes, beautiful puddings or a hundred or so freshly made canapés to intersperse with your own work: it won't raise the price too much, but will cut your workload and raise overall standards. If you don't have a good local deli, Waitrose offers a party catering service, called By Invitation. Visit the ordering point in a store, choose from a catalogue of menus, and it's ready five days later.
- Order in a take-away: for small parties, Indian, Chinese or fish and chips make a great late-night supper. Negotiate the price, based on advance booking and a bigger-than-usual order.
- For an easy pudding, mini Haagen Dazs are great, and come with their own spoon! Present lots of different tubs on a bed of ice. Alternatively, could you persuade an ice cream van to come and visit at the right moment?
- Create a visual feast of sweets, cakes, petits fours and meringues. Devote a whole table to it, work to a colour scheme, and use plates and cake stands at different heights, tall jars of candy, and a tower of prof-iteroles (*croquembouche*) for impact.

CAKE

If you're confident enough to bake your own cake, find a recipe from a sound, tried-and-tested source like *The Good Housekeeping Cookery Book* (Ebury Press), or invest in a copy of *Chocolate Cakes For Weddings & Celebrations* by John Slattery (Murdoch), or *Romantic Wedding & Celebration Cakes* by Kerry Vincent (Murdoch). Otherwise, cheat:

- Buy three sizes of plain white iced fruit cakes off the shelf at Waitrose or Marks & Spencer, stack on top of each other, and decorate with flowers or wrap with broad bands of ribbon in complementary colours.
- Make your own cake, but have it iced and assembled professionally.
- Create a meringue tower: make and store as many small round meringues as you have guests. On the day – and not before – someone (other than the bride) just needs to stack up a pyramid of meringues with

Self-catering

'We'd planned to do all the food at our wedding. In the end, we just made the cake and puddings. It was pretty stressful, but it was worth it.' Couple, 33 and 34.

'My mum and lots of her friends spent weeks making all the nibbles and dishes to accompany a hog-roast barbecue. Everything went smoothly, and it saved a lot of money.' Bride, 29.

a wide base, using whipped double cream as 'cement'. No more than a few hours ahead, poke daisy stems into the cream around the tower, so the flowers sit flat against the sides.

- Buy lots of prettily coloured mini fondant cakes, tie with different ribbons, and pile up on a multi-layered old-fashioned cake stand. Or do the same with fairy cakes, decorated with Love Heart sweets.
- If you need to transport your cake, assemble tiers after moving it, not before. Entrust a friend with last-minute finishing touches.
- Specialist cake-makers' shops are full of ingenious equipment and devices for making, assembling, decorating and transporting cakes. They'll hire out tins and other equipment, and give advice, too. Blue Ribbons Sugarcraft Centre offers a nationwide mail order service, or look for other stockists in *Yellow Pages*.
- Don't leave it to chance: bake a trial quantity of any recipe for tasting before doing the real thing, and have a trial run so that you're confident about assembly and packing in good time.
- Don't forget that a cake may wilt in the heat: put it out as late as possible, and choose one that's more sturdy in high summer.

DRINK

Planning and buying
- If you don't know much about wine, go to a good wine merchant and ask for advice, or enlist the help of a knowledgeable friend.

- Keep an eye out for discounts on good wines and buy while the stock is plentiful.
- Don't spend a fortune on wine unless you're sure your guests will appreciate it. People assume that wine is only moderately priced at weddings, whatever you spend.
- Avoid popular labels: everyone knows how much they cost.
- Don't buy wine with a supermarket label on it, however good. It just won't seem right.
- Quantities:
  - How much you'll need is, of course, totally dependent on how much your guests drink, and how long they'll be drinking for.
  - The oft-quoted guide of half a bottle of wine per head with a meal, plus one-third of a bottle of champagne for toasts, is a starting point, but I've yet to go to a wedding where consumption wasn't closer to twice that.
  - As a ready reckoner, you'll get about 6 glasses from a bottle of champagne or wine and 25 measures from a liqueur or spirits' bottle.
  - Beer, cocktails and other drink are even more difficult to calculate: there's no real substitute for sitting down with your guest list and working through who you think will drink how much of what!
  - Soft drinks go at a rate of between half and one litre per person.
  - Buy on a 'drink or return' basis, and you won't have to worry too much about quantity. Only chill as much as you need, because you won't be able to return bottles once labels have floated off into the ice bucket.
- Going overseas will save money, but do take account of the extra costs, such as the fact that you'll have to over-buy and won't be able to return unopened bottles, the possible need to hire a van, and the Channel crossing. Shop around for a good fare; prices can vary by hundreds of pounds for no apparent reason.
  - Before a Channel crossing, plan exactly what you'll buy when you get there, and ring to check they have it in stock.
  - If you go for the Calais outlet of a UK store, such as Oddbins, you may be able to find the wine to try here first.

- You can place an order direct via the Sainsbury's Calais website: it will also calculate the cost-saving for you.
- Do your research: read *The Channel Hopper's Guide* (Passport Guides), go to their website, or visit the Day Tripper website, which is crammed with shopping and Channel-crossing information.
- You could even drive the extra two or three hours to the Champagne region, and buy direct.
- Buy beer in small bottles and mineral water at the same time. It's ludicrously cheap.
- Cross-Channel limits are:
  - Wines: 90 litres
  - Spirits: 10 litres
  - Beer: 110 litres
  - Champagne: 60 litres
  - Fortified wine: 20 litres
- Work out the logistics of getting drink to the wedding venue: wine merchants will deliver countrywide, but if you've bought in France you'll have to organise that yourself.
- If you plan on servings cocktails or coolers, invest in a good recipe book, such as *Party Drinks* by Ian Wisniewski (Conran Octopus).
- If you want to forget the hassle but enjoy really good wine, you could entrust the whole exercise to The Pure Wine Company, whose wines are all organic. Give them a menu and let them worry about the rest.
- Buy ice rather than making it yourself; order in advance.

Money-wise: What to expect
DIY wedding food: a saving of 25–60%
Home-made wedding cake: about £120
Wine from France: a saving of 30–50%

Contacts
Blue Ribbons Sugarcraft Centre: 020 8941 1591; www.blueribbons.co.uk
Channel Hopper's Guides: www.channelhoppers.net
Day Tripper: www.day-tripper.net

National Association of Farmers' Markets: 01225 787914;
www.farmersmarkets.net
Oddbins: 0800 328 2323; www.oddbins.co.uk
Pure Wine Company: 0808 1003123; www.purewine.co.uk
Sainsbury's at Calais: www.sainsburys.co.uk/calais
Waitrose By Invitation: 0800 188884; www.waitrose.com

chapter thirteen

speak easy:
make them laugh, make them cry

Speeches can be a highpoint for wedding guests (as long as they're well done) and a nightmare for the speakers. In fact, weddings offer one of the best public speaking gigs going: you're on a high, your audience is on a high, everyone wants to hear what you've got to say, and at the end of it, everyone will clap and cheer, however bad you thought you were!

WHO SAYS WHAT

Each speech should form part of a show, leading from one to the next with momentum. They should be no more than about ten minutes long apiece, unless they are *very* good – even if you're the best man. As Bob Grosse, Secretary of the Guild of Professional Toastmasters, explains, etiquette sets the pace and structure very nicely:

First, the bride's father speaks to express good wishes. He

- Thanks everyone for coming, acknowledges the distances travelled and says how pleased he is that everyone is here for such a happy day.
- Says some nice things about his daughter and how proud he is: mentions her childhood, schooling, interests or career, and compliments her on her choice of husband.
- Continues with kind words about the groom: how the couple met, how he got to know and like him and how glad he is to welcome him into the family.
- Welcomes the groom's parents into the family.
- Finishes with some light-hearted advice to the groom, passing on the benefit of X years' experience living with his daughter.
- Closes with a toast to the bride and groom, in reply to which ...

The groom speaks to express thanks

- To his new father-in-law for his kind words and good wishes.
- To the bride's parents for their support, for allowing him their daughter's hand in marriage, and for providing a wonderful wedding reception (if they did).
- To his wife for marrying him and being such a wonderful bride, possibly recounting one or two anecdotes of their courtship.
- On behalf of both his wife and himself, to everyone at the wedding for sharing the day and for their gifts, making a toast to 'absent friends'.
- To people who have contributed to the wedding itself: this could be to specific individuals such as the clergyman for a moving and enjoyable service, a friend who has made the cake.
- To friends or family who have offered general support over the years.
- To his best man for his help and support.
- To the bridesmaids for their help with the wedding and for looking so special.
- Closing with a toast to the bridesmaids, on whose behalf ...

The best man speaks

- To thank the groom for the toast and compliments to the bridesmaids.

He then:

- Congratulates the couple.
- Thanks anyone who has helped him in his role on the day.
- And, 'while he's there', reveals a little of the groom's character to the guests who may or may not already know him.
- Aims to amuse and entertain the guests in the process (this is the tough bit, of course).
- Reads two or three of the most interesting or entertaining telegrams or messages sent by absent friends.
- Closes, if he wishes, with a toast to both sets of parents. Strictly speaking, say the Guild of Professional Toastmasters, it is not for him to toast the bride and groom: that is considered a special honour and the privilege only of the bride's father.

The bride's speech

- Fits in best after the father of the bride, thanking him for his kind words.
- Is made by almost half of all brides.
- Thanks everyone who has supported her on a practical and emotional level, making particular mention of her mum and other close family or friends on either side.
- Pays tribute to the couple's own children or stepchildren, if any.
- Is personal, heartfelt and not an opportunity for comedy, unless you know you can carry it off.
- Pre-empts her husband's chivalrous words about her, with a few about him, before passing over to her husband, who can thank her and her father for their kind words ...

Speaking for the bride

'My father and I decided he wasn't going to speak at my wedding, but at the last minute, I wanted someone to say something "for me". My girlfriend had written a really funny poem about shopping and fashion for my hen night – and I'd kept it with me. I asked her to read it straight after the best man's speech – and it stood up to the competition!' Bride, 27.

Speechless

'We didn't have any speeches. No-one really wanted to do it, so we all spent the time one-to-one instead, circulating the tables and taking round our guest book. I'm so glad we did – especially when I hear other couples saying they didn't have enough time to talk to everyone.' Groom, 28.

DOING IT DIFFERENTLY

If tradition doesn't work for you, work out what does:

- One change in approach is a series of five or six three-minute toasts, poems, eulogies or speeches from people who are chosen specially for their ability and knowledge of the couple. Time limits are strict.
- An entire speech can be given in the form of a poem. As well as sounding wonderful, and being very entertaining, delivery is much easier.
- Don't deliver a speech, run a trivia quiz instead. Put paper and pens on the table before the meal, then pose questions about the bride, the groom, their romance and the wedding. As in a pub quiz, each table passes their answer sheet to the next for marking. Relevant anecdotes can be told as you give out answers.
- Additional speakers, such as father of the groom, bride or bride's mother, usually speak after the bride's father and before the groom.
- Anyone can speak in place of the bride's father, but someone from her parents' generation will have a good perspective.
- If the best man is a great organiser but not a great speaker, a second can be appointed to do the talking.

☺☹ *'I was so nervous during the meal that while I was busy nagging the groom and best man not to drink too much before the speeches, I was glugging back the red and getting completely plastered. I heckled them right the way through their speeches, and thought I was hilarious. The next day, I was absolutely mortified. Heckling just isn't me, and everyone had worked so hard on their bit, I would have done anything to turn the clock back. I can't even think about the video, never mind watch it.' Bride, 32.*

SPEECHES AT SECOND WEDDINGS

Can be just as good, if not better, but

- Try not to duplicate speeches made at the first wedding: many of the guests will have already heard those childhood anecdotes. Concentrate mainly on the present and the future.
- Make a point of including children of either partner in the speech.
- Do not mention an ex-husband/wife or their parents, unless it can be done with genuine affection.
- If appropriate, sensitively acknowledge a first spouse who has died.

COMPOSING YOUR SPEECH

As long as you give it enough thought to make your words personal and heartfelt, and enough practice so that you feel confident and everyone can hear you, you can't go very wrong.

Give yourself plenty of time
Leaving it to the last minute is simply asking for trouble. The best speeches come from months of gathering material, weeks of writing, hours and hours of practising and rehearsing. Our best man's speech was so extraordinarily good, people still ask me for a copy of it; he worked steadily and determinedly on it for nine months.

Set goals
Start by setting out a few clear goals before you write your speech. Measure your material, the speech itself and the delivery against them. They may be:

- To give some (flattering) insight into the kind of person the groom is (for the best man), or the kind of person the bride is (for the bride's father).
- To pay tribute to both groom and bride.
- To amuse and entertain.

Gather material

Now gather the information and thoughts that will provide the raw material on which to base your speech. Possible avenues of search include:

- Mums, who invariably keep a box of treasures: newspaper cuttings, school reports, essays, letters and postcards.
- Quizzing friends and family. Meet up for a drink or two, and ask anyone who has them to bring along some photos to start the ball rolling. Take copious notes – or a tape recorder.
- History: What was happening the year the groom/bride was born? Newspaper headlines, the pop charts and fashion trends can all inspire quips about the person he/she became.
- Quotations: Anything she/he's said in the past which now seems very auspicious. Or, having identified certain traits in your subject, find relevant quotations from literature or current affairs. Quotations' books are plentiful on most subjects, or go online to Quotation Central.

Write the speech

By the time you've gathered some juicy material, you'll probably be itching to get started. To start, just get things down on paper, any old how. The most important things about the content of a speech, says speechwriter Chloe Hardy, is that it should suit the audience and have structure: a beginning, a middle and an end.

- **The first thirty seconds** of your speech are probably the most important. You must grab the attention of the audience and engage their interest. You could raise a thought-provoking question, make an interesting statement, or recite a relevant quotation.
- **Then introduce yourself:** What your relationship is to the subject, and how long you've know him/her and how well, with examples.
- **Set out the points you want to make:** As best man, for instance, you could cover:
  - How you and the groom met or sealed your friendship.
  - Stories about his schooldays, youth or early career.
  - A particular trait for which he is well known, such as being an avid football supporter, a keen cook, or a little extravagant.

- How the couple met, and any insight from the early days.
- Tales of the proposal or preparation for the wedding which might be a revelation, steering clear of the stag night.
- Why you think they're made for each other – making specific reference to the bride – and are sure they're destined for a happy future.

Get everything you want to say on to paper, and illustrate each point with anecdotes. Mix mockery with sincerity. Aim to raise a smile, not crucify with embarrassment.

- **Now go back and organise the points in a logical sequence,** so they link together and build on each other. Don't make countless points – just say a few things well.
- **The close of your speech** must contain some of your strongest material. Summarise the main point(s) of your speech, provide some further

---

From the expert: The golden rules of speeches and toasts

Bob Grosse, Secretary of the Guild of Professional Toastmasters

On speeches: 'Nothing blue, nothing suggestive, nothing racist, nothing about previous girlfriends and no bad language.'

On toasts: 'When you ask guests to raise their glasses, don't forget to ask them to stand up first!'

On the bride: 'Don't express too much amazement at how beautiful the bride looks!'

From the experts: Humour

Speechwriters Occasional Words

'Every one of us has had to endure a speech where the guy thought he was funny. Painful, isn't it? The simple rule about using humour is this: keep it low key, make it smart and make it quick. Another valuable rule is to personalise your humour – draw from your own experiences and your natural humour will come through. Tradition suggests leading off a speech with a joke. We say wrong! If your joke bombs, you've lost your audience before you've even begun.'

food for thought with a mention of the certainty of happiness to come, and wish the bride and groom well.
- **Go back and read it:** Does it meet your goals? Is it all relevant? Rewrite it, concentrating on getting the language and sentence structure right.
- **Finally, check:** Is it too long? (Ten minutes is about right for a best man's speech.) Does it break any of the golden rules?

REHEARSING AND MAKING YOUR SPEECH

Experts such as Bruno Barton and speechwriters Occasional Words share the benefit of their experience:

Preparation
- Write or print your speech in large lettering on to A5 cards (postcards are too small).
- Use as many cards as necessary, without cramming too much text on to each.
- Number them in case you drop them.
- Highlight or underline key words and phrases in coloured ink.

Practising
- Take time to become comfortable with the words you're going to say; your speech will improve dramatically. Practise as many times as necessary to get phrasing, pauses and timing exactly right. An hour for every minute of the speech is not too much: that's ten hours' practice for a ten-minute speech!
- Don't be afraid of going stale. If you can speak off the cuff, congratulations. The rest of us need practice and cue cards.
- Read the speech aloud to yourself at the same pace you'll read it to the audience. Identify any lines that don't sound right and rewrite them. Each time you practise, speak it properly. Use the intonation, pauses and voice modulation that you do in normal speech – not a brief, monotonous run-through. Do it in front of a mirror.

- Speak clearly, project your voice and take *plenty* of time. Time yourself.
- Use visualisation techniques: imagine an audience of the size that you'll speak to. Get used to that image, project your voice to the back of the room, make eye contact with imagined people all round the room. It helps, too, to visualise the applause and triumph when you've success-fully completed your mission.
- When using your cards, read a phrase, look up, deliver it, and look down for the next phrase.
- Practise in front of a friend, to help get over stage fright. Choose some-one who you feel comfortable with and ask for constructive advice and criticism.

On the day, before you speak
- Deal with sweating, shaking and a racing heart by taking long deep breaths, repeatedly. Try taking a breath for four counts, tensing your toes, and then releasing for four counts while you breath out. Repeat, tensing and releasing the muscles in a different part of your body with each breath. Work from your toes to the top of your head. You can do all this at the table while you wait to speak.
- Have no caffeine and just one drink.
- Remember that you are amongst friends and everyone is ready to enjoy what you say – even if it's not the most fantastic thing they've ever heard!

Beating stage fright

'I was due to make the best man's speech at a friend's wedding, but I just didn't believe I could do it. I'd tried speaking before, and it was disastrous. Then someone suggested a simple technique to help take away the fear: pick a subject you're passionate or enthusiastic about (football/Kylie/a great book – whatever gets you talking), and stand up and talk about it – at random – for a minute, in front of a friend. Don't give it any thought, just say what comes into your head. You'll be amazed how the words flow, and how good it feels to be making a speech.' Best man, 25.

21st-century dilemma: Should you use high-tech equipment?

This is a speech, not a business presentation. That said, a few visual aids can polish it up, entertain, and take the attention away from you for a moment. Ensure, however, that you're fully familiar with the equipment, and it doesn't take over or interrupt the flow of the speech. A PA system and microphone is a must in a large marquee, say the experts, because there are no acoustics, and you might want one anyway in another large venue, if there's a danger of not being heard. Get a 'dynamic' microphone: you'll need to hold it close to your mouth, but it doesn't feed back in that horrible way.

Delivery

- Be confident: this is a good speech and you're ready. What's more, you've been asked to do it because you're the best person for the job.
- Stand up and wait for silence. Begin when you are ready.
- Stand straight and project your voice out towards the audience. Make eye contact with individuals and smile occasionally. Keep breathing and relax your limbs. Put your visualisation techniques into practice.
- If you stumble over some words, don't panic. Move on if it was a small error, correct yourself confidently if it's necessary.
- If a tremble kicks into your voice, focus your efforts on speaking distinctly and at an even pace.
- Deliver each phrase with the measure, time and emphasis it needs. Stop to allow laughter to die down. Don't accelerate if laughter doesn't come. It doesn't matter. You're not just saying things to be funny, you're saying them because they make an interesting point.
- Speak up, and ask if everyone can hear you all right if you're not sure.
- Finish strong, in your choice of words and delivery. Avoid the impulse to gather your papers or slump into your seat. Wait a few moments, keeping your eye on the audience, then ask them to stand and make the next toast.

BRING IN THE PROFESSIONALS

Speechwriting experts can take the pain out of the whole episode. Some will write it for you, some will coach you in delivering it, and some will even make the speech on your behalf! As a halfway house, some also provide a basic template for each kind of speech, into which you slot the right dates, names and places, together with personal amusing anecdotes. *See* **Contacts** below.

Money-wise: What to expect
In the money-eating world of weddings, it's good to know that one of the highpoints is free! If you choose to pay:
Speech templates: about £30
Personally written speeches: about £200

Contacts
A Speech: 01472 237973; www.aspeech.co.uk. Malcolm Perkins' personal speechwriting service.
Crisp & Cheerful: 0800 389 8568; www.crispandcheerful.co.uk. Wedding speeches.
Occasional Words: www.occasionalwords.com. Canadian website rich with good advice.
Presence in Poetry: 020 8402 1374. Speeches in the form of a poem.
Quotation Central: www.quotations.com. Paid-for online resource.
Sparkling Wedding Speeches: 0121 444 3131; www.sparklingspeeches.co.uk. As well as providing a personal speech, Bruno Barton will critique your performance before the day. Basic speech templates are also available at www.finespeeches.com.
Speechtips: www.speechtips.com. Online speechwriting guidance from a US site.
Word Power: 01603 700547; www.wordpower.co.uk. Personally written speeches.

section
five

look fabulous and stay sane

The ultimate guide for a gorgeous, happy couple

chapter
fourteen

a stunning couple

In the general gorgeousness stakes, women have lately surrendered some of the limelight to their beautiful men. With credit possibly due to the likes of Brad Pitt and Jennifer Aniston, Jude Law and Sadie Frost, fashion *and* beauty have become a couple thing. And it's a great formula for weddings. No longer confined to formalwear 'uniforms', there can be as much antici-pation about his choice of dress as there is about hers. But while you're thinking about a collective look, don't be tempted to cross that fine line from well-partnered style to killer-coordinates, like Posh and Becks in their purple satin combos, topped off with Brooklyn's coordinating Stetson.

WHAT'S YOUR LOOK?

The only rule (or common sense) is that what you wear is appropriate to your own occasion. To be on the safe side, let the celebrant know what the dress code is, particularly at a religious wedding. Inevitably, the bride's look leads and the groom's will follow, save the occasional exception (like mine, where

From the experts: Where to buy
Brides magazine

For a comprehensive contact list of shops and suppliers for bridal wear, accessories, specialist services like shoe dyeing, and hair and beauty experts, the Brides *magazine address book is superb. It's free with the magazine every year and a permanent fixture on their website. Contact details are on page 224.*

he wasn't going to let anything come between him and his best excuse yet for a bespoke Ozwald Boateng suit and a pair of shiny Prada slippers).

For the girls, the question is simply White Dress or Not? The best laid plans to be original often end up on a road which goes something like this: 'Oh no, I'm not going to have a wedding dress, I'd prefer something, you know, a bit different ... trendy, maybe – or a bit glam ... Although ... I might just look at a few, you know, proper white dresses, just to see ...' And then, nine times out of ten, we've reached the point of no return.

The good news is that the fairy-princess look is enjoying a revival. Not only has the classic white dress entered new and stylish territory (as a flick through any wedding magazine will reveal), but some of the chicest labels have lately done the whole innocent-and-feminine thing big time. So you can do it with your fashion head held high.

If you find you *do* have the tenacity to stick with something less predictable, you have my greatest admiration – and couldn't have picked a better time to do it: the options are wide open, and mega-stylish, too. Glitzy evening gowns are perfect for weddings, for instance, and so is an all-white take on the retro, pencil-skirt-and-heels look.

For the boys, the first (and most obvious) thought is of traditional morning dress. A well-fitting morning coat, at the right kind of occasion, does indeed look very fine, but it's very much a uniform, and more men than girls now seem to throw tradition to the wind. Suits – finely tailored or casual – are the natural alternative, and there are many other options besides.

For shared style, consider:

TRADITIONAL WHITE

For her: Straight or full, beaded, embroidered or plain, bare-shouldered or long-sleeved; Queen Victoria's original fashion statement still goes strong.

For him: Morning dress is traditional – unless you're entitled to wear military uniform – but a classically tailored suit works too. This is also the place for ivory or cream brocade/silk damask coats or waistcoats – if you can avoid the 'Footballer weds' look.

ELEGANT CLASSIC

For her: The traditional wedding gown grows up with grace – into Grecian drapes, strapless columns and simple sharp lines.

For him: A classically tailored or sharp suit.

END OF INNOCENCE

For her: Sexy, body-hugging white dress (think Kylie-esque starlets in Julien Macdonald gowns at London premieres).

For him: Narrow-cut pants and slim-fitting Seventies shirt.

WHITE TROUSER SUIT

For her: Super-sharp or soft and fluid; Bianca Jagger will always be credited with this enduring trend.

For him: If it's hot, or overseas, and you have a strong sense of style, you might successfully carry off a white or cream suit of your own (I wish you luck, though, I must admit). A neutral or dark colour might be safer, if you could give the tie a miss.

OSCAR NIGHT

For her: Dazzling glitz and glamour, all sparkly and slinky: think Minnie Driver, Jennifer Aniston and all the other girls who do the red carpet so well.

For him: Black tie, or a really edgy deep-hued suit. White tie is more flash, but can be fun. Brad Pitt, Will Smith or Pierce Brosnan make pretty good role models; don't do a Russell Crowe, though, with that sheriff look!

COSTUME

For you both: Think Twenties, Fifties, Edwardian, Georgian and Elizabethan
– whether the wedding is themed or not.

COLOUR

For her: Pick the shade that suits you best – from soft blue to scarlet – and
use it for details, decoration or the dress itself. Bear in mind that big
expanses of really bright colours like purple or red will dominate photos.

For him: Don't be tempted to copy the look wholesale, unless you're pitching
for the cover of *Hello!* magazine. Better to choose black or grey attire, and
work in almost-matching shades to hers in your shirt, tie or buttonhole.

BOHO

For her: Skimpy, bias-cut or hippy-chic dress trimmed with feathers or beads.
For him: Nehru-collared or nicely crumpled suit; no tie.

BLACK

For her: Fashion's perennial favourite colour is totally unexpected at a wedding, so as a style statement, you just can't beat it. It's super-flattering,
of course, and you'll be able to wear it over and over.

For him: Depending on how dressy the dress is, a black shirt and tie, or a
snugly fitting black crew-neck (think Brad Pitt, again, if you can bear it)
adds a twist to the classic black suit.

Contacts on page 224 lists all phone numbers and websites for shops and
services in this chapter.

Girls first

We girls all want the same thing for our wedding … don't we? A bride's
absolute happiness on her wedding day could depend on just four vital things:
- That our choice of dress (or otherwise) is seen to be exactly what it is …
a masterpiece of exquisite taste and original thought.

- That it is *not* a fat day.
- That it is *not* the day you get a great red beacon of a spot.
- That it is *not* a bad hair day.

CHOOSING THE PERFECT DRESS

The options
From cheap and chic to top whack, in that order. For phone numbers and websites, *see* **Contacts**; for price guides, *see* **Money-wise: What to expect** on page 223.

- **High street everyday clothes:** Zara, Mango, Jigsaw, French Connection, Oasis et al are fantastic for pretty but special summer dresses, evening wear and well-cut trouser suits, and Topshop (fashion's Mecca) is bargain-heaven. Shop at the start of the season for plenty of choice, sizes and colours.
- **High street bridal wear:** Monsoon have some fabulous wedding dresses, and so do Debenhams, whose range has included designs from Jasper Conran, Pearce II Fionda and Ben de Lisi for just a few hundred pounds. Bhs is cheaper still and great for simple dresses.
- **Dressmaker:** If you know exactly what you want, that it will suit you, and you have a good dressmaker, you could save yourself a fortune. Some brides make their own, but even as a semi-confident seamstress, that scared the living daylights out of me. Don't try anything sneaky like taking the dressmaker to see you in the dress you want her to copy. It's a bit dodgy. For a list of professional dressmakers, contact Butterick's. For more on dressmaking, go online to Sew Direct.
- **Designer day or evening wear:** Ready-to-wear and diffusion lines from leading designers can still work out cheaper than a full-blown wedding dress. Look in big department stores for Armani, Ben de Lisi, Ghost, Donna Karan and more: pre-Christmas is best for evening wear (or just after, in the sales).
- **Almost new:** Once-worn wedding dresses can be a great buy, as can ex-samples. Try Déjà Vu, Modern Bride, The Bridal Gown Exchange, The

21st-century dilemma:
Dare a man ever enter a wedding dress shop?

You don't have to keep your dress a secret from your husband-to-be and yes, for the record, there's no law against taking him, or another male friend to shop with you. It's meant to be bad luck, but that may mean nothing to you, and his could be the only opinion you really want. Do warn each shop you plan to visit with your man, though: while some, like celebrity designer Neil Cunningham, have gone on record as being all in favour, others need a chance to get used to the idea!

From the expert: Investment dressing
Hilde Pollet, wedding dress designer

'It doesn't really make good sense to wear your dress just once. If it's being created especially for you, work with the designer on finding shapes, colours and fabrics which you can wear afterwards, too.'

Wedding Dress Exchange and Designer Bridal Wear. If you need to get one altered, Designer Alterations specialise in just that. End of season sales (January and July) are a good time to buy ex-samples from general bridal wear shops.

- **Hired evening and wedding dresses** are worn only a few times, so most look like new.
- **Theatrical dress hire:** From Angels, Royal National Theatre Costume Hire and Carousel Costumes.
- **Ready-to-wear bridal wear:** There are few ready-to-buy wedding dresses, which is why you need plenty of time. Most are now either:
- **Altered-to-fit bridal wear:** Try on a sample, and the dress is ordered in the standard dress size closest to your own. It's then altered for a much-improved fit. Minor design variations may be possible.
- **Made-to-measure bridal wear:** Again, you try on a sample, but the dress is made from scratch to your measurements. You may have more scope to customise a dress to your ideal and the fit should be perfect.

From the expert: Shop alone
Monique Lhuillier, Hollywood dress designer
'I always advise my clients to go shopping by themselves first. Really be true to yourself and pick gowns that reflect your personal style, rather than bringing along a lot of family members who perceive you in a different way and influence your decision.'

● **One-off and couture design:** Whether you go direct to a designer for a one-off wedding dress, evening dress or other outfit, the process is the same – and may involve several thousand pounds. The designer will create an original design in the perfect fit, giving you the freedom to have whatever you want. For women who aren't used to buying clothes this way (most of us) it's a huge leap of faith, however, to commit thousands of pounds to something we haven't seen. There will be a toile, or mock-up, in calico, which helps to refine your ideas before the thing is made up for real.

☺☺ *'I knew exactly how I wanted my dress, and I let the designer talk me out of it. I didn't really like what I wore and wish that I'd found someone else with more enthusiasm for my own style. I still regret not sticking to my guns.' Bride, 30.*
☺☺ *'My dress looked like a nightie. I don't know what made me choose it … I think I thought it would look trendy!' Bride, 26.*
☺☺ *'I found the whole wedding dress shopping thing really embarrassing. I felt really self-conscious. In the end, I went on impulse with a friend when we both had truly terrible hangovers. I found a dress I loved, and figured that if I looked good in it feeling – and looking – like I did just then, I'd be all right!' Bride, 27.*

Sharp shopping
Whatever you choose, from high street frock to couture gown, this should be one of the most blissful shopping experiences of your life, so make the most of it.

- **Set a budget:** In no other area of the wedding will you be more tempted to break the rules. There is no 'right' price for a wedding dress: see above for shopping routes in order of cost. At each shop, make your budget clear from the start.
- **Make appointments:** Almost all shops are 'appointment only'. If you can, do a weekday: Saturdays, lunchtimes and late-night shopping are often *heavily* booked. If you don't have a particular designer or shop in mind, contact the Retail Bridalwear Association, or look in the *Brides* magazine address book.
- **Give yourself plenty of time:** Six months is not too long, three months is getting tight for made to measure. You also need lots of shopping time: days to scout and refine your ideas, and more to settle on the dress of your dreams. Then there's all the fittings ...
- **If you're really short of time:** You may be threatened with price premiums to have things done quickly, but they're rarely justified, so beware. If you can't find an off-the-peg evening or wedding dress from the high street, a bridal shop might order a standard size quite quickly (miss out the alterations), or you may be lucky with an ex-sample or second-hand dress that's ready to go.
- **Have an idea of what you like,** but no more than that. Never buy on your first trip, and be open to suggestion. Choose your shopping partners carefully. Go alone on your first foray: sisters, best friends and mothers know you too well to think laterally. Enlist advice after that, but stick to your principles.

Dressing for weddings abroad
Choose:
- Something cool – or warm – enough. It's easy to forget just how hot the Caribbean is, or how cold the snow, when faced with something stunning in a dress shop.
- Shoes to suit the terrain: lace-up boots are a good option for snowy ground; avoid very high heels in the sand.
- Clothing which will travel well. Ideally, it should pack small enough (without being crushed – pack in a rigid box with acid-free tissue) to take as

hand-luggage. Make arrangements in advance with the airline: if you can't keep it in the cabin with you, ask for it to be loaded last and unloaded first.

● Insurance which covers the dress for *all* eventualities. The small print is particularly crucial here.

Second weddings

Grown-up wedding dressing has never looked so good – but a low-key approach is not obligatory.

Pregnant brides

Whether you plan on discretion or showing it off, a bump is now one of the most stylish bridal accessories. The choice of clothes is almost limitless; depending on your shape, cleverly cut couture, a fashionable empire line, a clingy, funky silhouette or fluid, flattering trouser suit can all work well.

Fit to flatter

Until I bought my wedding dress (blissfully, I must say, at Bridal Rogue Gallery), I really couldn't see the point in those buying-guides. The kind that says, if you're tall and thin, wear something really nice and trendy, and a smug look on your face; if you've got a massive backside, don't feel *too* humiliated – just avoid skin-tight, see-through mini-skirts. Tell me something I *don't* know …

I must confess, though, that once I'd betrayed the Something A Bit Different sorority and gone all Proper White, I found them quite useful, because I was trying on the kinds of clothes I'd never worn before. So here's my version, courtesy of my many figure faults and some of my best-looking bridal friends.

● **If you have a very full bust:** Lucky, lucky you. I spent my wedding day in a magnificently structured corset whose capabilities went woefully unchallenged. But since one of my best friends hates her bust, I've seen the misery of that, too. A trouser suit with a long-ish jacket looks great on her shape, especially as big busts tend to go hand in hand with good, long legs. Dress shapes that suit are well fitted and long (but not too tight) in the body, and a wide neckline that covers (most of) the cleavage and fans out across the shoulders. If you still want a classic wedding dress, a dark bodice is flattering.

- **If you have a very small bust:** Don't crush it flat! I had my boned corset made to measure *around* my padded bra, and it worked a treat. Those things have a construction all of their own, so no-one knows what goes on underneath. If you feel very bony, a stole looks good, or try some cleavage-enhancing underwear.
- **If you have dumpy legs:** A long, slightly A-line dress over high heels is a must. A little train adds to the illusion of length. People will think you're leggy. Miraculous.
- **If you have a thick waist:** A pointy-down V-shape waistline for you. Make sure it's just below the waist, not on it, or you'll end up looking like you've got freakishly wide hips instead.
- **If you're a classic pear:** Wedding dresses are great for us, because they fit well; most high street clothes are so strangely cut, they make things seem so much worse. A slim-bodiced, wide-skirted dress, *à la* Davina McCall, will have them all thinking you're reed-slim. For a narrower silhouette, a soft A-line with a train falling from the waist covers a multitude of sins. Forget bias-cut. Completely.
- **If you have plump arms:** Everyone hates the top of their arms, according to 90% of the dress shops I went to. Choose long sleeves reaching onto the hand in a slim, but not tight fit. If you want to go strapless, a wrap with a clasp flatters more than those little bolero tops.
- **If you're small:** You're feminine and dainty, and I'll bet you've got small feet too. So what's your problem? My daintiest friend said that full dresses looked ridiculous on her, but since she couldn't decide between a girlish little strappy number and a slim column, both of which looked truly amazing, I didn't feel too sorry for her. Overly high heels are counterproductive – you could look all shoe and no body.
- **If you're a little larger** than the average Barbie doll, this is your moment. Having something made to measure will be sheer heaven. You can choose boning to define and enhance your shape, a skimming A-line skirt which cares nothing for what's underneath, and details that

make you feel gorgeous. Go for a simple, streamlined silhouette, and maximise good features like a pretty cleavage or small waist. The only problem is trying them on: ring bridal shops in advance to see if they have samples in something more realistic than a size 10 to avoid a disheartening experience.

- **White, ivory or cream?** Everyone will push ivory on you. At least try white – it suits some people much better.

ACCESSORIES

Don't overdo the accessory thing. Bags, wraps, veils, tiaras and bracelet/necklace/earring sets can be so beautiful and beguiling, you forget that wearing them all at once is not a good move. Best for cheap and chic jewellery, hairclips or tiaras: Hennes, Selfridges, Fenwick and Accessorize.

Your bouquet – should you have one – will obviously marry up with the look of your dress, provide a theme for the buttonholes and attendants' flowers, and even hook up with the venue decorations, too. For more on flowers, *see* Chapter Ten.

Headdressing
Even if veils aren't your thing, most brides want to wear something on their heads. It usually gives the look polish and moves you into another – bridal – world, even if it's just a flower tucked behind your ear or sparkly hairclip.

- **Veils:** One of the big do-you, don't-you questions. Lengths vary from short to ridiculously long, and the only way to decide what and if is to try it with your dress. Wearing 'just a short one' isn't always a compromise, though: because it's short, it sticks out, and because it sticks out, it may be considerably more noticeable than a long one which just hangs neatly behind you.
- **Tiaras:** I just love tiaras. Really, that's why I wanted a long white dress. They're so pretty and twinkly and girly, and they can be made however you want them. They look fantastic hanging over the mirror of your dressing table forever more, so they're well worth the money.

- **Hats:** The obvious partner to a trouser suit, a cute or wide-brimmed hat can also shift a simple wedding dress into an altogether funkier league. Stetsons, berets and matador hats, too, have all been done to great effect.

Shoes

The style is down to you, but comfort is essential.

- Choose a shoe type which you've worn comfortably in the past. First-time spike heels and laced-up ankles can be challenging.
- You're going to be on your feet for a *long* time. A slightly more solid heel, less pointy toe or proper ankle strap will make all the difference.
- Get your shoes before the final alterations on your outfit or dress, so the length is exactly right.

Celebrity inspiration

Famous brides can spend £100,000 (or more) on their version of the long white gown:

Keely Shaye Smith *married Pierce Brosnan in a simple strapless dress topped with a fitted lace coat by Richard Tyler.*

Courtney Cox *married David Arquette in a fabulously elegant, slim-cut, long-sleeved, cowl-necked gown by Valentino.*

Jennifer Lopez *wore romantic lace, also by Valentino.*

Sara Cox *chose Vivienne Westwood's trademark high-class courtesan corset look.*

Madonna's *still-secret dress was designed by friend Stella McCartney.*

Catherine Zeta-Jones *wore a sculpted, beaded, sleeveless dress by Christian Lacroix.*

Jemima Goldsmith *wore a slim silhouette and fitted jacket by Bruce Oldfield, topped with a wide-brimmed hat.*

Victoria Beckham and **Davina McCall** *both wore the tight bodice and full skirt of Vera Wang, the designer of choice for celebrity brides.*

Kate Winslet *wore a plunging beaded gown by Alexander McQueen for Givenchy.*

- Cover the soles with masking tape so you can take them back if they hurt before the wedding.
- Wear them around the house for a few hours, two or three times, to get used to them.
- If you plan to dye your shoes after the wedding, don't Scotchguard them. The dye won't take properly if you do.

What lies beneath

Few wedding dresses allow for sexy underwear; most require something sleeker and more functional (and a quick change later if it's going to make him happy).

- **Shaper-tights:** If you're bum- or thigh-conscious, these are just so worth it, whether you're wearing a dress or trousers. Make sure you get a good strong pair with support all over the tummy, bottom and thighs. Not only will you go down half a dress size, but your bottom won't wobble as you walk up the aisle and they'll smooth out any knicker-line, too. The difficulty is getting them in ivory, cream or white: if anyone you know is going to the US, ask them to get you a pair of Donna Karan's, because they're the best and come in all the right shades.
- **Tummy-shapers:** If a flat tummy eludes you, these are miraculous. They come in 'big pant' and cycling short varieties.
- **Strapless bra:** Unlike most, the Wonderbra version actually stays up and gives you some oomph, too.

White mischief

Not so traditional looks:

Billie Piper married Chris Evans in a sarong, bare midriff, white shirt and flip-flops.

Rachel from Cold Feet wore a hot pink-on-white floral print.

Cindy Crawford wore a thigh-length white slip of a dress – by John Galliano – and bare feet for her beach wedding.

And Bianca Jagger launched a thousand white trouser suits and wide-brimmed hats.

- **Bust-enhancers:** Gel bra inserts, stick-on moulded cups and stick-on supports (the underwear industry's answer to the old Sellotape trick) can work wonders. Try La Senza and Maxcleavage.com.
- **Lace a corset upwards** to **maximise** your *décolletée*.
- **Lace a corset downwards** to **minimise** a larger bust.

BEAUTY BRIEF

The one vital rule is: *Don't do anything new the day before your wedding*. I worked as a health and beauty journalist on women's glossy magazines for years, but it never became any less horrifying when people rang up – as they did from time to time – to say, 'Help, I had a perm yesterday, and it's a disaster, and I'm getting married tomorrow.' Trial runs and product tests should be done with weeks to spare, months for a new hairstyle or colour. Breaking this rule is just asking for trouble.

Shape up

If you're happy with your shape, whatever it is, great. Lots of brides, however, put a diet at the top of their 'to do' list, even if they're already slender. Anxieties about shape and size are naturally amplified by the thought of buying that ultimate item of clothing, and by the time you've been through a few trying-on sessions and imagined yourself walking up the aisle, all eyes on your rear view, you're one of the lucky ones if you can resist attempts to change.

I know you've heard it all before, but permanent lifestyle changes like steady exercise and healthy eating are the only route to weight loss that stays off. Give yourself plenty of time: a stone lost over a year through simple, sustainable changes is much healthier, and far more likely to be gone for good, than half a stone lost in a fortnight.

EXERCISE PAYS

Exercise makes you feel *so* much better: take it from one who's just resumed her pre-wedding running efforts after being sat on her backside for six months writing this book! As well as releasing feel-good hormones (endorphins) and burning off calories, a moderate amount of steady exercise can redistribute body fat so that clothes fit better in the most gratifying way.

Try to:

- Do some kind of aerobic exercise for half an hour four times a week.
  - Sustainable exercise, like a daily brisk walk, is infinitely more conducive to weight loss than frenzied, sporadic gym sessions: there's no build-up, no learning curve. You get maximum benefit from day one; you can do it any time, working it into your day such as by walking to work; and it's not hard, so you won't dread it and put it off.
  - Swimming, running, exercise classes and other sports are obviously just as beneficial, if not more so – as long as you do them regularly.
- Work out with a friend to keep motivation up, and find something you really enjoy.
- Protect yourself against injury by doing things properly and building up slowly. You'll get no benefit if you have to give up after a week because of a twisted knee.

EAT RIGHT

Eating healthily will dramatically improve your well being, looks and ability to cope under pressure, whether or not you're trying to lose weight.

- Make small but significant changes to your diet. Your mainstays should be:
  - Complex carbohydrates, such as wholemeal bread and cereals
  - Low-fat protein, in the form of lean meat, fish, beans and pulses
  - The whole range of green and brightly coloured vegetables
  - Plenty of fresh fruit.
- Take a multivitamin and mineral supplement.
- Drink loads and loads of water. Ask anyone who does it: the effect is dramatic.
- Minimise intake of:
  - Animal fat and fried food
  - High-fat dairy food
  - Refined carbohydrates: white flour and sugar
  - The baddies: salt, alcohol, caffeine and processed food.

CHEAT

The success of these slimming miracles is largely in the psyche of the user, I suspect, but the following may help your shape a little and boost your confidence a lot:

- Salon body wraps: they're expensive, and you'll probably need a few to see any results, but some people swear by these in times of crises.
- Slendertone: enjoying a revival; users say this is a great supplement to exercise when you just can't stand the thought of another sit-up, or have a particular trouble spot.
- Cellulite and slimming creams: I've done almost all of these, and I still have no idea if they work.
- Miracle underwear: this works, without a doubt. You can buy things to hold in your tummy, snap in thighs, support your bottom and flatten your chest. I don't even think they're particularly uncomfortable; others say they're a killer. More underwear cheats on page 206.

Skincare

If you're not doing it already, start a daily routine: remove make-up and cleanse thoroughly, then follow with a toner and a good dose of moisturiser. Most skins benefit from a gentle exfoliant twice a week, too.

It's worth paying a visit to your favourite skincare counter for an updated assessment of what your skin needs. Almost all the skincare brands now offer a one-to-one consultation, and even a mini facial, for about a tenner, which you get back on any product you buy. Don't feel you have to buy any more than you really need.

SPOT OF TROUBLE

Every girl's nightmare: the Big Spot on the Big Day. These are the rules:

- If you're prone to spots, now's the time to get to the bottom of the problem, if you haven't already:
  - Talk to your GP or a dermatologist if it's full-blown acne or any other clinical skin problem: you may need prescription-only treatment. Otherwise, see a good independent beauty therapist. As ever, do it in plenty of time. Even if you hit on a solution, it could take a few

months to do its work.

- Keep a log to calculate when in your monthly cycle you're likely to get spotty. If it hits bang on your wedding day, can you shift your cycle with the contraceptive pill?
- Keep a food log, too: it's a myth that chocolate causes spots, but food sensitivities in some people can trigger a break-out. Find out if that's true for you.
- Boost your intake of zinc and vitamins A, C and B6 – especially if skin problems are hormone-related.

- If your spots are the kind of random one-offs that everyone gets from time to time:
  - Don't, don't, don't squeeze:
    - If it's the day of the wedding, you can guarantee that squeezing will make it worse. Not only will it make it go bright red and swell, but you'll also break the skin, onto which make-up will not stick, so you won't even be able to conceal it.
    - If it's got to the end of its life, but it just won't go away, and you have some time in hand, go and get a beauty therapist to zap it for you.
  - Dab it with whatever works for you (but find out what it is in good time before the wedding: a medicated or drying treatment ointment, toothpaste, tea-tree oil or one of the many cosmetic blemish rescues on the market).

- When you make up, don't over-conceal, or you could end up drawing more attention to your spot, not less. Some make-up artists simply paint on regular foundation, mixed with liquid concealer, with a soft brush, and then dust with matt powder. When you touch up, gently remove the make-up on and around the spot and start again so powder doesn't clog up with a new layer of foundation.

Body beautiful
SILKY

Start working on rough skin on your back, knees, elbows and tops of arms: rub down with a rough towelling mitt, loofah or exfoliating body-scrub two or three times a week. Moisturise every day and you'll soon see a difference.

THE GOLDEN QUESTION

The modern tanning debate heats up where weddings are involved. Some people swear by a light tan, others say it looks tarty against a white dress. The real variety (sun- and sunbed-induced) is deeply frowned upon – and rightly so – but some people with acne and eczema depend on the healing power of UV and find it too much of a temptation at this crucial time.

The safe, fashionable alternative, if it's colour you're after, is a fake tan. Have it applied professionally and don't even consider it without a trial run weeks ahead. Ask for a very light tan; it'll probably fade to the right level after two or three days. Hot on the heels of the celebrity favourite, St Tropez, is the spray-on Fantasy Tan; available at salons.

Staying pale is still very stylish, too, or warm skin tone with a final super-light dusting of bronzing powder (not too glittery) on shoulders and cleavage, after making up.

If your wedding is in the sun, take special care not to over-tan – or worse, burn – before the ceremony. When you get your photos, you'll really regret it.

SMOOTH

The hairy bride is not the best look right now. If you decide to start waxing, bear in mind that it could take two or three six-weekly sessions before legs seem really smooth.

Make-up

Even if you're confident with your make-up, a lesson is a great way to update your look and customise it for your wedding day.

- Make-up counters are a good way to get a free lesson (even if you pay, you'll get the money back on any purchase) but only go to consultants whose own make-up you like. Have several sessions, if necessary. Ask the consultant to write down how products were applied as well as what they were.
- If you can afford to splash out, get a photographic make-up artist to give you a lesson, or come to you on the day. (The *Brides* address book lists several.) Have a trial run first.
- Always choose a natural look, with a little extra eye and lip definition.

Give high fashion a pass: heavy eyeliner, sparkly make-up and unnaturally dark or light lips are instantly dating.

- Mascara should be waterproof, but some irritate, so test in good time.
- Matt make-up is always more flattering and looks better in photographs.
- Application is everything, so invest in the right tools: foundation is best applied with a latex sponge; a giant brush is perfect for powder; good eye-shadow brushes are the only way to blend properly for a professional look; lashes really benefit from eyelash curlers before mascara, and a lash comb afterwards. The Body Shop has it all and is good value.
- Add shimmer only in small doses: a flick of iridescent pencil close to the top lashes, a suggestion of bronzing powder around the hairline, temples, cheekbone and jawline, a dot of shimmery gloss in the middle of the lips.
- Work out the safest way to make up without risking your clothes. Unless your dress has to go over your head, the trick is to make up everything but your lips, then dress, then add lipstick last. Ideally, put something protective over your clothes until the last minute.
- *Don't* paint your nails on your wedding day. It's too risky.

On-the-day, make-up rescue capsule
Pack up the following to keep handy all day:
- All your lip cosmetics.
- A powder compact and brush.
- Concealer: the wand variety.
- Some tissues and cotton buds.
- A few ready-to-use cotton buds: dip three or four in eye make-up remover, then seal them individually with cling film. Do the same with your foundation. Use them to tidy up smudges and touch up blemishes during the day. Convenient, small and less risk of accidents.
- Put in a little pouch with your essential wedding day kit; *see* page 300.

Brows and lashes

If it's new to you, have a good professional brow shape (nothing drastic) six weeks before, to check you like it. If so, book in another session there and then to fall three days before the wedding. Pluck any stragglers the day

Beauty secrets

'Just before our own, I went to a friend's wedding. The bride just smiled and smiled all day long – her eyes were all sparkly and her happiness was really genuine – she looked fantastic for it. I set my sights at that.' Bride, 24.

before. If lashes are fair, get them tinted when you have your brows plucked. You'll get away with less – or no – mascara.

Hands and feet

Get in the habit of looking after hands (and feet if they're going to be on show). Start with a manicure to get a good nail shape, then every week:

- Trim and smooth nails with an emery board to help nails grow strong.
- Push back cuticles with a rough towel after a bath.
- Smooth rough skin with a pumice stone.
- Use a good dose of hand-cream or moisturiser, whenever you remember.
- Paint nails with a multi-purpose base coat, strengthener and top coat.

Teeth

As well as looking after your teeth properly, and seeing the dentist and hygienist twice a year, help yourself to a dazzling smile by cutting out tea, coffee, smoking and red wine. Cosmetic tooth-whitening will set you back a few hundred pounds, and can temporarily aggravate sensitive teeth, but the results are good and can last for years. Allow several weeks for treatment, more if teeth are sensitive.

HAIR

Care, cut and colour

It's never too soon to work out what you're going to do with your hair: the wretched stuff grows only in its own sweet time.

- If you don't already have a hairdresser you love, find one fast.
- Have a preliminary planning session, to get the length, cut and colour right in good time.

From the expert: Getting ready

Deborah Campbell, hairstylist

'If the hairdresser or make-up artist is coming to you, make sure directions are really clear, journey times checked, time allowed for setbacks, and get a contact number in case they're late.'

- Work out a series of appointments, working backwards from the day itself, so your hair can reach its peak for the day. Most people find that their colour is best after about ten days, a cut after a week or so.
- To get hair into really good shape, have a trim every six weeks, condition regularly and keep heat-styling to a minimum.
- Have at least one full run-through of your final wedding style.
- Does your hair look best the day it's washed or the day after? Don't be persuaded to wash it on the day if it takes 24 hours to settle.

HAIR UP VERSUS HAIR DOWN

One of the biggest debates. In favour of up:
- You'll feel really special.
- It's glamorous.
- It's the best base on which to anchor flowers, jewels or a tiara.
- It's very 'bridal'.
- It shows off good bone structure really well.

In favour of down:
- You'll feel much more you.
- You won't have to worry about your hairstyle falling out.
- You can really show off pretty, natural hair.
- You won't wonder who that stranger is in all your wedding photos.

PUTTING IT ALL TOGETHER: THE BRIDE'S COUNTDOWN

Six months before
- Shop for your dress and schedule fitting sessions. Let them know if you're losing weight.

- Decide how you want your hair, find the right hairdresser, and work towards the length, cut and colour you want. Book all your appointments, especially for the wedding day itself. (*See* timings below.)
- Start the nutrition and exercise regime you plan to follow right up to the day.
- Get to work on your skincare (face and body).

Three months before
- Go for a make-up lesson and book a make-up artist if you're having one.
- Start weekly nail care.
- See the dental hygienist. Begin teeth-whitening, if you're doing it.

Two months before
- Get your shoes so they're ready for your final dress fitting.
- Choose all your accessories, and order any that are being made to order.
- Trial any treatments: lash dye, brow shape, fake tan.

One month before
- Have everything waxed as needed.
- Perfect your make-up if you're doing your own.

Three weeks before
- Final dress fitting.

Two weeks before
- Final appointments for hair-cut and colour.

One week before
- Collect your dress (or sooner if it's ready).
- Have a full run-through: get your hair done and time it, if you haven't already; go home and do your make-up, time it; try on your dress with the right underwear, accessories and shoes. And yes, time that too. Make a note of anything you need that's missing and go get it, now.

Two/three days before

- Have final lash and brow treatments.
- Check bookings for the day.
- Have any self-tanning treatment.
- Waxing.

The day before

- Have a manicure and any other (pre-tested) treatment which will relax you.
- Pluck any eyebrow stragglers.
- Lay out everything you need and put together your portable make-up kit to take with you on the day.
- Unwind with the pre-sleep routine on page 222.

On the day

- Once showered, start getting ready an hour before you need to. That'll allow for hitches, and for getting ready photographs. These average times are a guide only; work to your own from your run-through. Don't forget to build in time before you leave for family pictures, too.

The usual order is:	Average time
1. Hair done to almost ready	1 hr
2. Make-up done except for lips	1 hr
3. Spritz of perfume (make sure it dries completely)	1 min!
4. Dress	30 mins
5. Finalise hair and add any headdress	15 mins
6. Make up lips	10 mins
7. Hand everything you need to your chief bridesmaid to carry with her on your behalf: make-up kit, speech, other necessities (*see* page 300)	4 mins
8. Ready!	
Add: hitches, getting ready snaps and travel time to the ceremony	1 hr
Total getting ready time	**4 hrs!**

Gorgeous grooms

Things are somewhat easier for grooms, although you could undoubtedly learn a little from the sections above. Here's what you need to think about:

WHAT TO WEAR

After consulting with your bride on the look you're collectively going for, what you choose to wear at your wedding may depend on what you wear to work every day. If a smart suit is your daily bread and butter, it might be more special to dress down, rather than up; if you rarely have the chance to wear something smart, a simple well-cut suit will be a pleasure and a treat; and if you're a bit of an unfulfilled show-off, dressy costume or the-whole-works formalwear is probably quite a temptation. If you're marrying in overseas heat, dress down. More ideas on page 196.

Getting your gear
Depending on your budget ...

- **Hire:** Have no fear of ill-fitting, shabby old stock. Currently on offer are fine-quality formalwear, including morning dress and frock coats, Nehru jackets, top hats and tails, evening dress, Highland wear – even designer suits. Most big high streets have a well-supplied Austin Reed, Young's Hire, Pronuptia or Moss Bros, and probably an independent formalwear shop, too. Online, at Groomservice and I-do.uk.com, you can 'try on' outfits with their interactive mannequins, then find a stockist.
- **Off-the-peg/ready-to-wear and altered-to-fit:**
  - For suits:
    - Save yourself a fortune with M&S or Next.
    - Upgrade to a hip, high street label like Ted Baker or French Connection.
    - Go designer: menswear in good department stores include a good selection of Armani, Hugo Boss, Calvin Klein, Paul Smith et al, and diffusion lines, too. Debenhams' collection is good value.

- Go for uber-style from the edgiest designers: try Ozwald Boateng, Tomasz Starzewski, Marc Wallace and William Hunt (of the deep collars and big ties worn by David Beckham).
- For formalwear:
  - The dressy variety – frock coats and embroidered waistcoats – is best at Favourbrook and dedicated wedding-wear shops.
  - For classic and traditional, try Hackett, Austin Reed, Gieves & Hawkes or any men's tailor.
- **Bespoke/personal tailoring:** The home of men's formal dress and classic tailoring is in and around London's Jermyn Street and Savile Row, but

Celebrity grooms: Does money buy style?

Dave Stewart wore white suits for both of his weddings – but did he get away with it? The second time he completed the outfit with a pair of Birkenstocks, a floral garland and a circlet of flowers on his head ...

Elton John decided on a straw boater and pink bow tie ...

David Seaman went for the footballer's classic: ivory brocade frock coat ...

Michael Douglas reportedly spent longer in make-up than Catherine Zeta-Jones on the morning of their wedding. Yuk ...

But Jamie Oliver (thank goodness) looked just right in his pale blue Paul Smith suit, tieless pink shirt, Patrick Cox snakeskin shoes – and pale blue Cadillac.

Etiquette issue: Is it 'proper' to wear morning dress?

These days, morning dress for a wedding is as much a fashion as a politeness, especially when the 'real' formalwear of this century is simply a smart suit and tie. Depending on what you want to wear, you can argue it both ways: because morning dress is still the convention at a wedding, it's perfectly good to wear it. But because, strictly speaking, it's improper for an afternoon-into-evening occasion, the groom who doesn't want to wear it has a good defence! Wedding party and guests should follow the lead of the groom, though, but be sympathetic to those who feel uncomfortable.

there are outposts at shops and department stores around the country. Having a one-off made is a decidedly pricey route, but if you're really confident about what you want, why not make the ultimate sartorial investment? You'll get a lot more wear out of it than a bride gets from her dress, and it's likely to cost less.

The trimmings

For men who are often starved of a good dressing-up session, weddings can be a tempting orgy of waistcoats, ties, cravats, handkerchiefs, cummerbunds, top hats and more. Like your bride, it's important not to get carried away; limit accessories to two or three. Have a colour theme, by all means, but vary the way you use it with slightly different tones and prints. If you want to treat yourself to some more durable trimmings, how about a made-to-measure shirt, smart belt, elegant cufflinks and a great pair of shoes (wear them in beforehand, with masking tape on the soles).

☺☹ *'I thought a brightly decorated waistcoat would be original, a stamp of my own personality on an otherwise traditional look. A year later, I wish I hadn't worn one, to be honest. Every groom does the same thing. It's not original at all. And certainly not my style.' Groom, 26.*

GROOMING

Forgive me if I state the obvious in this section: male grooming expertise does vary. As for the girls, *don't* try anything for the first time with only days to spare. If you plan to do some body work, read pages 207–8.

Hair

It really is worth investing in a good hairdo:
- If you don't have a good hairdresser/barber already, find one.
- Aim to get the cut right by at least six weeks before the day.
- Have a final cut a week before the wedding to give your hair a chance to settle down.

- Don't even think about doing something very different – cut, colour or curl – for the wedding. You'll always cringe at the photos.
- Stress can lead to hair problems like itchy scalp, dandruff, even oiliness, so get them sorted out in good time if they strike.

Skin

For glowing skin:

- Get into good skincare habits well before the wedding. Starting the week before means one thing: spots!
- Cleanse your face properly every day: a soap-free cleanser is best if skin is dry.
- Moisturise after your daily shave.
- Exfoliate with a scrub (like Clinique's) a couple of times a week.
- Treat yourself to a couple of pampering sessions: London's Porchester Spa has male-only sessions, making it a particularly safe retreat from wedding planning. Enjoy steam rooms, sauna, Jacuzzi, swimming pool and icy plunge pool – and come out radiating good health! The Refinery, also in London, is the first all-male health spa, where the full works are on offer: including massage, shave, haircut, waxing and manicure.

Nails

I think men benefit more from a manicure than women do: I'm not big on male preening, but nice hands are definitely very sexy. Otherwise, trim and shape nails with an emery board every couple of weeks – and just before the wedding.

Teeth

Follow the tips on page 213 for gleaming white teeth. Whitening treatments are not just for the girls!

PUTTING IT ALL TOGETHER:
THE GROOM'S COUNTDOWN

Three months before
- Have a look at the bride's countdown, and realise how easy you've got it …
- Decide on your outfit: if you're having a suit made or altered, allow plenty of time.
- Have a manicure.
- Find a good hairdresser.
- Start a skin-boosting programme.

Two months before
- Reserve any hire clothes.
- See your dentist.

Six weeks before
- Have your last but one hair-cut.
- Wear in new shoes.

One week before
- Final hair-cut.
- Ring to check on hire clothes.

Two days before
- Trim and shape nails.
- Collect hire clothes and try them on again.
- Check accessories, the rings and paperwork. It should all be lined up and ready to go.

On the day
- Allow yourself plenty of time to get ready. Keep a buttonhole back when the best man takes them off to the ushers.
- The full wedding countdown is in Chapter Eighteen.

Both of you, feeling good

What's guaranteed to make you both look fabulous on your wedding day is a relaxed mind, and a blissfully happy look on your face! If you can take off to a spa together for a few days before the wedding, it's a great way to unwind, look great – and have some quality time together. Even if you can't, focus on staying relaxed and well rested over the pre-wedding months.

RELAX AND SLEEP

You should, of course, be getting plenty of sleep. Not only will it help you look your best, but the stress, work and pre-wedding celebrations mean you need more than usual:

- Take regular exercise. Walking is perfect, combined with gentle stretching before and after.
- Follow the balanced eating suggestions on page 208, and eat no less than two hours before bed.
- Learn a relaxation technique: the classic one is to tense each part of your body in turn to the count of ten, then relax it to ten more counts. Start with your toes and work up to your head. Take ten minutes to concentrate on this every day; you can do it anywhere.
- Cut out caffeine altogether and limit alcohol to one unit a day.
- If you must smoke, don't do it late in the day: nicotine is a stimulant. Take lots of vitamin C.
- Yoga can help control anxiety with deep breathing and inner balance; a few sessions can make all the difference.
- Get into a good bedtime routine. Get up and go to bed at the same times every day. Before bed, have a bath with a sleep-inducing aromatherapy oil, such as lavender, chamomile or neroli, drink some chamomile tea, and read something dull for a few minutes. Don't watch the television: it's stimulating.
- Make sure the room you sleep in is warm enough, but has a flow of fresh air, too.

Reasons to be nervous
Prince Charles & Lady Diana Spencer's wedding was watched by 750 million people worldwide. That's 150 million more than watched man's first walk on the moon.

- Try natural remedies for nerves, anxiety and sleeplessness, such as Rescue Remedy, White Chestnut or Mimulus, all by Bach Flower Remedies, from health stores.
- If you're feeling really anxious, see your doctor. General information and advice on stress counselling is available from the International Stress Management Association (ISMA).

DEALING WITH NERVES

If you're worried about jitters on the day:
- Follow the advice above to try and get a good night's sleep.
- If you can't sleep, don't worry. The adrenaline is more than enough to carry you through the day.
- Do the basic relaxation exercise described above as often as you need to. No-one will notice.
- Carry some Bach Rescue Remedy with you. Put a few drops on your tongue at crucial moments: before the ceremony, before the speeches.
- If you sweat excessively under pressure, ask your GP for a prescription-strength antiperspirant, which will be extremely effective. Try it out for a while before the wedding; and take care not to overdo it.
- It's easy to say, but don't worry. There's so much goodwill around you at your wedding, the air is literally thick with it, and all the normal symptoms of nerves – blushing, shaky voice, tears – aren't just normal on a wedding day, they're endearing.

Money-wise: What to expect
High street bridal wear: £150–£500

Theatrical dress hire: about £80+
Wedding dress hire: about £400+
Made-to-measure bridal wear: about £700–£2000+
One-off and couture: about £1,500 to several thousand
Formalwear hire, basic trousers and coat: about £40+
Men's designer suit: £450+
Classic tailoring or bespoke suit: about £700+
Full works formalwear/dressy frock coats: about £800+

Contacts

Angels Fancy Dress: 020 7836 5678; www.fancydress.com
Austin Reed: 0800 585479; www.austinreed.co.uk
Bridal Gown Exchange: 01746 783066; www.bridalgownexchange.co.uk
Bridal Rogue Gallery: 020 7224 7414
Brides magazine: see their address book at www.bridesuk.net, or free once
*   a year with the magazine*
Butterick's: for a list of professional dressmakers, send £1 to Professional
*   Dressmakers List, Butterick Co Ltd, New Lane, Havant, Hants, PO9 2ND*
Carousel Costumes: 01926 881356; www.carouselcostumes.com
Debenhams: 020 7408 4444; www.debenhams.com
Déjà Vu: 01483 203545; www.dejavubridalwear.co.uk
Designer Alterations: 020 7498 4360; www.designeralterations.com
Designer Bridal Wear: www.designerbridalwear.com
Dream Dresses: www.dreamdresses.co.uk
Fantasy Tan: 01707 643031; www.fantasytan.co.uk
Favourbrook: 020 7491 2337; www.favourbrook.com
Gieves & Hawkes: 020 7434 2001; www.gievesandhawkes.com
Groomservice.co.uk: 08000 384042; www.groomservice.co.uk
Hackett: 020 7819 6800; www.hackett.co.uk
I-do.uk.com: www.i-do.uk.com
International Stress Management Association: 07000 780430;
*   www.isma.org.uk*
Lords Formal Wear: 020 7363 1033; www.lords-formal-wear.com
Marc Wallace: 020 7731 4575; www.marcwallace.com

Maxcleavage: 0870 33 33 904; www.maxcleavage.com
Modern Bride: 020 7935 3726
Monique Lhuillier: www.moniquelhuillier.com
Moss Bros: 020 7447 7200; www.mossbros.co.uk
Ozwald Boateng: 020 7437 0620
Porchester Spa: 020 7792 3980
Pronuptia: 01273 563006; www.pronuptua.co.uk
Refinery: 020 7409 2001; www.the-refinery.com
Retail Bridalwear Association: 0121 321 3121; www.bridal.org.uk
Royal National Theatre Costume Hire: 020 7735 4774;
    www.nationaltheatre.org.uk
Sew Direct: www.sewdirect.com
Slendertone: www.slendertone.co.uk
St Tropez: 0115 922 1462; www.sttropeztan.com
Tomasz Starzewski: 020 7235 4526
Wedding Dress Exchange: 020 8473 4416
Wedding Warehouse Sale: 01476 565691
William Hunt: 020 7836 0809
Young's Hire: 020 8327 3010; www.youngs-hire.co.uk

chapter
fifteen

your dream team

Some couples (somewhat irreverently) just go it alone. You can see why: a hoard of irregularly shaped friends, cousins and siblings in mix-and-match silks and accessories, cluttering up the occasion and doing nothing of any great use, could be at odds with a couple's idyllic nuptial vision.

But they could be missing out. The system of best man and ushers, maid of honour and bridesmaids can be one of the most effective – and enjoyable – of all wedding traditions. You just need to bring it bang up to date. Only the tiniest weddings run smoothly without the support of a small army and on the day, you want to be a bride and groom, not administrative officers, so delegation is vital.

Think of it as two teams – male helpers and female helpers – with the best man and maid of honour heading them up. If you're doing your wedding unconventionally, ambitiously or on a shoestring, you're going to need more help, not less. Never mind handing out the service sheets, we needed people to light 300 tea-lights, sew 140 lavender bags, pull the petals *very* gently off dozens of roses, and heap our children with hours of attention when we couldn't. If it makes more sense, you could give helpers new titles – or none at all – and rewrite all the traditional job descriptions, too.

MAKING THE CHOICE

You're going to rely heavily on this band of brothers and sisters, so choose friends who have their wits about them, and are responsible and accountable. The best man and maid of honour titles will probably fall to people you're especially fond of; just don't expect them to be something they're not on the day. That said, many a questionable best man has come into his own when the heat was on, to be utterly dependable in making arrangements, or sincere and touching in his speech.

Child attendants are gorgeous to look at, and older ones will usually take their roles very seriously and be a credit to their proud parents. Younger ones are a law unto themselves, though, so if you can't face the thought that they may go completely off plan, forget the idea. But if you have children/stepchildren of your own, a starring role is the perfect way to help them feel important and enjoy the day.

Don't be pressured into choosing someone you don't want: it's an honour to be asked, not a right. Obviously, asking two of your brothers to be ushers, but not a third, might be a little below the belt, but enthusiastic candidates for leading roles may come from all sides, and you need to be firm. Be prepared with convincing reasons: money (lack of); the desire for the minimum of fuss and paraphernalia.

On the flip side, your invitation may be a worry or unwelcome pressure, so only appoint people who are really keen. Some women are horrified at the prospect of being 'frump of honour', whatever the dress, and many men would do anything to avoid making a best man's speech. There are solutions; *see* Help Is At Hand over-page. Young attendants may feel most anxious, so check it's something they really want to do, and reassure them that if they don't want to be in the procession, that's fine. (It probably won't affect the outcome, but makes dropping out less traumatic for everyone.)

It's customary now to present gifts to all your helpers, either during the speeches, or at a private moment before or after the wedding. With the full line-up of bridesmaids, best man, ushers and page boys – plus a bouquet each for the mums – this can be quite a shopping list: people realise this, so if you're on a budget, a thoughtful gesture, such as a book or framed photograph, or something you've made yourselves, will be appreciated.

WHO DOES WHAT?

With the change in the way weddings are done, comes a change in the help you need, and the standard 'who does what' needs a little rethinking: traditional roles and responsibilities undoubtedly have their place, but modern planning is largely about common sense and team work.

The bride

Almost all she had to do, in a time long gone, was to look beautiful. The modern – invariably working – bride now often creates the wedding almost single-handed, taking on practically everything that everyone else used to do: mother, groom, bridesmaids, best man and all. It's not surprising that wedding planning can unhinge the sanest bride. (*See* Chapter Sixteen.)

The groom

If he's going with tradition, it falls to him to organise legal matters, most of the marriage ceremony, honeymoon, transport to and from the church and transport from the reception, buy the wedding ring and a gift for his bride, plus, of course, deliver an eloquent speech. In an ideal – 21st-century – world, he does this and plenty more besides, as an equal member of the planning partnership. Some are extremely competent as sole or chief wedding organiser (one of Hollywood's biggest wedding planners is male); others admit to doing absolutely nothing at all.

HELP IS AT HAND

For suppliers' phone numbers and web addresses, *see* **Contacts** on pages 224 and 243.

Father of the bride

● **Traditional duties:** Just the walk down the aisle with his daughter on his right arm, giving her away, his speech, and the money – many fathers still expect to pay for much of the wedding (*see* Chapter Seven for who pays for what).

- **Modern role:** Together with his (probably working) wife, he's likely to make a contribution to the couple's own wedding fund, if he can. He may walk the bride down the aisle alone or with her mother, or the couple may arrive together, without either parent. Many fathers now also provide practical or logistical help. Another senior member of the family or long-time friend may of course take on all or some of his role.

- **What to wear:** While morning dress is still commonplace for all leading men at formal weddings, it's not unusual for a bride's father to feel more comfortable in a smart suit, and the groom's choice will normally dictate the male dress code. It might be a fitting compromise, however, if he sets a traditional dress code for older guests, while the groom leads a modern one for his peers. Male guests can then dress as they prefer. Just make it clear on a note with the invitation. (*See* Chapter Fourteen for more on men's clothing.)

Mother of the bride

- **Traditional duties:** Although the bride's mother takes no part in the ceremony, her traditional position is central to the whole occasion, as both hostess and wedding planner for the greater part of the day. The guest list, invitations, service sheets, reception venue, food, drink, flowers, cake, cars, entertainment and photography are all hers, historically, as is a key role in the choosing of the bride's and bridesmaids' dresses.

- **Modern role:** The best mothers (in my happy experience) now set themselves firmly in the role of bride's deputy and advice-giver, (the *welcome* variety), while the bride herself takes on her mother's previous role of project leader. Some couples are still happy to leave the bride's mother to do the lion's share of the work, but she should then also enjoy some control and credit for the day's success.

- **What to wear:** They're all so young-looking now that many mothers rightly see their daughter's wedding as a wonderful excuse to invest in some very stylish clothes. Wedding magazines are plumped with ads promoting purpose-designed 'mum wear', and it seems a shame, when there are so many contemporary stores and labels – designer, diffusion and high street – just perfect for the occasion. Try upmarket boutiques like Whistles and L. K. Bennett, as well as leading designers. On the high street, try stores like Episode, Hobbs, M&S Autograph and Debenhams for their own designer diffusion lines. Of the two mothers, the bride's has first call on outfit colour, but she should choose early. It's no longer taboo to wear white when you're not the bride, but any considerate mother will check first. Hats, once obligatory, are now a matter of personal choice - but usually irresistible! Bear in mind that big brims get in the way of kisses and the photographer's lens.

Best man

- **Traditional duties:** Besides getting the groom to church on time, the best man's purpose has been to give support and assistance to the groom in general. In preparation, that means he should help choose and manage the ushers, help the groom to organise the ceremony, service sheets, transport and honeymoon; to organise and return, if necessary, clothing for the groom, ushers and himself, and, of course, organise the stag party. On the day itself, he collects the service sheets for the ushers to hand out; collects and distributes the buttonholes; he usually witnesses the register; and takes charge of the ring, well-wishers' messages for reading at the reception, plus documents for the wedding and honeymoon. He carries the cash with which he settles the church fees, waits beside the groom for the bride's arrival, produces the ring at the appropriate moment, and accompanies the chief bridesmaid in the recessional. He takes care of transport logistics for the bridal party, checks that guests have transport to the reception, then, with the ushers, accompanies the bridesmaids there. During the reception, he will act as toastmaster, requesting silence for grace, calling on speakers and, of course, make his own speech (*see* Chapter Thirteen). He will finally ensure that the groom has his change of clothes, transport, documents and anything else the couple needs for 'going away' – and that they catch their plane. He'll usually be last to leave the reception, taking any gifts with him. There's more, but that's most of it!
- **Modern role:** Many best men now see themselves doing just two of those things: organising the stag party and making the speech. Yet if you

followed some traditional guides to the letter, the role would be so huge that a couple might feel it's simply too much to ask of one person. Plus, there's even more that a best man may find himself doing at a modern wedding: the photographer usually relies on him to gather people for group shots, and he's the natural choice to liaise with and pay bands/entertainers on the day, to help to organise guests' parking, to keep everyone to schedule throughout the day, and to deal with many of the niggling details and admin that arise, such as ordering taxis home for guests, queries from suppliers and contractors, and taking any last-minute phone calls for the bride and groom. He may need to gather up any unopened drink for return after the wedding, and keep safe – or even have developed – any disposable cameras. It is often more practical that a team of the bride's friends should take on some of his responsibilities, and the appointment of a toastmaster would also greatly reduce his role.

- **Who to choose:** Traditionally, a single man of the groom's choosing. In reality, a married best man may be more *au fait* with what's required of him and, since the bride may rely on him as much as the groom, the choice should be shared by the couple. A best man can of course be a best woman, and often will be a reliable sibling (usually the one closest to you in age) or friend, or possibly two or three of them. If the role in its entirety is too much for one person, or you have more than one candidate sibling, it may make perfect sense to appoint one in charge of looking after guests, another in charge of support and admin, and a third to make the speech. Resist the temptation to award the role as an accolade or compliment to someone who is simply not up to the job. It calls for: a strong sense of duty, the ability to organise and get things done,

Their wedding

'Our five-year-old son was best man. Not to be sweet, but because that's who I wanted to help keep me calm and grounded on the day, and wait beside me before the ceremony. Other people were dubious about trusting him to produce the ring at the crucial moment, but I knew he'd get it right.' Groom, 29.

confidence as a public speaker, and a degree of charm in dealing with your guests. Second marriages sometimes feature the groom's son as best man; even if he's a child, he can be given part of the role and take on duties appropriate to his age.

- **Style counsel:** Taking his lead from the groom, he may dress as formally or informally as the wedding dictates, usually in a matching or toned-down version. A shirt and tie or buttonhole, linked into the wedding theme or colour, is a low-key way to demonstrate his status and link him to the wedding party. *See* Chapter Fourteen for men's dressing.

Ushers

- **Traditional duties:** To guide guests to their seats (left-hand side of the church for the bride's/right-hand side for the groom's), save the front rows for the couple's families, hand out service sheets, help ensure all guests have transport from the church to the reception, escort the bridesmaids during the day, and generally support the hosts in looking after the guests.
- **Modern role:** As well as attending to guests, a team of the couple's friends may find themselves with a whole range of responsibilities before or on the day, such as to help with lighting or hi-fi equipment, light candles, move flowers, offer drinks, make introductions in lieu of a formal receiving line, help gather people for photographs, keep things running on time, receive gifts and put them in a safe place, manage the delicate issue of confetti-throwing, pass around the guest book for signing, encourage use of throwaway cameras and, if necessary, join the jolly band who clear up the venue the next day.
- **Who to choose:** Any spare siblings on either side, together with your close, current group of friends – female as well as male – are most likely to be able to help (as long as they're reliable!). They'll know your friends and family, be able to keep an eye out for guests who seem a little lost, will have seen you through the complications of planning the wedding and understand any practical needs. Old friends and more distant relatives, such as cousins, are less likely to be really helpful ushers, but it may be friendly to ask them if you plan to have quite a few.

- **Style counsel:** Men may dress as the best man, complete with button-holes, but girl ushers look good dressed up, without being bridesmaid-ish, in a trouser suit or shift dress, with corsages to match buttonholes.

Maid of honour

- **Traditional duties:** Her finest hours all pertain to dresses: first the choice and fittings for the bride's, her own and the bridesmaids', and then, on the day, dressing the bride and of course modelling her own. But there's a little more to it than that: a hard-working, hands-on chief assistant to the bride, she involves herself in many of the wedding preparations and on the day, guides and instructs bridesmaids, pages and flower girls. She arrives out-side the church ahead of the bride, and waits to greet her and arrange her dress, veil and train, then follows her in procession down the aisle, takes her bouquet for the duration of the ceremony, helps her put back her veil, and accompanies the best man to the vestry for the signing of the regis-ter. At the end of the ceremony, she returns the bouquet and walks back down the aisle on the best man's left side. Later, she helps the bride to get ready to go away, and may take care of the wedding dress.

- **Modern role:** As well as being a fine-looking complement to the bride, and witness to some of the biggest shopping trips in a girl's life, the modern maid of honour now turns her hand to the hen party with as much gusto as the best man does the stag. I don't think any of those are her most important tasks though. Her reason for being, in my book, is to counsel and support the bride during those deeply stressful wedding plans, and this 'bride's best friend' really comes into her own on the morning of the wedding. From the moment she wakes on that day, the bride has to re-set her mind entirely and surrender control of the wedding. While she gets ready, her maid is her hands, voice, eyes: running errands, dealing with last-minute thoughts or worries, delivering messages, and keeping her environment calm and uncrowded with tact and diplomacy. The maid of honour may hear a last run-through of the bride's speech, or fill her in on any wedding-morning gossip and news. She'll make the morning fun, reassure her that everything is running to plan, and keep the bride's nerves at bay (with the help of a glass of champagne). During the day, she'll fulfil any traditional requirements, and continue to ensure the bride has everything she needs (bouquets for presentation to the mums, her speech, her sobriety) and of course keep a constant eye on the bride's hair and make-up, touching up with an impressive bag of tricks (*see* Chapter Eighteen) whenever necessary.

- **Who to choose:** Need you be told? It's what best friends/sisters are for: as long as you both agree on how you see the role. If you have more than one sister, it can be tricky: don't pick just one unless there's a very good reason (she's the only one close to you in age/the only one who's not yet had the job). Having more than one maid of honour, or none at all, is fine. You can either have a collection of bridesmaids to share the job, or do away with the idea altogether and privately ask your best friend to be your right-hand girl on the day. She'll still be flattered and you can give her a nice present in lieu of a dress. You can't sack a bridesmaid for being pregnant, or pretty much anything else for that matter. Don't nominate a maid of honour on the basis that you think you should, or your mother insists, or someone is sulking. You'll regret it.
- **Style counsel:** *See* **Bridesmaids** below.

Bridesmaids

- **Traditional duties:** Besides cooperating with dress fittings and being decorative, bridesmaids are there to support the bride and maid of honour in her responsibilities above, follow them up the aisle and down again, look after younger attendants, and accompany ushers.
- **Modern role:** Pitching in on the multitude of tasks that are general team preparations and on-the-day logistics (*see* **Best man** and **Ushers** above.)
- **Who to choose:** As many or few as you wish of your closest friends. It's customary to equal the number of ushers, for pairing up (formally or otherwise!). Don't worry about them looking nicer than you: they really won't. Again, don't appoint under pressure (no-one should *expect* to be a bridesmaid), but do consider everyone's feelings. And even if you're not close, asking your future sister-in-law is a nice gesture, and should help you get to know each other better.

- **Style counsel:** As brides get older, so do their maids, and if ever blousy or frilly frocks *were* a good idea, they certainly aren't now. And who says bridesmaids have to wear long dresses: what about knee-length outfits, suits, and wide, fluid trousers? As a basic rule, bridesmaids should dress as close to their own style as possible. If she'd never want to see the outfit again as long as she lives, don't make her wear it on your wedding day. I don't subscribe to the notion that being a bridesmaid is a one-way treat that must be repaid by wearing any vile thing the bride or her mother chooses. To the contrary, it can be stressful and expensive, and bridesmaids should be treated with consideration. The issue of money raises it ugly head again here (bridesmaids historically pay for their own dresses), but even if the bride is paying, is it really *nice* to make unwelcome demands in return? Bridesmaids, in turn, need to be accommodating, though!

  The designs of many modern bridesmaids' dresses, such as Watters & Watters, are thankfully grown up, simple and elegant. Or for a thoroughly modern approach, why not:

- Choose a single colour: a natural halfway house, everyone simply chooses their most flattering silhouette, but all in the same colour. Bring the look together with matching pashminas and kitten heels.

- Nominate a mini collection at a high street store, then let everyone choose for themselves: shops like Episode, Hobbs, Oasis and Zara often present dresses, skirts and trouser suits in a distinct group of matching fabrics and styles. Go early in the season, when stock is good, and ask staff to locate additional stock from other branches – many routinely do this for weddings.

- For a very unstructured wedding, simply pick a style or role model: Say 'trouser suits', or 'Oscar night', then have just one unifying factor, such as a wrap, or buttonhole.

- Go for black: it really does make for the most elegant line-up.

- Put all the bridesmaids in the same dress, but in a set of harmonious shades – such as coffee, chocolate and cream.

- Accessorise with greatest caution: if you find yourself giving serious thought to Dorothy bags, give yourself a serious talking to, instead.

Expert advice: Give puffed sleeves a pass

Colin Cowie, Hollywood wedding planner

'If Princess Diana didn't look great in big puffy sleeves, no bridesmaid's going to make it!'

As a general rule, 'real' shoes and bags look better than those varieties created just for weddings.

- *See* the bride's dressing section in Chapter Fourteen for more ideas and contact details.

Flower girls and child bridesmaids

- **Traditional duties:** Simply to look pretty, and scatter flowers in the path of the bride.
- **Modern role:** Still to look pretty. And behave reasonably well for their age – quite a lot to ask of a young child who may feel anxious and disoriented.
- **Who to choose:** As long as you're not looking for military order, anyone who fits the bill. It can get complicated if you choose one young niece and not another, so find a category that works for you: such as god-children only or your own children only. Fascist dictats like only blonde/good children are not the best; if that's your (secret) reference point, invent another one for public use!
- **Style counsel:** Girlie stuff is OK here, but bad taste isn't. Even young children resent dodgy clothes, and teenagers will never forgive you. Simple day-dresses with little white plimsolls are a very sweet modern alternative to flouncy frills, especially in duplicate, and stores like Jigsaw Junior and Monsoon Girl have lots of pretty but funky dresses just made for little 21st-century bridesmaids. Look, too, in catalogues like Vertbaudet and Mini Boden, for pretty but simple outfits. Fairy costumes can have a pleasing kind of kitsch about them: go for a single pale colour, with ballet shoes instead of the twinkly plastic variety. Try John Lewis and toy shops. If you're feeling particularly benevolent, you could let your fairies

carry a pretty wand instead of flowers. Heavy bouquets will get a fast refusal from tinies.

☺☹ *'For bridesmaids, we had two little nieces, who looked absolutely beautiful, but my sister did all the work – without any of the glory.' Bride, 24.*

☺☹ *'I only wanted little girls, not grown-up bridesmaids. But my sisters cried, even when I told them I was worried they'd just look prettier than me (they're identical twins and gorgeous), so I had them both in the end.' Bride, 29.*

Page boys or ring-bearer
- **Traditional duties:** As for flower girls. In addition, the ring-bearer, um, bears the ring (safely attached to a cushion or hymn/prayer book).
- **Modern role:** Same.
- **Style counsel:** The traditional page's garb seems a bit unkind, I always think, if the child is more than about three. Tone it down, or choose a more everyday option, like long linen shorts, a shirt and a tank top. The fancy dress option can work well: mini maharajas look very endearing, for instance, but don't let your imagination take you too far down a road that will make you *very* unpopular.

Young attendants
'We had three very little bridesmaids. To help them down the aisle, we lined it with familiar faces – and sat their parents near the top. We asked them to hold hands and follow the bride – all they really had to do was make it to their mums' waiting arms. They were perfect!' Bride, 32.

Dylan Brosnan, three-year-old son of **Pierce Brosnan & Keely Shaye Smith**, wasn't altogether convinced about his formal wedding attire. They reached an eleventh-hour compromise: the suit went on, but was matched with his much-loved leather biker boots.

Etiquette issue: Who pays for attendants' clothes?

Traditionally, bridesmaids and male attendants pay for and keep their own clothes, but that's a custom which is out of date and rarely fair or relevant, now. The cost is a considerable imposition to place on a friend, especially when the bride and groom dictate the choice and cost of the outfit, so it's become more commonplace for the couple to pay. Hired clothing is always paid for on the attendants' behalf. The important thing is to be upfront so that no-one has any nasty surprises, and if you expect people to pay for their own clothes, let them choose something they can wear again. One compromise is to share the cost: the couple pays for the dress, for instance, and the atten-dant pays for accessories which can be worn again.

MORE HELP

Toastmasters

'Brides spend months preparing their wedding. They've got it all planned down to the minute, and on the day ... they're *busy*!' Toastmaster Nick Grant may be stating the obvious, but he has a point. Even your mother, best man or best friend might not have the experience to take the reins as the two of you step into your starring roles, and anyway, are you comfortable burden-ing them with the task? If your wedding is sufficiently formal for a toastmas-ter (they can be very low key but they do wear that uniform), it may be an investment worth making. They can:

- Advise on timings, toasts, speeches, dress code, correct form and pres-entation during the preceding months.
- Provide 'front-of-house' hospitality: greeting guests, guiding them to the reception and drinks, organising a well-run receiving line, announcing guests, the meal and the new bride and groom.
- Deal with gifts, assist with organising people for photographs, and cir-culate the guest book.
- Call guests' attention to seating arrangements, and any special notices, such as no smoking, as well as advising guests of arrangements after the meal.

- Say grace, announce speakers and toasts, and the cutting of the cake.
- Read cards and messages, and handle gifts and bouquets for presentation.
- Liaise with all other parties on the day: caterers, videographer, band or DJ.

Wedding consultants

If you're very busy, and time is money, a wedding consultant could make perfect sense. It's a natural step in the new wedding culture, where modern brides may be 'cash-rich, time-poor', her mother less involved, her ideas new or unusual, and expectations considerably higher than they might have been a decade ago. In the US, planners come as standard in about 70% of weddings. 'Over there, it's the second call a bride makes,' says planner Dominique Douglas, 'after calling her parents.'

Aside from a religious ceremony, which is still best arranged by the couple, a wedding consultant can fix virtually everything. Venue-finding, catering, original entertainment, buying and wrapping thank-you gifts, handling RSVPs and giving travel or accommodation information to guests can all be part of the service, '... and we often do quite a bit of counselling, too,' says specialist Sophie Lillingston. The idea, as Hollywood wedding planner Colin Cowie puts it, is that a couple should feel like 'guests at their own wedding'.

What's more, a professional planner could – like a good accountant – earn you back their fee. Not only do they leave you to get on with earning a living, and save you costly experiments (*see* **Hidden costs** in Chapter Seven) but they also:

- Know the best suppliers and who's good value for money.
- Represent repeat business for a contractor, incentivising them to offer you a better price and a more reliable service (usually, suppliers have virtually no incentive to keep your custom).
- Get several quotes for each aspect of the wedding, and negotiate them against each other.
- Protect you from expensive mistakes.
- Ensure you get everything you've paid for.

FINDING A PLANNER

Even if you don't want – or can't afford – a full-blown planning service, many provide one-off guidance or help in a specific area:

- Ask around for personal recommendations.
- Look in wedding magazine features and classified sections, or at the *Brides* magazine online address book.
- The most established, experienced names crop up again and again, like Sophie Lillingston at Lillingston Associates and Doug Showell and Liz Sexton at Alternative Occasions.
- Perfect Start at the Wedding Design Company is a one-off meeting offering expert guidance to set you on the right track.
- Alternative Occasions will provide a one-off appointment for brain-picking or trouble-shooting.
- Alternative Occasions and the Wedding Design Company also offer an on-the-day service to manage last-minute preparations: they'll check over your plans before the wedding, then see it through till you go away. They can also add a styling or design service.

Other vital roles

Other high-profile or meaningful tasks can be an important part of any wedding; allocated sensitively, they can avert distress where there's potential for disappointment. It's also a simple but touching way to involve special friends, or capitalise on one with a special talent. They could:

- Do a reading.
- Sing at the ceremony or play music.
- Say a prayer, or grace.
- Light a candle during the ceremony.
- Write a poem or eulogy for the ceremony or speeches.
- Be a witness.
- Make the cake.
- Make favours.
- Help with flowers and decorations.
- Walk the bride down the aisle.
- Take on some administrative responsibilities.

With a little help from my guests

'I was delighted to help at my friend's wedding. I never expected, or wanted, to be a bridesmaid, but I was really flattered when a couple of little things cropped up just before the day, and the bride asked me to keep a check on them. It was just nice to be useful – and take a bit of stress off the bride and groom.' Guest, 37.

'My best friend's mum had always wanted to be a voice-over artist, so we asked her to do the reading. She was fantastic – and loved it when people asked if she was an actress!' Bride, 28.

- Chaperone guests who need special attention.
- Help the photographer to identify people – or round them – up for pictures.

PARTY PARTY

Your friends will be expecting some pre-wedding celebrations. If you want a serious booze-up, rich with lewd sexual innuendo, that's your prerogative. The low-key, grown-up alternatives may be more your style: some people give the whole thing a miss, or have a joint party, dinner or weekend away with a few close friends. It's amazing how many people stand their ground over the wedding plans, then bow to pressure on stag/hen parties. As ever, do what you want – not what everyone expects of you.

The sensible bit
- Whoever is planning the event, it should be in full consultation with you unless you specifically say that you want to be surprised, shocked or humiliated!
- Avoid putting in charge the kind of person who will disregard the need for common sense.
- You don't *have* to invite members of your family-in-law-to-be, but you can guarantee it will cross their minds. If you decide against it, a second

celebratory drink or supper party just for the girls/boys of the new extended family might work.

- Does anyone really have to be told that a shaved eyebrow takes months to grow back?

What's your style?

Some party choices are decidedly girly, some are pure testosterone. Many hip couples are doing it together and anyway, (almost) anything he/she can do, you can do better …

- Lap-dancing clubs are the hot place to go, for women as well as men.
- Myla, the cult lingerie brand, will do an at-home party: tagged 'designer sex', Myla is more *Sex and the City* than sex shop. Women-only events are to discover – and buy – extremely sexy, very beautiful lingerie, plus perfumed body products and designer sex toys, all over a glass or two of good wine. Kate Moss shops in the Notting Hill store, so it must be good – send him there for a little gift shopping or he can order online or by phone.
- Arrange for the spa to come to you: turn your flat into a retreat, with aromatherapy candles, incense, fruit (and champagne) coolers, and arrange for a beauty therapist to spend the day doing treatments for all your girlfriends.
- Before booking a restaurant, check out 'Tabletalk' online at Toptable to find out where all the A-list celebs are dining.
- The where-to-be-seen London venues include Attica, Teatro and the Stork Rooms.
- Book a Party Bus for between 20 and 70 people. It will go to several clubs, playing dance music all the way. There's no queuing, and everyone gets VIP entrance.
- Adrenalin rush: sailing weekends and extreme sports beyond your wildest dreams at Elemental Adventure; rally driving at Brands Hatch is just one of the boys-and-toys ideas at Octagon Motor Sports.

Money-wise: What to expect
Wedding planner: about £1,500+
One-off consultation with a wedding planner: about £200+
Toastmaster: about £250
On-the-day wedding consultant: from £600
Bridesmaids' outfits, average spend: about £370

Contacts
Alternative Occasions: 01932 872115; www.stressfreeday.com
Attica: 020 7287 5882
Colin Cowie: www.colincowie.com
Debenhams: 020 7408 4444; www.debenhams.com
Elemental Adventure: 0870 7387838; www.eladv.com
Guild of Professional Toastmasters: 020 8852 4621;
    www.guild-of-toastmasters.co.uk
Jigsaw Junior: 020 8392 5658: www.jigsaw-online.com
Lillingston Associates: 07000 710131
London Guild of Toastmasters: 01737 212999;
    www.toastmastersguild.org.uk
Mini Boden: 0845 357 5021; www.boden.co.uk
Monsoon Girl: www.monsoon.co.uk
Myla: 08707 455003; www.myla.com
Octagon Motor Sports: 01474 872331; www.octagonmotorsports.com
Party Bus: 0800 731 3838; www.partybus.co.uk
Toptable: www.toptable.co.uk
Teatro: 020 7494 3040
Vertbaudet: 0500 332211; www.vertbaudet.co.uk
Wedding Design Company: 020 7553 7103; www.yourweddingdesign.com

chapter
sixteen

is everybody happy now?
negotiating the emotional minefield

No prizes for working out that a wedding is right up there with divorce, death, moving house and Christmas as one of the single most stressful events in your life. In fact, says Professor of Psychology Ben Fletcher, it can even carry health risks. So be warned …

From parents' guest lists to the pain of paying for it all, wedding planning is tough. Not only are you desperately trying to juggle your own expectations with everyone else's, but there's so much to do, and so much importance placed on it. It's a big public show – and you only get one crack at it.

Even in this modern day, the symbolism surrounding a wedding is deeply ingrained in our souls: the major life transition, leaving the security of the old family and becoming a new one. 'Planning the day that represents all, that is bound to rattle some raw emotion,' explains psychologist Lori Bisbey. So where is it felt most?

YOU'RE ENGAGED …
AND NOT EVERYONE IS DELIGHTED

'We make such a big deal of weddings,' says Lori Bisbey, who's also co-author of the book, *Rites of Passage* (Kyle Cathie). 'Everybody's supposed to want it and everyone's supposed to be happy for you.' But it doesn't always work out that way.

Friends/sisters/cousins (even the really nice ones) may:
- Feel the pressure to do it themselves – even if they don't want to.
- Finally express their doubts about your choice of partner.
- Envy the fact that you're the centre of attention.

Colleagues may:
- Decide you need one last taste of what you're giving up.
- Be worried that you won't pull your weight for the next few months.
- Be delighted that they've got something to use against you in the battle for promotion.

Parents may:
- Worry about the cost.
- Be unable to accept that you're not a baby any more.
- Be unable to accept that you're officially having sex.
- Not like your choice of partner – and feel bound to remind you at every opportunity.

The answer is much the same – whatever the problem:
- Don't flirt with anyone and do pull your weight at work.

That did it
Joan Collins' fifth husband, *Percy Gibson*, is 32 years her junior – and critics wanted to know if she thought the age difference would be a problem. 'Look, I'll tell you about the age thing,' she retorted, 'if he dies, he dies!'

- Refuse to get boring about the wedding.
- Don't give anyone reason to think you're smug.
- Don't tell people if you two have a row.
- Don't get drawn into arguments.

WELCOME TO STRESS CITY

What happens to us brides?

With all the egalitarian will in the world, weddings lay much at the door of the bride. They're built around core female instincts (the raising of babies in a secure environment variety) and fairy-tale heroines (does anyone even know the prince's name in Snow White, Cinderella or Sleeping Beauty?). So inevitably, girls are going to take this thing pretty seriously. 'Even if you've already left home and don't plan on having children, it's firmly tied up with that at a social – and historical – level,' says Ben Fletcher.

OBSESSION, PERFECTION AND LIST-ADDICTION

Men can, and sometimes do, plan weddings as well as women – if they want to. But since women tend to be more organised and more multi-tasking (research proves it), they can feel compelled to take control. My lists were so many and so long, with lists of lists, and sublists too, that I felt deeply embarrassed if anyone saw them. For the unlucky majority (and their poor long-suffering partners) attention to detail, an inclination to double-check and the urge to Get Things Done can take on a new dimension. If a year ago you had a healthy passion for fashion, and now you think fifteen girls in the same damson neck-ruff sounds just great, you may need to re-connect with your pre-wedding self.

EMOTIONAL FRAGILITY

Many brides-to-be end up one sharp word away from losing it. Besides feeling the enormity of the occasion so keenly, we take on the lion's share of the work, and then find ourselves in constant and often fraught discussion about it. Everyone wants a piece of you, and a piece of the wedding, and a chorus of voices telling you they're making allowances for you 'because you're obviously stressed' does *not* help. Some brides get a bit spoilt, too – which can only mean more friction.

Stress counsel

Top wedding stresses – for brides *and* grooms – and advice from the experts on what to do about them:

GENERAL
- Set out your principles right at the beginning; measure and try to solve problems against those.
- Identify what's causing your stress, then deal with it. You don't *have* to make a speech/wear a silly dress/formalwear/invite children if you don't want to. *See* page 222 for more on relaxation and stress management.
- Listen to a maximum of two opinions, on anything. Any more is confusing.
- If things are chaotic, take a day's holiday and get organised. Draw up a schedule of tasks, with deadlines, and delegate as much as you can.
- Look after yourself physically: *see* Chapter Fourteen.
- If suppliers/caterers/dressmakers make you panicky by saying you don't have enough time/money to get what you want, don't just take their word for it: get a second opinion.
- If people sulk or cry – because they're not a bridesmaid, for instance, or so and so says they won't come if someone else is invited – too bad. Appease, where appropriate (a would-be bridesmaid could do a reading instead). It's unlikely to work, but at least your conscience will be clearer.
- Do remember to show an interest in other people's lives, however stressed or absorbed you are.
- If you're falling out with everyone around you, ask someone *reliable* for an honest opinion. Apologise, and change, if necessary.
- If your hormones are your downfall, avoid PMT or a badly timed period by setting your wedding date tactically. See your GP about strategic use of the Pill to manipulate your start date, take vitamin B6 or Evening Primrose Oil if you don't already, and ask for stronger painkillers if you think you'll need them.

● Read *The Conscious Bride: Women Unveil Their True Feelings About Getting Hitched* by Sheryl Nissinen (New Harbinger) for greater insight and understanding about what's going on inside your/her head.

NERVES

The fluttery-tummy feeling of love is nothing compared to the intestinal roller coaster of writing all those cheques and thinking about the speeches …

● Remember that everyone's wishing you well and will have a great time whatever happens.

● Remember that everyone fluffs their vows, and people will love it if you cry (specially if you're male!).

● Read the advice on relaxation, sweating (and spots!) in Chapter Fourteen.

● Think through your main worries and make contingency plans.

● Come to terms with imperfection.

● Do some extra work on your speech: read Chapter Thirteen.

MONEY WORRIES

The toughest problems can hinge around the *source* of the money. Donators of cash invariably expect something in return – and that's usually control. It may help to:

● Cut the cost drastically by making your wedding small, different or overseas. *See* Chapter Three for a revised approach, if it's not too late.

● Pay for it all yourselves, if you can afford to, although proud fathers can take this badly (*see* The Parent Trap on page 254).

● Manage your money well. Decide how you're going to spend it, then don't be led astray. Mismanaged funds (and debt) invariably lead to resentment.

FORGET ABOUT THE WEDDING ALTOGETHER

You might think you don't have time, but the following might force your mind on to other things and get the wedding into perspective:

● Do some charity or volunteer work.

● Give blood.

> ### From the expert: Planning should be a pleasure
> Sophie Lillingston, wedding consultant
> *'Enjoy the planning – the day itself is over so quickly – and give yourself plenty of breaks. Set yourself targets, and when you've met them, just stop for a while. Pick up your wedding file again when the next tasks are due to be done.'*

- Borrow someone's children for a day.
- Do something that's physically challenging *and* rewarding: a sponsored walk, a major session in the gardening.
- Have a de-cluttering session: wardrobe, kitchen cupboards, junk room. It's unbelievably liberating.

LOVE IN A PRE-WEDDING CLIMATE

With a wedding looming on the horizon, things are not always a fanfare of romance. 'Public commitment ceremonies change a relationship,' says Lori Bisbey. 'People spend a lot of time thinking about things they're never going to do again, and they may worry that things will change between them.'

If the two of you seem to fall out over everything
Grim as it may seem, this does occasionally happen to everyone, except Mr and Mrs Perfect-to-be.

- There's a great saying about marriage: 'You're both going to get angry, just don't get angry at the same time.' Work with that one …
- Make deals and stick to them:
  - How you'll handle money
  - How you'll handle both sets of parents
  - How much you'll talk about the wedding
  - Who will do what and by when.
- Take time out: *see* **Pre-wedding relationship rescues** on page 251.
- Remember Mars and Venus? We girls must stop talking incessantly

Men as wedding planners?

'He did most of it. He's much more organised and energetic than me. He did a far better job than I would have done.' Bride, 27.

'He barely did a thing. I minded at first, but realised that he just wanted to stay out of my way so I could have whatever I wanted. It was more out of generosity than disinterest.' Bride, 38.

'Every time I did something to try to save some money, she went and spent twice as much.' Groom, 26.

about every tiny detail; you boys have got to stop trying to fix things and just *listen*.

- If you're falling into the tender trap of bride and groom stereotypes ('Why won't he get off his backside and do some of the work?' versus 'Could she be any more obsessed?') take Sophie Lillingston's advice: 'There's really no point in making a groom do things he's not comfortable with. Get him involved in things he'll enjoy, and then leave it at that.'

If you're having doubts

A bout of pre-wedding anxiety can make you question even the most solid relationship. 'Lots of people feel unsure before they get married,' says Ben Fletcher. 'It's a very private stress, difficult to discuss with your partner, but one that usually goes away.' What if it's more than that? 'You have to listen to your feelings, which is very hard when you feel backed into a corner,' adds Lori Bisbey, 'particularly if you're marrying someone people don't like. No-one wants to be told: I told you so.' If your worst wedding nightmares are coming true, and 'nerves' do not account for a growing fear that things are not right:

- Weigh up the history of your relationship against your current feelings. Is this a temporary blip, or something you've seen, but tried to ignore, before?
- Give airtime to both voices – 'problem' versus 'no problem' – to see if one is louder.

- Talk it over with someone sooner rather than later, while there's time to think.
- The clichés are true: better a broken engagement than a broken marriage, or worse, broken family. 'There's no such thing as a simple, quiet divorce,' says Lori Bisbey.
- Publicly, you can call it a postponement, if that makes it easier. Who knows, things might work out. Just make sure your partner knows where things stand.
- Even if close family are disappointed, keep in mind that they'd feel much worse if you took them through a wedding under false pretences.
- Marriage Care offers free telephone help to couples at any stage of their relationship; Relate offers face-to-face counselling. *See* **Contacts**.

Pre-wedding relationship rescues

If you simply need a boost, the following might remind you why you decided to get married in the first place:

- Prepare for the marriage – and not the wedding. Discuss your happiest dreams for your life together, and cover some practicalities too.
- Arrange proper dates again. If they're the cheap variety (walk, cinema, half a pint) so much the better.
- Go away for a weekend: a cheap B&B works just as well as a plush hotel.
- Write your vows together – or study the words you'll be saying – then start putting them into practice. Respect, patience and love are essential during the stressful pre-wedding months, as well as for the rest of the marriage.
- Space matters: don't just allow it, create it for each other. Get him football tickets; fix lunch and some serious retail therapy for her and a friend.

The wedding that wasn't

'We went to a wedding of a very confused friend who realised her mistake with just minutes to go. She went through with the wedding, but I found out later that she'd refused to sign the register! The couple then pretended to be married for a year, mainly to spare their parents' feelings, and then pretended to get divorced!' Guest, 36.

- A short ban on wedding talk is obvious, but works wonders. Make it a regular slot in your diaries.
- Choose your song: even if a first dance isn't you, naming 'your' song is still special.
- Importantly, if you're prone to flaming rows and stony silences which worsen under stress, work out in advance how to make peace fast … you may need it just hours before the wedding!

Don't forget each other on the day

It's the most frequent cry – 'We barely saw each other all day!' – and a great disappointment for some. To savour every moment:

- Discuss what you're expecting of each other on the day. It's a social occasion, of course, but understand how much each needs the other to focus on them. Some are happy to spend the day catching up with friends, others expect their partner to have eyes only for them. Reach a compromise.
- Consider a table for two, instead of a top table. Some people feel uncomfortable, but others say it was the best chance they had to concentrate on each other for a few minutes.
- Everyone will tell you to plan a few moments alone at the wedding, to step back, look on and take it all in. Chances are you'll still forget: ask someone to make sure you do.
- Concentrate on and enjoy your vows. They'll be over before your feet have touched the ground, and they're what the day is all about.
- If you're seriously hoping to have sex on your wedding night (the majority don't), you could try a month of abstinence beforehand. Some couples say it works …
- Grooms would be well advised to give a good (but spontaneous) reaction to The Dress.

SECOND WEDDINGS

Over a third of weddings in the UK are second marriages for one or both partners. In some ways, they're far less stressful, because you have more freedom to do away with convention: you're probably paying for it yourself, and parents had their chance to have their way the first time around.

In other ways, second weddings are much more stressful: there's likely to be a larger, and possibly more sensitive, wedding cast. Ex-partners and your own children need careful handling, and bride and groom might have very different expectations of the wedding itself, when it's the first wedding for one and the second for the other.

A quiet occasion might be the answer, but if you want a full or traditional wedding, there is absolutely no reason not to. Many churches will marry divorcees, so if you want a religious ceremony, persevere (*see* Chapter Eight). And if you think people will find your choices inappropriate, don't invite them.

IF YOU HAVE CHILDREN OF YOUR OWN

'A wedding doesn't have to be stressful for children of the bride or groom,' says Ben Fletcher, 'but it can be, if handled the wrong way.' At worst, it can be upsetting or confusing: 'Many children of divorced parents hold out the hope that Mummy and Daddy will get back together, but when one of them remarries, that's it,' says Lori Bisbey. They may feel it's disloyal to go to the wedding of a parent, but be unhappy about being excluded too. Even if it's the children's own parents who are getting married, the experience can be daunting. For the vast majority, though, it's a very happy occasion. The expert advice is:

- Ensure that children are a negotiated part of the plans. 'Don't put them on the spectators' side,' says Ben Fletcher. Invite them to be included in the ceremony itself – but don't force it.
- If you can, involve the other parent in preparing the children for the wedding, or even invite them, if you know it will be a success: it will help children to feel less torn.
- Allow children to air their feelings.
- Explain what will change and reassure about things that won't.
- Help them to understand what it's about, at a level appropriate to their age.

- If you need it, there's professional help available for all childcarers, including stepparents and grandparents, at Parentline Plus. *See* **Contacts**.

THE PARENT TRAP

The trouble with weddings now is that no one knows what's 'right'. Abandoning the traditional wedding formula (bride's parents in charge) has much in its favour, but peace and harmony isn't it. Rewind a century or two, and I'll bet brides never argued with their parents. They may have felt a bit resentful about having to marry their father's wart-covered business associate, but at least they didn't have tense negotiations over the seating arrangements, favours and guest list.

Mothers and daughters: Why the clash?
Weddings certainly exacerbate mother–daughter tensions. A mother has her own set of dreams for your day, and hers are tied up with some difficult stuff: losing her little girl, feeling old, wanting to make a good impression on her own friends. 'There's an inevitable clash of expectations, desires and wants,' says Ben Fletcher, 'and you may have to act as mediator between your mother and your husband-to-be. All that's a recipe for massively heightened

How their mothers shaped up
'My mother did absolutely nothing. Because I was upset about it, my sister and I took her out for lunch to try to talk about it, but all she wanted to do was talk about her holiday. After the wedding, she got loads of thank-you letters. She did have the decency to hand them over, though!' Bride, 36.

'We're not a specially close or affectionate family, but my mother and I got on particularly well while we were planning the wedding. We had some anxious moments – but they were all happy ones!' Bride, 25.

'A friend of my mother told her that all a bride-to-be wants from her mum is to hear that everything she's doing is wonderful. She worked hard at that one – and it was probably a tough call!' Bride, 35.

Losing a son ...

'Despite the fact that we married in France, and paid for the whole thing ourselves, my mother-in-law completely hijacked our wedding. She rang the cake-maker to change the order from chocolate to fruit cake, without telling anyone; she invited all her friends without even asking us; and paced up and down outside the town hall for half an hour before the wedding, sobbing because she couldn't find her son to "say goodbye".' Bride, 26.

The celebrity mother-in-law

Weddings – and marriages – all around the film world are reported to have floundered in the face of a formidable mother-in-law:

Sylvester Stallone's *wives, including the current* **Jennifer Flavin**, *have certainly felt the pressure from his infamous mother, Jackie, with repeated reports of fights and fall-outs.*

Minnie Driver *says that the break-up of her engagement to Josh Brolin wasn't the fault of her future stepmother-in-law,* **Barbra Streisand**, *but the press think otherwise.*

Raquel Welch *sent jaws to the floor when she arrived at the wedding of her son Damon to Rebecca Trueman, daughter of cricketer Fred, wearing a few pieces of scanty black cloth in lieu of a dress.*

sensitivity on both sides.' As Lori Bisbey puts it, 'The scope is there to disagree in big and glorious ways!'

Mothers and sons

You could be lucky. Despite unflattering stereotypes, mothers-in-law on both sides can be highly popular, providing an oasis of rationality and practical, no-strings-attached support. In the modern climate, parents of grooms are often rightfully included as much, if not more, in the planning (and indeed financing) of a wedding.

Problems classically arise when mothers are struggling to let go of their sons. If they're not involved in the wedding arrangements, they don't have that distraction: they can't throw themselves, and their emotional turmoil, into practicalities as a bride's mother often does. For the unhappy few, the result can be unresolved resentment, interfering and attempts to steal the limelight.

Dealing with problem parents

'Time and again, it's a payment issue,' says psychologist and twice mother of the bride, Kathleen Cox. So first ensure that the money issue is crystal clear: who's paying for what, and what's expected in return. If you feel comfortable taking your parents' cash, you still need to be specific, even if that means agreeing exactly what the decision process will be and which areas are personal and for the couple alone to decide. If there's potential for tension, assign funding to a specific area, like flowers, so that the strings are attached only to that. Once money is sorted:

- Agree with your partner that you'll put each other first. Solidarity is an essential display between the two of you, and to the outside world.
- Agree with your partner in advance precisely how much control you want parents to have.
- If parents are disappointed for any reason, such as in your decision against a religious ceremony, or in refusing their money to go it alone:
  - Stick quietly to your guns, explaining without arguing.
  - Try to reassure them that their feelings – and role – are important.
  - Find other ways to make them feel needed and important, without being patronising.
- Whoever is best at smoothing the path should take the role. Sit back while your diplomatic partner works his/her magic.
- Enjoy your parents' involvement, and use it. Benefit from their help, don't suffer it.
- Set precedents about married life right from the beginning. Don't spend every Sunday at either set of parents' home unless you plan to keep that up.
- The mother who seems disinterested may simply be waiting to be asked, or feel hurt. If you want her involved, enlist her help.
- Be specific: the same words can mean different things, and different words mean the same thing, so you need to clarify any agreement or discussion.

And you thought yours was complicated!

'I'm English, my husband's mother is Hindu and his father is Muslim. All we really wanted was a civil wedding and a reception that paid small tribute to both our cultures. The reality wasn't going to be as simple as that: first, for my mother-in-law, we had a Hindu betrothal ceremony, followed by a marriage blessing. I wore a sari and had my hands painted with henna. Two weeks later, we married the way we'd planned – at a register office in York. I wore a red dress, my husband wore a Nehru-collared suit, and we celebrated with a black-tie party for 120 people at Castle Howard nearby. The next day, we went to a pre-wedding party my father-in-law had arranged, and a Muslim ceremony the day after that: in full ceremonial dress, we were married (yet again) before 200 of his family and business associates! Finally, we went to Pakistan a few months later for a big wedding reception, organised again by my father-in-law, because my husband's grandmother had been too frail to come to the Muslim ceremony here! After four "weddings", the presents alone had to be seen to be believed: in all we received 56 whisky glasses, seven crystal fruit bowls, a ship in a bottle, several silver-plated tea sets – and much more besides. The amazing thing was, I barely got stressed about any of it!' Bride, 31.

- The mother who is a complete nightmare should be given no slack. Keep as far away as possible. If she's the groom's mother, tradition is your friend, so use it. She has no business trying to hijack your wedding, so you can tell her politely to back off. 'A difficult mother was always going to make trouble,' says Ben Fletcher, so don't blame yourself.
- If parents are hijacking the guest list, stand firm. See page 40.
- Be appreciative of your mum's efforts. 'There's a tendency to arrive for the weekend, deposit a list of orders, and leave again!' says Kathleen Cox.

Divorced parents and stepparents

Traditional etiquette doesn't provide well for complex family set-ups: it says that even divorced parents should sit together at the church, and in the stan-

Clever dressing

Viscountess Serena Linley paid the ultimate compliment to her now late mother-in-law, Princess Margaret: she re-created the princess's wedding dress to wear for her own marriage to Margaret's son, David, three decades later. A timelessly beautiful design, it looked as right in the 90s as it did in the 60s.

dard arrangement at a top table, with stepparents seated elsewhere, regardless of most circumstances.

It has to be more civilised to seat *everyone* with the same degree of consideration – both at the ceremony and at the reception – to prevent anyone from feeling sidelined, and to protect already fragile family relationships. Generosity is the order of the day: however acrimonious a split, most can put their feelings aside for just for one day. A bride who is very close to her stepfather may find it difficult to decide who will give her away, and who will speak for her. Look at the alternatives in Chapter Eleven and Chapter Thirteen.

KEEPING EVERYONE HAPPY

Modern manners

It's an expensive business being a guest at a wedding (*see* page 39) and time-consuming at that. No-one minds, of course, unless they feel like rent-a-crowd. Simple touches make them feel loved and valued; it's important to consider practicalities, too:

- Include essential information with your invitation: maps, a list of accommodation, transport and road directions. Cover anything else – from the rules on smoking and confetti to dress code. If you're doing anything unusual, or unconventional, let people know.
- If you're asking people to bring a guest, avoid writing 'plus one' or 'and guest' on the invitation: get the name, instead.
- Make requests considerately: the jury's out on whether to include details of your gift list (although etiquette says don't), and your wedding may not be the right type for young children, but clipped orders like 'Gift list at

John Lewis' and 'No children' are not good manners and look particularly awful in print.

- Send out invitations well in advance to give people plenty of time to get organised, especially if they have to book accommodation.
- Don't send out last-minute invitations: people will know they were on the C list. If you want to stagger the invitation process, bring it forwards a few months instead.
- Think of ways to make out-of-town guests feel welcome – or even have a pre-wedding drink or dinner the night before (no-one will expect the bride and groom to stay long or late). A small gift, or even a handwritten card, in their room will go a long way.
- If the wedding means an overnight stay, don't expect people to come alone, especially if they don't know anyone.
- Make sure everyone can see and hear what's going on. That's what they're there for. Plan decorations, acoustics and room layouts accordingly.
- When you set the time for your wedding, consider people's journeys and their stomachs. Suggest a pre-wedding pub lunch venue if necessary.
- Don't leave guests standing for too long outside the church or reception venue waiting for you to have photos done. They should be welcomed, given a drink, and shade or shelter, before you go off. If you can give them something to eat, that'll give you a little longer, but don't leave your own wedding for hours.
- Include guests in some photos to make it a shared experience – and get much more interesting pictures.
- However dreamy an outdoor wedding sounds, in the UK you have no option but to plan for rain, with indoor reception facilities and umbrellas. Wet guests are unlikely to be very happy. Make sure heating is adequate, too.
- Too much sun is just as bad, so make sure there is plenty of shade in summer months. Chinese parasols and fans are a cheap and pretty solution.
- Don't ration drinks. If money's tight, better a pay-bar than nothing at all, or choose drinks that stretch, like punch.
- Think of all dietary needs: kosher, vegetarian, pregnant women and all. Include a line on the reply card asking special requirements.

- When you do the table plans, remember that people almost always prefer to sit with their friends.
- Even close friends become rather reverent when you're the bride and groom, so the onus is on the couple to make contact and be friendly with everyone.
- If you have extra guests for the evening, look after them. Greet them, then provide some food and a couple of drinks. A pay-bar is OK once you've done that.

Handfasting

'Our wedding was quite New Age, so we put in a note with the invitation to let people know what to expect, then added, "If you must laugh, do it at the back – oh and please don't wear a hat." No-one laughed, and everyone had a great time!' Bride, 37.

Outdoors

'We were determined that the ceremony was going to be outside, come what may, so we printed "please bring an umbrella" on the invitations. It wasn't exactly sunny, but it didn't matter a bit.' Bride, 29.

Humanist

'There was a lot of confusion about our wedding: loads of people seemed to have the strange idea that humanism meant naturism – and we were going to have a nudist wedding! We spent a lot of time beforehand explaining what was going to happen – and that it was really going to be quite an ordinary occasion!' Bride, 24.

Guest appreciation

'I was so stressed out about us at the wedding, it hadn't occurred to me that without the guests, it's not so different from any other day. When I arrived in church it really hit me: they were all there, they'd travelled hundreds of miles, made so much effort to look really good – and all for us.' Bride, 27.

- Don't burden people with costly obligations:
  - They don't have to join your pre-wedding parties. Sound people out politely rather than pressurising.
  - Put plenty of cheap presents on your gift list.
  - Include cheap but nice accommodation for overnight guests. The expectation that everyone will come and stay at your luxury hotel with you is not reasonable.
- Departures are important: guests don't like hanging around uncertain about whether you're going to make an exit, and older generations will feel uncomfortable leaving before the bride and groom. See page 170 for how to handle it.

☺☹ *'I was invited to an evening reception of a wedding a few years ago. When I arrived at the allotted time, the bride and groom were nowhere to be seen, there was just a pay-bar and some slices of limp, barely unfrozen pizza to eat. I wondered why I was there.' Guest, 24.*

Other people's children at your wedding

THE 'NO-KIDS' DILEMMA

It's a tricky one: kids could really add to your day, or they could ruin it. As a mother, I like children at weddings (as long as the situation is right) but I also deeply sympathise with couples who want to keep the occasion adult (as long as they do it with tact).

- In their favour, children can add a wonderful 'perfect world' dimension to your wedding. They provide charm, surprises and a cute subject for photos.
- They can also be vile, noisy and messy. For an evening or black-tie party they rarely work.
- If you'd like them there, don't worry too much about how children will behave. Their parents are your friends, so they'll act considerately. If a baby starts crying during the ceremony, the mother will take it outside – with an usher's help, if necessary. It's likely that you won't notice children much during the day anyway.
- Decide in good time because it will affect your plans: venue, readings, time of day, entertainment.

If you decide not to invite them, treat parents with courtesy:

- Word the invitation clearly and politely. Leave the children's names off the invitations, and follow with a phone call or add a personal note to clarify, and check that everything is OK.
- Give them plenty of warning.
- If your wedding is far from home, they may not be comfortable relying on a local babysitter that no-one knows, so don't push them into it.
- Think before you present your decision not to invite children as a benefit to parents. It could strike the wrong note.
- Decide in advance what you're going to do if people ask to be made an exception. Work out the most tactful approach for your friends – and what you feel most happy with.

KEEPING KIDS HAPPY

It's a simple formula: happy children = happy parents. If the parents are the two of you, it's even more important.

- Appoint someone who isn't a guest to keep a very close eye on them: younger children and toddlers need a higher proportion of adult care than older children.
- Lay on entertainment if you can, and schedule it to take care of the most child-unfriendly times, such as during the meal and speeches. *See* page 165 for entertainment ideas.
- Give children jobs and games to do: keep them busy with disposable cameras or confetti to hand out and use; a treasure hunt; a quiz about the day. Set up a video room if possible.
- Wedding crèches are an additional cost, but can be well worth it. Try Crèchendo or the Mobile Crèche Company. Some will even bath children and put them to bed so parents can stay on and party! Before booking, check directly with parents to find out what's suitable for their children.
- Do a children's table serving familiar food like sausages or pasta, and follow with sweet tea-party treats and a children's cake. Decorate chair backs with balloons, and pile up colouring books, crayons and comics on the table.

- Be age-sensitive: don't lump teenagers with young children. They'll soon join in on kids' stuff if they feel inclined!

AFTERWARDS

The turmoil can reach new heights *after* the wedding: use Chapter Nineteen to steel yourself for the practical as well as the emotional upheaval.

Contacts
Crèchendo: 020 8772 8140; www.crechendo.com
Mobile Crèche Company: 01423 797440; www.mobilecreche.co.uk

Emotional support
Relate (the former Marriage Guidance Council) provides counselling to couples at every stage of a relationship. General information: 01788 573 241; counselling via your local branch (in the phone book); www.relate.org.uk
Marriage Care is a charity which provides expert relationship guidance, whether you're married or not. Their national helpline gives free support and counselling over the phone, from 11am until 3pm, Monday to Friday, on 0845 6606000; www.marriagecare.org.uk
Parentline Plus offers free emotional help and guidance to parents or carers on any subject, including stepparenting and other special circumstances: 0808 8002222; www.parentlineplus.org.uk

section
six

memories to last a lifetime

Catch them while you can ...

chapter
seventeen

photos, videos and mementos

Now you might think that all your planning and dreaming is for one thing: your wedding day. But you're wrong. Because from the moment you wake up the day *after* you wed, you'll realise that what you were really planning for was your *memories* of your wedding. For the rest of your life, that's what your wedding will be: glorious, happy memories (and the start of a wonderful marriage, of course).

While I'm not suggesting that the entire day should be given over to the photographer – we've all been to *that* kind of wedding – it is important to devote ample time and thought to preserving the magic of the day before it's too late. Weddings, after all, are a kind of madness. You spend ten times more money, time and energy on a single day than you would ever consider spending – even in moments of drunken insanity – under any other circumstances. But you do it, and it's wonderful, and worth it, and afterwards, your memories will be with you forever and ever. Or so you hope ...

There are two big problems with wedding memories: firstly, many couples don't have any in their heads at all. The day passes as a fourteen-and-a-half-second out-of-body experience, and you wonder if it really happened at all. Whole hours will be lost from your life – on the day you want most to keep them. Secondly, many couples are disappointed with their wedding photos. I don't think the photographer is always to blame (although sometimes she/he is), but when those all-important pictures come back, they may not be quite what you hoped.

So it really is important to make sure you get the photographs you want, and to back them up with other well-planned memory aids, such as a box of wedding mementos, a video or guest book. For more ideas, *see* page 278.

PHOTOS FIRST

Four essential steps should get you great pictures:
- Find a photographer with sufficient talent, expertise and experience with a camera; usually a professional, sometimes an exceptional amateur.
- Be clear about the style of pictures you want: posed or 'fly on the wall', black-and-white or colour.
- Be very clear about the specific shots you want covered.
- Know how to look your best in photographs.

Choosing the photographer
Suggestions from experts like the Guild of Wedding Photographers UK include:

FINDING THEM
- Start in plenty of time: many photographers are booked 12 months ahead.
- Ask friends and contacts for personal recommendations.
- The Internet is a fantastic resource; many photographers' sites carry a good selection of pictures.
- Look in wedding magazines (both features and small ads) for styles you like.

- Bear in mind that any pictures you see have been carefully chosen and skilfully edited; not every one of their pictures will be that good!
- Contact professional organisations (in **Contacts** at the end of this chapter) for lists of photographers in your area; their websites may also carry examples of their members' work.
- Talk to people who have used these photographers for their wedding. Even if they're recommended, ask for negative comments as well as positive ones – aspects which could have been better.

JUDGING THEIR WORK

- See at least three preferred photographers who are free on your wedding date. The photographer should show you a considerable amount of work. Examine it carefully.
- See lots of pictures from the same (recent) wedding, not just the best of lots. Do the pictures tell the story of the wedding day fully? Is there a good mix of portraits, groups and story-telling pictures? Are the groups tidy, with everybody looking happily at the camera? Do the prints show detail?
- Check the calibre of indoor pictures closely – you may have no choice if it rains – and discuss the wet-weather options.
- Look at *all* the pictures – if you only like half of them, you'll probably only like half of your wedding photos, too.
- Don't get too bogged down with the choice of album – that's the one thing you can put right *after* the event.
- Similarly, don't be too impressed by modern technology and elaborate photographic treatments: they're a great tool but good pictures have to be the starting point.
- What happens if the photographer is ill on the day?

From the experts: The right choice

Damien and Julie Lovegrove, wedding photographers

'Check out the work of the photographer(s) who'll actually be doing the pictures on the day (not just the company that employs them). Get to know them and be sure you like them.'

From the expert: Get the best from your photographer

George Dawber, wedding photographer and national president of the Master Photographers Association

'Don't let the fear of an outdated photographic style make you go too far the other way. A high-quality, classical wedding picture, well-lit and beautifully posed, is timeless and anything but old-fashioned.

'Communicate with your photographer – and keep communicating. He needs to know what your expectations are.

'Ensure that anyone who will be in group photographs or portraits is asked before the day itself to take responsibility for being in the right place at the right time. It's not the pictures themselves that take the time, it's tracking down the people who should be in them!'

● Find out exactly what's included in the price. Some include photography, prints and an album in one price, and charge for subsequent prints. Others charge only for their time, with all prints as extras. Still others hand over the proofs and the negatives for you to sort out. Be sure to clarify and compare like with like.

Getting the style – and shots – that you want

● Your photographer should meet you beforehand to plan the day's schedule and draw up a list of shots and a timetable. Arrive at a plan which you feel sure you'll be satisfied with and the photographer believes is practical, agreeing what will be covered when, what proportion of time and shots should be given to groups and portraits, and how much to candid/story-telling/reportage shots.

● Portraits and groups should take no more than a couple of 20- to 30-minute sessions. A session before you leave for the ceremony is a good time to cover some family portraits: pictures of the bride with her mother, father, even bridesmaids – everyone will be looking perfect and it's not taking up time from the wedding itself.

● Make copies of the shot-list: give one to the photographer in good time, together with a note covering any other points agreed. Give a copy to

From the expert: What is reportage photography?

Brent Jones, wedding photographer

'It's a very misunderstood word. The pictures are completely unrehearsed, and unset up. It takes more time, because you're waiting for the moment, instead of faking it, but the pictures have real feeling, a view of the characters. I think they're better for it. It takes trust, though.' It's not a good option for people who want to plan the majority of shots in advance.

    your best man or other helper, and keep one in your wedding file.

- Words like 'reportage', 'fly on the wall', 'traditional', 'formal', 'informal' and 'posed' mean different things to different people. Better to spell out what you mean, show examples of what you like (ideally from the photographer's portfolio) and explain why. Your photographer should advise you on the best places to take photographs.

Your wedding shot-list

Don't go mad – this many shots would take too long, and you may want just the bare minimum of posed pictures. Choose what's important from the list below, add any extras that are personal to you, and err on the side of caution.

THE BUILD-UP

- Getting ready shots of bride and groom, including details like shoes, tiara and cufflinks
- The groom and guests at a pre-wedding drink
- Groom and best man
- Groom with best man and ushers
- Groom with his family
- Guests and bridal party arriving
- Bridesmaids
- Ushers

BRIDE, FAMILY AND BRIDESMAIDS READY TO GO TO THE CEREMONY

- Bride with mother

- Bride with parents
- Bride with family
- Bride with bridesmaids
- Bride and father getting into car

THE CEREMONY
- Bride's arrival
- Bride with father
- Bride and father walking up aisle
- Bride and groom at start of ceremony
- Exchange of rings
- Signing the register
- Procession out of ceremony
- Bride and groom outside
- Confetti shots
- Wide shot of activity outside venue
- Bride and groom getting into car
- Flowers and decorations

GROUP SHOTS
Any not covered before the ceremony, plus:
- Bride and groom with their own children if they have any
- Bride and groom with bridesmaids
- Bride and groom with best man and maid of honour
- Bride and groom with best man and ushers
- Bride and groom with maid of honour and bridesmaids
- Bride and groom with groom's family
- Bride and groom with bride's family
Three/four generations, such as:
- Grandmother, mother, bride and daughter
- Youngest and oldest guest with bride and groom

RECEPTION
- Location shots

- Bride and groom arriving
- Guests arriving
- Receiving line
- Candid shots of guests
- Candid shots of bride and groom circulating
- Bride with close friends
- Groom with close friends
- Everyone at the wedding, guests and bridal party
- Tables and decorations
- The cake

Reliving it

'When we got back from honeymoon, we went straight to my parents' house, where they had the photos back from the photographer. I have to admit that I sat up almost all night, just looking at them over and over again! It was like being reunited with an old friend. Two years later, I still pore over them from time to time. I love them. They're priceless.' Bride, now 29.

Formal photographs

'We were sure we wanted formal photographs for our wedding, although lots of people expressed surprise at our choice – I think they think we're quite trendy! After a long search, we found a photographer whose style was per-fect for us – very classic, elegant, structured shots with a slightly retro feel. We were so happy with the results: most were black-and-white, and there was a Fifties-movie look to them which actually looks quite cool!' Groom, 34.

Double-check

'We gave two close friends (who had no other responsibilities) a copy of the photographer's list of shots and put them in charge of checking that we got every picture we'd asked for. We asked the photographer before if he minded – but he was great about it – maybe he appreciated the help with rounding people up! It was one of the best things we did, because he nearly missed a couple of really important shots.' Bride, 23.

- Cutting the cake
- Speeches and toasts
- First dance
- Bride throwing bouquet
- Bride and groom going away

Being photogenic

To help yourself to look good in pictures:

- Before the wedding:
  - Get out all your recent photos and pick out the ones you like. What's the common theme? Grinning or smiling gently? Photographed from an angle, or straight from the front? Chin down slightly, eyes looking very slightly up, or head held high (double chins work in mysterious ways!).
  - Be vain: spend time in front of the mirror practising those poses you like and working out your best smile. Do you look best with teeth showing or not? Then practise standing tall without looking stiff.
  - Learn how to make up for the camera: do *not* pile it on, but subtly define features and add a little natural-looking colour. Go for matt textures, not shine, and waterproof mascara. Get an expert to show you what suits you best, then go home and photograph it to see how it works on film.
  - Avoid very shiny fabrics for your dress.
  - *See* Chapter Fourteen for more on flattering clothes and make-up.
- On the day:
  - Relax. It really helps if you like the photographer, who should make it easy to laugh and smile.
  - Don't be photographed in direct or overhead sunlight (a good photographer will know this anyway).
  - Do the model thing: between shots, relax your face, look away from the camera, and close your eyes. Just before the next round of pictures, look at the camera, open your eyes, put on a fresh smile, and pull your whole body up tall. Widen your eyes and look straight at the lens for every click of the camera.
  - Stand up tall and close together. Sitting is rarely flattering to the

body, although sitting and leaning slightly forward is flattering for headshots.

- Keep alcohol to a minimum.
- Ask a friend/bridesmaid to warn you when to top up make-up and tidy hair.

Photo rescue

You can correct some problems:

- The latest technology means that it's sometimes possible to add some-

When photographs go wrong

'We tried to book the then Wedding Photographer of the Year six months before our wedding. He wasn't available, but one of his team was. He assured us that the pictures would be exactly to his style and standards, so we agreed – and paid £2000 in advance. When the proofs of our wedding pictures came, we were horrified: they were absolutely awful. They'd been shot on the wrong film, so everything was yellow; there was a black outline round everything; there were things growing out of people's heads, and worse. When we said we weren't happy, he refused to acknowledge there was a problem, and said the pictures would be fine once they'd been treated – but wouldn't let us have them, unless we agreed in advance that we would deem them acceptable. Despite the fact that we have successfully sued the company, been awarded compensation, and had them struck off the professional register, he has refused to give us the finished pictures, a refund, or compensation, because he says we sued under the wrong name. He still has our £2000 and our pho-tographs. We've re-shot some pictures with another photographer at our own expense, but there was no hope of rounding up all our guests: many had come from the US. We're going to sue again, because we're just not the kind of people to be taken for a ride: we want our wedding photographs, we want recognition of what's happened, and we want compensation. This has been complete hell. The stress and misery it caused meant that for months I could not bear to think back to the wedding at all. Thank God I work in TV – at least we had a fantastic wedding video.' Bride, 29.

Book of memories

'My brother made us a photo album, using copies of all the guests' own photos, captioned with lines from our vows, fragments of conversation and sections of the speeches. He spent hours with the video, copying it all down. We treasure it even more than the official photos.' Groom, 30.

one in to a photo to complete a group – or remove them, or remedy faults such as closed eyes or poor exposure. Discuss with your photographer or photographic shop. Digital photography is particularly malleable in this way, but even the conventional kind enjoys some of the benefits of the digital age.

- The original photographer – or an able amateur – could retake some pictures without having to mock up a wedding: if there isn't one with your mother, for instance, re-create a 'getting ready' picture, or for a group shot of your bridesmaids, have a 'dress-fitting' session.
- If you're not happy with pictures of the two of you, use it as an excuse to have a portrait done after your honeymoon when you're looking gorgeous, tanned and relaxed.

THE VIDEO

Should you, shouldn't you?

Time was when wedding videos were a bit of a joke. Too many unwelcome glimpses of TV's *You've Been Framed* gave them a bit of a bad name. But we've moved on: the man with the camera is such a familiar sight at weddings that people barely notice him any more, and the results are greatly improved. For people who have no idea what happened at their own wedding, a video is like putting together the pieces of a jigsaw puzzle.

You don't have to have a video, of course. Many people can't bear to watch themselves on a TV screen, or find it a slightly too real medium, preferring the fuzzy magic of their personal memories, and some of us feel overly conscious of a camera. You could even be forgiven for thinking they were still a bit corny. Plus, it's yet another thing to pay for.

Choosing and working with a professional videographer

- Seek personal recommendations or look in magazines as you would choosing a photographer. The Association of Professional Videomakers can suggest someone in your area.
- Watch a number of full-length examples before deciding on someone you like.
- Assess the videographer and his work in some of the ways you would a photographer's (*see* page 268).
- The filming should be clear, steady, well focused; the editing seamless.
- Be very clear about the aspects of the wedding you want covered, including any private moments or personal reactions.
- Agree in advance what kind of finished film you want, how it will be edited down: some couples like quite a 'raw' film, others prefer that it should show only the 'perfect' moments.
- Discuss background music and titles. Can you choose your own – or give music a miss?
- Establish what the price includes, how much additional copies cost and any other possible extras.

Advice for the amateur

The DIY solution is a great way of getting a fun reminder of the day for next to nothing. Don't expect slick, professional results – just a rough-and-ready recording – unless your amateur is especially gifted.

- Use an up-to-date video camera, hired if necessary from a photographic shop.
- Know your equipment and film something beforehand. Familiarise your-self with the zoom, basic switches like on/off and standby, and loading and unloading film. Play back the film, take a critical view of your work and see how it can be improved.
- Visit the venue in advance and work out where you're going to stand for good shots of the ceremony, the speeches, the cutting of the cake.
- Stand steadily, feet apart and arms in a comfortable position.
- A tripod is helpful when filming the same scene for a long period (during the ceremony or speeches), but continue to look through the camera the *whole*

time. The light may change, or people may move without you realising.
- When filming, leave a 'frame' around the subject, and leave space above people's heads.
- Take your time and hold shots for a while. Record more than you think you'll need.
- Follow action and movement steadily and slowly.
- Use your zoom sparingly and slowly. Zooming too fast results in loss of focus.
- Check the camera, film, settings and sound from time to time. Mistakes are hideously easy to make. Terrible-but-true horror stories include an entire ceremony filmed in strobe, another glared out by sunlight, speeches recorded without sound, and an entire day's shooting made without film in the camera.

SPREADING THE WORD

You can show your photographs or video to the rest of your guests and absent friends, without inviting them all over (again):
- Yourcast.tv will put your video – or even your invitations – online.
- Confetti will put online (for a small fee) the pictures from disposable cameras bought from them.
- Special Occasions Webs will set up a site for you with its own web address, displaying a large number of photos for a year.

THINGS YOU'LL BE GLAD YOU KNEW

- During the specific time you've allocated to pictures, make that the priority. You don't want a photographer blowing a whistle, a videographer obscuring everyone's view, or your guests getting restless during your photographs, but the combination of sensitive, professional people and a good dose of refreshment for your guests should provide plenty of opportunity for wonderful pictures.

- Appoint someone to retrieve disposable cameras and to go round picking up pieces of memorabilia before they're swept away: a confetti box/a place card/a piece of ribbon, etc.
- A guest book is a great idea, but it moves slowly as people read the messages already written. Appoint someone to take it round and speed it along, or better still, try one of the other approaches below.

MEMENTOS THAT MATTER

After the photos, there are many other ways to ensure that all that happiness is wrapped up safely to revisit whenever you need to.

- A memory box: make a treasure trove of all those little bits and pieces which the less sentimental might cast into the bin. If you're feeling creative, you could cover a box in a fabric remnant from your dress, or your bridesmaids', and trim it with ribbon. Alternatively, order a simple wooden box, incorporating a personal detail, from the Memory Store. Put in it anything evocative or which might make you smile (or raise an eyebrow!) in a few years' time, such as:
  - An invitation
  - Letters of reply or thanks after the wedding
  - Wedding cards and gift labels
  - Your pre-wedding 'to do' list or diary
  - A champagne or wine bottle label
  - Confetti
  - Service sheet
  - Fabric swatches
  - Transcripts of the speeches
  - The words of your vows
  - CD of the music played at your wedding ceremony, or for your first dance
  - A wedding favour or detail
  - Ribbons from flowers or decorations
  - A dried buttonhole

- Your own two place cards
- The sixpence from your shoe
- Ask your guests to write messages.
  - Put a pile of small cards on each table, with a pen, and a box or bowl to put them in once messages have been written.
  - Get a book which can be disassembled (or make one with card, paper and ribbon), take the pages out, put one or two on each table for signing, and reassemble later.
  - At a small wedding, a Polaroid camera could be used to take pictures of people as they arrive at the reception, and their picture handed to them to sign and leave in a box.
  - Cut squares of fabric in your wedding colours: ask people to write on them and when you're old you can make them into a patchwork quilt!
- Put disposable cameras on every table. Write a tag to invite people to take pictures and leave the camera behind.
- Have a photo album covered with fabric from your dress or waistcoat, paper from your service sheets and invitations, or flowers from your bouquet; from Ever After Albums.
- Keep your bouquet (or retrieve it!). Some flowers, like roses, dry well hung upside down in an airing cupboard. Alternatively, have it preserved professionally. For preservation without pressing, get it quickly and in pristine condition to Flowers Framed Forever (whose style is clean and modern), or to Petals & Lace. Pressed For Time will press and frame. All contacts are listed over-page.

Money-wise: What to expect

Photographer, average spend: about £630

Video, average spend: about £450

Personal websites for online video or picture display: about £150+

However, prices for photographers vary so much that there is no benchmark, and price is no indication of quality. The price may depend on the total time the photographer expects to spend at your wedding, the approximate number of photographs to be taken, and the number of prints.

The following are all quotes from couples' recent weddings:

'Our photographer cost £2000. The pictures were so bad, we wrote the cheque for only half the bill. He didn't even try to get the remainder of the money.' Bride, 29.

'We paid £250 for a great set of pictures in a basic but nice album.' Bride, 24.

'We paid £450 for hundreds of really good 6x4 inch prints and all the negatives. We organised our own prints.' Groom, 35.

'We paid £400 for loads and loads of pictures, but not one of my mother. She's still quite upset about it!' Bride, 29.

'We had no photographer, just lots of friends with good cameras. We have a great wedding album.' Bride, 26.

Contacts

Association of Professional Videomakers: 01529 421 717; www.apv.org.uk

British Institute of Professional Photography: 01920 464011;
   www.bipp.com

Confetti: 0870 840 6060; www.confetti.co.uk

Damien & Julie Lovegrove: 01275 853204;
   www.lovegrovephotography.com

Ever After Albums: 01458 830 886; www.everafteralbums.com

Flowers Framed Forever: 020 8878 1811; www.flowers-framed-
   forever.co.uk

Guild of Wedding Photographers UK: 01225 760088; www.gwp-uk.co.uk

Institute of Videography: 0845 741 3626; www.iov.co.uk

Master Photographers Association: 01325 356 555; www.mpauk.com

Memory Store: 0115 969 1367; www.the-memory-store.com

Petals & Lace: 01371 873986

Pressed For Time: 01489 574668; www.pftuk.co.uk

Society of Wedding and Portrait Photographers: 01745 815030;
   www.swpp.co.uk

Special Occasion Webs: www.special-occasion-webs.co.uk

Yourcast.tv: 0207 586 1441; www.yourcast.tv

section
seven

get sorted

Take care of all the practicalities, lists and countdowns,
and you'll be free to have the day of your lives

chapter
eighteen

step by step, list by list:
planning for one perfect day

I'm an obsessive list-maker with perfectionist tendencies, a control-freak, cautious and meticulous about detail and organised to the point of ridicule amongst my family and friends (gosh, I sound lovely, don't I?). Planning projects and working with a team of people has been a core part of my job for many years, so it's not surprising that my wedding was ludicrously well organised – and took over my entire life.

I tell you this not to urge you to be the same, but to put this chapter into context, and suggest that you put any organisational advice (mine included) into context. I lapped up every word, tip, list or instruction that came my way ... and literally couldn't see the wood for the trees, or the wedding for the planning. Now that the dust has settled, I'm fairly certain I would have enjoyed it just as much, if not more, if I'd let go a bit. And if you decide that planning a wedding is simply not your bag, *see* page 239 to find out about handing it over to the professionals.

KEEPING THE WORKLOAD MANAGEABLE

Some people seem to organise an entire wedding in half a dozen phone calls; others install an extra half-dozen phone lines. I wish I'd been in the first camp; it's probably obvious that I was firmly in the latter. If you're the kind who just wants to fix it and move on, you can, if you:

- Delegate: there are people who are up to the job. List six close friends and family whose organisational skills you admire, then tell them how much you'd appreciate their help.
- Be specific: don't waste time on vagueness. Decide what you want, make it very clear, and finish the job. It's not aggressive, it's assertive.
- Let go: you cannot control everyone and everything, and you will exhaust yourself trying.
- Keep it simple: the grander your ideas, the longer they'll take. And the more there is to go wrong.

MAKING IT HAPPEN

Get organised

The trick, in my view, is to get all your planning tools and processes (listed here) on the go from day one (or as soon as is practical). Then add to them as you go along, so that every single thing you do, buy, appropriate or organise will be right where you need it: come the wedding, you're all squared up, packed up, set up and ready! This is what you'll need:

- **Wedding file:** An A4 box-file housing all your ideas, paperwork and correspondence.
- **Planning countdown:** A list of everything you need to do, and when. *See* over-page.
- **Budget planner,** to square up nicely (*see* Chapter Seven).

- **Guest list,** including RSVPs and contact details. *See* page 290.
- **Timetable of the day** showing exactly what's going to happen when, and who has to do what to make sure it does. *See* page 294.
- **Ceremony box** (or two) for all the bits and pieces required at the ceremony venue. *See* page 299 for more.
- **Reception box** (or two) for everything needed at the reception venue. *See* page 300.
- **Bride's dressing case** (or two) or corner of the bedroom: for all her clothes, accessories and beauty essentials (*see* Chapter Fourteen).
- **Bride's wedding day kit-bag:** Everything she needs to keep at hand, throughout the wedding day; for contents, *see* page 300.
- **Groom's dressing case** for all his clothes, grooming and accessories (*see* Chapter Fourteen).
- **Groom's wedding day kit-bag:** On-the-day essentials, including paperwork and rings; for contents, *see* page 300.
- **First night and honeymoon cases,** packed for both of you.

THE PLANNING COUNTDOWN

Build your own masterplan around the timetable below:

1 Scribble down absolutely everything you can think of that will need doing, planning, or sorting, including anything from the countdown below. Do it together, and incorporate all major tasks (such as venue and caterer) as well as all minor ones (such as wearing-in your shoes or putting tea-lights in candle holders). You'll still be adding to this list the day before the wedding.

2 On several sheets of paper – or in a big desk diary – divide up everything you have to do over the time that you have. Put things that are time-sensitive or urgent under specific dates or months.

3 Over the weeks, as you think of new items to add to your list (hundreds, probably) just slot them in where appropriate.

4 Every time you order something, mark the date on your countdown when it should arrive, and when it does, put it straight into the box or case where it belongs.

5   As you complete an item, tick it, but don't scrub it out: leave it visible for checking later.

Your countdown
Might look something like this ...

WHENEVER YOU CAN (EIGHTEEN MONTHS AHEAD IS NOT TOO SOON)
- **Basics:** Thrash out the core issues (Section Two):
  - **Type of wedding**
  - **Date** (with alternatives)
  - **Budget**
  - **Number of guests**
- **Announcements:** Tell people about your engagement, formally or informally (Chapter Two).
- **Ceremony:** Decide on a venue, then see the minister or celebrant to discuss the wedding ceremony, dates and legal preliminaries (Chapter Eight).
- **Key players:** Appoint your chief attendants – best man/woman (Chapter Fifteen).
- **Reception:** Book the venue (Chapter Five) and caterer (Chapter Eleven).
- **Photographs:** Book photographer and videographer (Chapter Seventeen).

NINE MONTHS BEFORE
- **Guest list:** Discuss and finalise with all concerned (Chapter Four).
- **Attendants:** Choose the rest of your helpers, plan their roles with them, and discuss clothing (Chapter Fifteen).
- **Flowers and decorations:** Appoint a florist and start working on anything you plan to make or do yourselves, including favours (Chapter Ten). Remember bouquets for mums if necessary.
- **Music and entertainment:** Book all performers for both ceremony and reception (Chapter Eleven).
- **Childcare:** Book childcare professionals, or plan amongst your helpers (Chapter Sixteen).

- **Honeymoon:** Book. Chapter Six lists tour operators and luxury travel specialists.
- **Wedding night accommodation:** Organise for you, and make up a list of hotels and B&Bs for your guests. At busy times, make provisional reservations for them, too.

SIX MONTHS BEFORE

- **Wedding cake:** Order (Chapter Eleven).
- **Bride's dress:** Choose a dress/dressmaker/outfit (Chapter Fourteen).
- **Clothing for bridesmaids and attendants:** Choose and order (Chapter Fifteen).
- **Transport:** Book or arrange to borrow special transport for the wedding party (Chapter Ten). Organise guests' transport.
- **Ceremony words and music:** Decide on readings, music, hymns, prayers and vows in conjunction with officiant (Chapter Nine). Give everyone involved copies of the relevant pieces and planned ceremony order so they can prepare.
- **Power supply:** Check with all suppliers/contractors what wattage/amperage they'll need; make necessary arrangements.
- **Bride's hair and make-up:** See your hairdresser, plan your look, and start on the full countdown in Chapter Fourteen.
- **Invitations, order of service and other stationery:** Print everything in one go, if possible, and send out invites as soon as you are ready.
- **Gift list:** Make arrangements with your chosen store (*see* page 305).
- **Speech:** Start gathering information and piecing it together (Chapter Thirteen).
- **Insurance:** Consider taking out wedding cover.

THREE MONTHS BEFORE

- **Menu:** Finalise with caterers (Chapter Eleven), or arrange to order supplies for any catering you'll do yourselves (Chapter Twelve).
- **Clothing for groom and male attendants.**
- **Passport and driving licence:** Allow at least six weeks for new documentation.

- **Wedding rings.**
- **Going away clothes.**
- **Wedding shoes and accessories.**

TWO MONTHS BEFORE

- **Thank-you presents:** Buy and wrap for family and attendants.
- **Honeymoon:** Organise visas, inoculations and traveller's cheques.

ONE MONTH BEFORE

- **Timetable for the day:** List out the schedule and tasks (*see* page 294) .
- **Team meeting:** Talk through the timetable, roles and tasks with all your helpers in good time.
- **Contact details of suppliers:** List all your contractors, their office and mobile phone numbers, and attach it to the timetable.
- **Numbers:** Call round for final replies; give caterers final head-count.
- **Bride's hair and make-up:** Have a full trial run.
- **Write thank-you notes:** As gifts arrive (*see* page 311).
- **Collect certificate or licence** to present immediately prior to the marriage ceremony itself.
- **Pre-wedding parties:** Don't have ladies' or stag nights in the last week!

THE FINAL WEEK

- **Rehearsal:** Think through each step of the ceremony and reception and familiarise yourself with locations.
- **Check traffic** route and any reports for any potential delays on the day.
- **Final calls:** Call the celebrant to confirm final details. Contact caterers, musicians, florists and other suppliers to check all is ready, that they have everything they need (address and directions plus, for example, order and timings for music at ceremony/play list for reception/decision re seasonal flowers/ribbons or fabrics you've supplied for bouquets). Ensure that they know who to contact on the day with any queries (*not* either of you!). If at any point you've made any changes, such as to time of ceremony, double-check *everyone* knows.
- **Finalise budget:** Chapter Seven.

- **Try on:** Dress up in your full outfits, accessories, shoes. Time it. Practise walking around, and how to hold your dress as you climb steps.
- **Dress:** Arrange for someone to take care of it after the wedding.
- **Perfect your speech:** Content and delivery.
- **Guest list and seating plan:** Chase up any question marks and finalise seating plan (ideally, it should be changeable right up to the day: *see* Chapter Eleven).
- **Honeymoon luggage:** Make arrangements to have it sent to your wedding night hotel.
- **Collect any hired clothes.**
- **Going away clothes:** Give them to your maid of honour/best man to take to the reception on the day, if it's not at home.

THE DAY BEFORE

- **Don't do any wedding work yourself:** This is the real world, where couples are rarely able to follow advice to shut up shop a week before the wedding. But if there's still lots to be done, spend your time delegating the following, not doing it:
- **Venue decoration:** Even if these are of your own making, an able team should be leading the effort at this point – not you! Put favours and place cards on tables (Chapter Ten).
- **Music:** Cue up recorded music; leave instructions for play.
- **The cake** should be set up at the venue as early as is practical.
- **Unwind:** Or keep busy if it stems nerves, but start to wind down in good time for sleep (Chapter Fourteen).
- **Have all your personal things ready:** As well as clothing, check speeches, gifts, etc are to hand. *See* **Kit-bags** for bride and groom.
- **Do nothing risky:** From a perm to quad-biking, today is not the day!
- **Check the weather forecast.**
- **Check in with all attendants.**

Counting down to a weddings overseas?

As well as much of the above:

As soon as you can

- **Research all the options:** Where will you go, how will you do it, and who will organise it? (Chapter Six).
- **Legal:** Check out the residency requirements/procedures, and begin arrangements for the marriage ceremony itself. Make any advance preparations, but be aware that some paperwork cannot be done too far ahead. (Chapter Eight).
- **Send save-the-date cards** to all your guests.
- **Make provisional bookings.**
- **Plan for guests' travel** arrangements, accommodation and costs.

Six months before

- **Photographer, florist, cake, music:** Discuss with tour operator or arrange your own.

Four months before

- **Finalise paperwork:** Make applications for any specific certification, including visas, and send photocopies of any original documents (birth certificate, passport, etc) for advance checking or approval (Chapter Eight).
- **Ceremony music, words and readings:** Have them approved in good time. Language issues could prolong any discussion (Chapter Nine).

Three months before

- **Transporting your dress:** Arrange with the airline, ideally to carry it as hand luggage.
- **Finalise travel** for you and your guests.
- **Insure** the wedding and travel.
- **Inoculations:** *See* page 64.

Two months before

- **Courier ahead:** By a secure and safe method, send to your hotel any items for the ceremony or reception that will be bulky to carry such as service sheets, place cards, table plan, favours.

ONE MONTH BEFORE
- **Order currency and traveller's cheques.**
- **Pack a document wallet with all the legal papers you could possibly need:** They must be originals, not copies.
- **Invest in some protective packing equipment:** This is not the flight on which to squash your shoes, or find that something's leaked! Give yourself plenty of time to pack.

THE GUEST LIST

Once you've decided on who to invite (dilemmas are tackled in Chapter Four), and the style of your invitation (Chapter Ten), you need to get the ball rolling.

Invitation wording

The formal invitation, traditionally sent out by the bride's parents as wedding hosts, reads:

Mr and Mrs Donald Bride

request the pleasure

of your company

at the marriage of their daughter

Clare Mary

to

Mr Adam Groom

at St John's Church, Wimbledon

on Saturday, 21st September 2002

at 2 o'clock

and afterwards at

The Lodge Hotel, Raynes Park

RSVP
Address

Where stepparents, divorced or widowed parents are involved, the names that appear at the top will simply be those who are acting as principal hosts. The traditional variants are these:

- If both parents are hosting, but your mother has remarried, her new name will appear alongside your father's: 'Mr Donald Bride and Mrs Doreen New …'
- If both parents are hosting and divorced, but your mother has not remarried, they will be 'Mr Donald Bride and Mrs Doreen Bride …'
- If a father is hosting alone, only his name will appear: 'Mr Donald Bride requests … at the marriage of his daughter ...'
- If a widowed mother is hosting alone, her married name will appear: 'Mrs Donald Bride requests …'
- If a divorced mother is hosting alone: 'Mrs Doreen Bride requests … at the marriage of her daughter ...'
- If the hosts are one parent and their new spouse, they will be 'Mr and Mrs Donald Bride … at the marriage of his daughter' or 'Mr and Mrs David New … at the marriage of her daughter ...'
- If both sets of parents are hosting: 'The pleasure of your company is requested at the marriage of Clare Mary, daughter of Mr and Mrs Donald Bride, and Adam, son of Mr and Mrs Benjamin Groom …'
- If another benefactor is hosting: 'Mr and Mrs Extremely Generous request … at the marriage of Clare Bride to Adam Groom ...'

You, of course, can word your invitations how you like, as long as no-one's feelings are hurt and their involvement, financial or otherwise, is properly considered. A friendly, fun or unexpected form of wording is a natural way to present the tone of your wedding:

- If the bride and groom are hosting, you could say: 'Clare Bride and Adam Groom request the pleasure of your company at their marriage', but consider any other wording that you feel is right from the informal to the blatantly casual, as in: 'We're getting married … come and celebrate with us', or 'The rumours are true … Clare and Adam are finally getting married'.
- If everyone is chipping in on the bill, either:
  - Make the invitation generic: 'The pleasure of your company is

requested at the marriage of Clare Bride and Adam Groom'.

- Word it as if from the two families: 'The families of Clare Bride and Adam Groom request the pleasure of your company at their marriage ...'
- Name young family members, such as the couple's own child/ren, as 'hosts'. Since they plainly aren't, the host remains unspecified.

- To acknowledge parental contribution in a generic invitation, you could name them at the bottom as addressees for RSVPs.
- For an invitation to the evening celebrations only: The hosts '... request the pleasure of your company at an evening reception to celebrate the marriage of ...' or, far more relaxed, 'We'll be celebrating our wedding on the evening of ... Please join us'.
- Dress code is not normally printed on a traditional invitation, unless it's black tie, but might be appropriate on a funky one.
- The word 'reception' smacks of formality: if it feels more natural to ask guests 'to a party', or to 'celebrate with us', then do.

Timing

- Invitations are traditionally sent out six weeks ahead; three months is now more realistic.
- A save-the-date card, sent as soon as you set it, is advisable – especially for busy times.

Ordering and writing invitations

- Order one invitation for every household, plus at least 20% spare to allow for errors.
- Allow several weeks for printing.

Celebrity invites

Gail Porter invited guests to her wedding to *Dan Hipgrave* of Toploader by text message.

Madonna & Guy Ritchie didn't sent invites at all. (Security, security!)

- Remember to include one for the minister and his wife, and one for the groom's family.
- Allow plenty of time for proof-reading before giving the go-ahead to print, and ask at least one other person to double-check for you. As well as looking for factual errors, make sure that layout, paper-stock and typeface are all correct.
- Order any other stationery at the same time: service sheets, menus, place cards, reply cards, thank-you cards.
- Handwrite the name of each individual guest on the top left-hand corner of the invitation. Only those named are invited; avoid saying 'plus one' or 'and guest' – if you want guests to bring a companion, get their name.

Enclosures

With the invitation, include any of the following that are relevant:

- A note, setting down any information such as dress code, confetti and camera use at the ceremony, minicab numbers, your policy on young children, and a request to reply by a certain date (but preferably nothing about your gift list – *see* page 307).
- A map and directions, ideally on one separate sheet, with journey time from a key location.
- A list of decent accommodation nearby: all price ranges.
- A reply card, asking people to specify any dietary requirements.
- A schedule of the day's events, if it's not following the standard pattern or people need to dress accordingly.

Managing replies

Keep close tabs on your guest list:

- As you address each card, make up a master list of each guest's details. This will be invaluable for checking details with them, writing thank-you notes, and communicating any change of plan.
- Draw one column each for:
  - Address, phone number and e-mail
  - Reply
  - Special dietary needs

- Gift received
- Thank you sent.
- Expect 10% to decline and another 10% to leave replying till the last minute.

The timetable of the day

Having planned a wonderful wedding, the couple who have created the whole thing will (most inconveniently) simply be unavailable to take charge on the day. The event itself is highly complex, with things going on 'on stage' and 'behind the scenes' – and will undoubtedly need steering, all day long, to keep things running smoothly.

Tradition recognises this (with its protocol, etiquette, mother in charge, time-tested procedure and team of assistants), but very modern wedding planning doesn't, dumping almost everything in the over-worked hands of the bride (and, hopefully, groom). As a solution, you could:

- Appoint a toastmaster: their function is to ensure that everything happens as it should. *See* page 238.
- Appoint a wedding planner: some experts will step into the breach for the last few days before the wedding, and stage-manage the day itself. There's a rundown of services on page 240.
- Make full use of your entourage: the best man, maid of honour, ushers and bridesmaids (or whatever you choose to call them) all have considerable responsibilities (*see* Chapter Fifteen). Discuss them together from the start.
- Draw up a timetable, complete with who does what when, for the whole day. It should serve as a foolproof instruction manual for everyone.

To create the ultimate wedding timetable

1 List out *all* the things that will need to be done throughout the day. Do this over a period of weeks: they'll pop into your mind continuously.

2 Consider who's the best person for each job, letting technically-minded or very sociable people do what they do best.

3 Start building up a timetable of the day, from first call to lock-up; the outline below is based on your average 2pm wedding, with traditional roles, as a starting point only. Timings are very rough: substitute your own.

Time	Bride and Groom	Who/what's needed	Behind the scenes	Helper in charge
-4 hrs				
	Bride starts to dress	Bride's case	Check bouquets and buttonholes arrive; distribute to appropriate locations	Best man
			Check ceremony and reception boxes are safely delivered to venues	Bride's mother
-2 hrs				
	Groom dresses	Groom's case	At reception location, make any final changes to the seating plan; ensure place cards and favours are on tables; check heating	Usher/helper
-1 hr				
	Groom and best man depart for wedding	Rings, speeches, paperwork and other essentials	Check photographer arrives at bride's location	Best man
	Bride ready	Bride's kit-bag	Check make-up and hair essentials, speech, spare tights, etc all included	Maid of honour
	Photos of bride and wedding party still at home	Bouquets, buttonholes and corsages to each	Round people up and check that all required pictures are taken; check photographer knows route to ceremony	Maid of honour

Time	Bride and Groom	Who/what's needed	Behind the scenes	Helper in charge
-45 mins				
	Ushers arrive at wedding, show guests to their seats (traditionally the bride's family and friends on the left-hand side, facing the front, the groom's on the right-hand side)	Service sheets	Ensure that all male attendants/female ushers buttonholes; ensure that musicians are in place; ensure that seats are reserved for the couple's parents and attendants; check heating	Ushers
-30 mins				
	Best man and groom arrive at wedding		Ensure that readers/sayers of prayers have texts to hand, and are conveniently seated; make any necessary payments to officiant and/or musicians	Ushers
-15 mins				
	Bridesmaids arrive		Prepare young attendants, and to receive bride	Bridesmaids
-5 mins				
	Bride's mother arrives	Usher to show her to her reserved seat	Cue music for entry of bride and groom	Usher
-2 mins				
	Bride and giver-away arrive and enter with attendants	Music; attendants to assist bride, hand her her bouquet	Watch over young attendants	Bridesmaids
Zero hour				
	Ceremony begins			

STEP BY STEP, LIST BY LIST

Time	Bride and Groom	Who/what's needed	Behind the scenes	Helper in charge
+1 hr				
	Bride and groom exit ceremony	Flower girls to hand confetti/petals/bubbles to guests	Oversee flower girls	Bridesmaids
	Photographs	List of desired shots	Round up subjects and check off list of shots	Best man
+1 hr 30 mins				
	Bridal party transported to reception	Wedding cars	Check that all guests have transport to reception	Ushers
	Arrivals at reception	Drinks	Ensure that all guests are looked after; liaise with and pay any musicians	Ushers
+2 hrs				
	Receiving line	Bride, groom, both sets of parents and possibly best man and maid of honour	Ensure progress is efficient	Ushers
	Group photos	Bride's kit-bag; list of shots	Check bride and groom freshen up for photos; last chance to ensure all group shots are taken	Maid of honour, best man
+3 hrs				
	Meal announced	Ushers to guide guests	Bride and groom in position to be announced into the room	Best man

Time	Bride and Groom	Who/what's needed	Behind the scenes	Helper in charge
	Wedding breakfast		Ensure that speeches and any gifts or bouquets are to hand; check microphone; ensure that the photographer and any stray guests know when speeches and cake-cutting are due to start	Maid of honour, best man
+4 hrs 30 mins	Speeches	Best man to announce and toast; bride's father, bride, groom, best man to speak	Hand props or gifts to speaker for presentation	Maid of honour, ushers
+5 hrs 30 mins	Cake-cutting	Best man to announce	Check that musicians/DJ have arrived and set up; make any payments	Ushers
	Best man to announce final arrangements – entertainment and guests' transport home		Arrange taxis for those guests who require them later in the evening; light any candles	Ushers
+6 hrs 30 mins	Party – first dance	Best man to announce	Check everyone knows it's about to start	Ushers
	Bride and groom prepare to depart	Going away clothes	Retrieve cases from safe storage and help couple to change	Maid of honour and best man
	Farewell celebrations		Ensure that everyone has transport	Best man

In the family

'We have a lot of sisters and brothers (I'm Irish!). I involved them in everything right from the start, so when the day came, everyone knew what was supposed to be happening without being told. We didn't worry about a thing.' Bride, 27.

My mobile phone

'Everyone in a key role needs to keep their mobile phone switched on in the last 48 hours: I don't know how people managed my job before we had them. I wish I'd remembered to turn it off, though!' Best man, 25.

The ceremony box

Get a large, strong box (the plastic storage ones are cheap and sturdy; available from Homebase).

- As things come in for the ceremony, simply put them straight in the box:
  - Service sheets
  - Spare copies of readings and prayers
  - Confetti, dried flowers or pots of bubbles, and boxes or baskets to present them in (*see* Chapter Ten).
- If you think of anything you need to take to the ceremony, but don't yet have, stick a Post-it note on the box to remind you.
- Organise for the box to be delivered, or take it yourself, to the ceremony location the day before, or entrust it to an usher to transport on the day.

The reception box

Do exactly the same for the reception. This box will contain:
- Any decorations, vases/containers, candles for the reception
- Favours
- Seating plan and place cards

- Spare copies of speeches
- Practical equipment: extension leads, scissors, Sellotape, pins, floristry tools, pens, paper
- Gifts for attendants and mothers
- Children's toys or crayons
- Menus and table names or numbers.

The bride's dressing case

Allocate a corner of your room to the growing stash of things you'll need to look ravishing. A small free-standing clothes rail, from Ikea or Homebase, may be a worthwhile investment if you have several bulky outfits to hang up.

The bride's wedding day kit-bag

A small – and ideally good-looking – bag should contain all the make-up essentials on page 212, plus:

- Spare tights or stockings, plasters, paracetomol
- Your speech
- Contact lens solutions/spare glasses if you need them.

The groom's dressing case

The groom can hoard up everything he needs in the same way as the bride.

The groom's wedding day kit-bag

As well as any personal grooming props (let's not leave him out), the groom must not be without:

- The ring/s
- Legal documents required for the ceremony
- Money to make any payments
- His speech.

If you have children

Put together (or pack up) the following as they come in:

- Their outfits for the day.

- Things for them to do the evening before and the morning of the wedding (favourite books, videos, toys).
- Special gifts to give them privately as a thank you for their help.
- A spare of whatever is their emotional crutch (blankets/teddies/comforters) – as if you needed telling!

And in the ceremony/reception boxes:

- Bribes: I know, I know, we shouldn't. But when a four-year-old looks set to refuse that walk up the aisle at the crucial moment, you'll be so, so glad you've got a sparkly new Barbie doll to put right at the top of it.
- More things to do: crayons, paper... whatever keeps them busy.

HOW TO FIND THE UNFINDABLE

Inevitably, you will have a great idea (a particular decoration/type of paper/food/favour) and then wish you hadn't, when you can't find the very thing you need to make it happen! The following can make a search much more fruitful. For references, phone numbers and web addresses, *see* **Contacts** at the end of this chapter.

- The Internet is, of course, a fantastic resource in the search for something unusual – but can be a fantastic time-waster, too. Give it a go.
- Wedding magazines are crammed with the latest information and suppliers.
- Other specialist magazines: interiors, music, craft, food and other publications carry a phenomenal amount of contact and stockist information. If you can't find what you need in the magazine, try calling them: most are glad to help.
- Don't overlook the telephone directories. If the wedding is away from home, the online Yellow Pages is a godsend for finding a resource outside your own postal area. Alternatively, get hold of a local *Yellow Pages* next time you're in the vicinity.

HOW TO PLAN AT WORK, WITHOUT LOSING YOUR JOB

The rules are fairly obvious, but in case you need reminding:

- Be discreet. Everyone will be expecting you to turn your office into Wedding Mission Control, so do everything you can to prove them wrong.
- Don't cry at work.
- Don't leave wedding magazines on your desk.
- Keep wedding talk to a minimum. People will think you're boring, and over-emotional, probably.
- Use your lunch hours for wedding tasks, but keep strictly to time.
- Use the journey to work for wedding planning and reading.
- Use your mobile phone for incoming and outgoing wedding calls, not your work number. Set it to vibrate instead of ring so it doesn't shrill out 'wedding' every time it rings, and pick the right time to make and take calls.
- Get a free web e-mail address, so your wedding e-mail doesn't come through the company's mail box.

TROUBLESHOOTING

I feel like a bit of a killjoy, filling your head with thoughts of what could go wrong on this, the happiest day of your life, but there are good reasons.

1 You might as well come to terms with the fact that not everything will be perfect.
2 You might be able to take preventive – or curative – action.
3 It's nice to know that these things happen all the time and that everyone who suffers them says it *really* doesn't matter. So if:

- **You have a massive spot:** I know ... It's the worst thing that could have happened ... *see* page 209.
- **The car doesn't turn up:** Send someone off for a quick recce: who has the smartest car (guests/family/anyone)? Tie huge tulle bows, ribbons or anything else festive to the windscreen wipers.

- **The traffic is bad:** Everyone else will be caught up in the same traffic, so it won't seem so bad. However, it's only common sense to check a week before for any potential traffic problems (football match/protest/road works) so you can warn everyone. If you're really late, ask whoever is already at the ceremony venue to keep the celebrant informed.

- **The cake is damaged:** Floral decorations can hide a multitude of sins, or someone could go and buy an impressive ready-made confection from a local patisserie (they may even deliver). If it's hopeless, skip the cake-cutting altogether – you can still serve it in slices.

- **It rains:** This is just real life – rain comes on average every three days in the UK. So be prepared, with indoor space suitable for reception and photography – and plenty of umbrellas. When the sun comes out, make a run for it (mid-meal if necessary) for pictures of the two of you outdoors.

- **You fluff your lines, dry up, cry or giggle maniacally:** All this is so normal, no-one will give it a moment's thought – except to think that it adds to the day. If nerves are really bothering you, read up on rehearsing your words in Chapter Thirteen and relaxing in Chapter Fourteen.

- **A supplier delivers poor products or service:** You're in a vulnerable position. Even if a problem emerges a few days before the wedding, you can hardly threaten to cancel, can you? And if you get into a fight, you'll feel wretched and worry that they're going to ruin your day. On the day itself, you're just not in a position to check up on them. Having everything in writing, a contract and wedding insurance are all good precautions. If there's a problem on the day, you'll need to draw it to the offender's attention at the time and make some record of it, too. That done, you may just have to be philosophical about it – until you can find out about your options after the wedding. *See* Insurance? on page 83.

- **You just don't feel happy:** The stress and anxiety are meant to slip away as you walk down the aisle, but what if they don't? And what if the two of you have had a row? Research shows that smiling actually chemically affects your mood (for the better!), so you may just have to fake some happiness while you wait for it to take effect. *See* Chapters Fourteen and Sixteen for advice on relaxing, feeling more positive and enjoying each other on the day.

- **You're ill:** If it's not too serious, adrenaline has an amazing capacity to carry you through. Make sure you have a good supply of your most used and most effective medicines for colds and flu, and take vitamin C and Echinacea daily for a week or so before the wedding. If it's more than that, see a doctor as quickly as you can: they're usually very sympathetic and will pull out all the stops if they can (with fast-acting painkillers and other symptom-management drugs they may not normally prescribe). Keep off the alcohol. If it's hopeless, get on to your insurers …

- **Someone is very drunk:** Tell someone to check they don't get out of hand; act quickly and decisively if they become aggressive, and find them somewhere comfy and enticing to go to sleep (with regular checks that they don't pass out).

- **Sex is out of the question:** Planning ahead can help: line up some mood enhancers, in the form of massage oils and candlelight (*see* page 242 for the latest in designer sex shopping), and abstain for a couple of weeks beforehand. But really, hardly anyone has sex on their wedding night. Don't worry about it. Do it tomorrow night instead.

Their wedding hitches

'Our DJ was a nightmare. He was literally covered in tattoos, did terrible voice-ups over the records and spent most of the time sitting on the speakers smoking fags. What could we do but laugh and make the best of it?' Groom, 26.

'I was really, really late: I heard afterwards that everyone at the church was getting anxious (my future husband most of all), and the best man's mobile phone rang. After he'd rung off, he put on a really serious face, and started: "I've just been informed … that the bride … is finally on her way." My poor husband!' Bride, 27.

'The car dropped us off at the church – and then left! We waited a while after the ceremony, but it never came back to take us to the reception. We had to beg a lift!' Bride, 28.

GIFT LIST

I have to say that I was shocked when we started work on our gift list. I naively thought my call (and the implied promise of a big spend) would be welcomed. I phoned quite a few shops, and I can confidently say that *only one* gave a response which I considered fitting. And by that, I don't mean jumping around in excitement … just being helpful, un-snooty, efficient and pleasant – and not crushing me with put-downs that my request was too soon, too late, or in any other way inappropriate. Subsequent service and delivery was excellent, too – which also transpired to be unusual. That said, I'm sure lots are very good; it's just that I didn't know about them. The following might help to get yours right:

- Most big stores are over-subscribed. The customer, it seems, is rarely king.
- Put your name down about six months before the wedding date to reserve a place.
- They'll tell you when to come back and actually draw up the list – usually around eight to ten weeks before the wedding. Ask about returns and exchanges before you decide on a store.
- Gift wrapping and free delivery are all very well, but not reason enough to choose a store. Service, the products themselves and the price range are much more important.
- The average spend, according to Goldfish Credit Card Company, is £67, but have a good mix of low-cost and more expensive items: groups of friends often club together to buy one big thing, and some people spend so much, you'll be gobsmacked by their generosity.
- Allow plenty of time in the store to draw up the list (a day or so) and work out before you go the kinds of things you're looking for. Don't overfill the list; you could end up only with low priority stuff.
- If you want lots of different or unusual things, an independent wedding list service will give you far greater freedom than being tied to one store.
- You might want a single, very expensive item, like a flat-screen TV or dining table and chairs. There are ways to achieve this:
  - Make the most of stores which help you do this, by telling guests who call that you'd like gift vouchers towards a single large item.

- Cheat, if your conscience will allow it: put the same £70 item on your list a dozen times. Keep one, and trade the rest for the large item you want. A multitude of visitors will be happy to see the Dualit kettle *they* gave you gleaming away in your kitchen.
- Go for classic things, like white towels, but don't choose a load of mumsy stuff because you're worried that trendy things will date. So does mumsy stuff. Just get what you really, really like.
- Put some really special and amazing things on your list. If you don't get that beautiful, oversized vase, ridiculously expensive leather waste-paper basket, or uber-stylish bread bin now, you never will. Practical stuff is great, but it won't give you the same warm wedding memories.
- Don't put very dull stuff on there: who's going to want to give you a baking tray?
- Gift departments tend to be incredibly busy, and getting through on the phone is a complete nightmare. Find out when's a quiet time to call, and how to order via fax or the Internet.
- If you're having gifts delivered, book the delivery date months before the wedding. Otherwise, you may not get them for a long time after.
- Check gifts as they arrive. If the order is complete, without faults or breakages, you'll be unusual.
- Keep a clear record of the gifts you've received, who from, and whether you've thanked them. Keep the list indefinitely.
- Write thank yous as quickly as you can.

Celebrity gift lists

Sophie Rhys-Jones & Prince Edward *reportedly requested a £42,000 silver tea service and a £3000 tea strainer. On the cheap side, we're told, they had soufflé dishes at £61 each.*

Victoria Adams & David Beckham *went to the other extreme, apparently, asking for nothing but M&S gift vouchers! That's posh.*

Etiquette issue: Announcing the gift list

It is not considered good manners to mention the gift list with the invitation, or enclose a card from the store where your gift list is held. Guests will ask of their own accord if they want to be guided (really, they almost always do). However, it is becoming increasingly normal to make reference to gifts in a letter accompanying the invitation, so if you feel you must, or that it is genuinely helpful to your guests, then you are certainly not the first. Just don't even contemplate printing details on the invitation itself.

Alternative gift lists

If you've been living together for years, you may have everything you need. (Although how anyone can resist a gorgeous new set of fluffy towels, crisp, chic bedlinen, matching china and glassware, and the latest wave of trendy kitchen stuff, when their house is full of the old tat they bought when they first moved in together, I really don't know.) The alternative is a gift list with a difference, providing anything from travel vouchers to adrenaline sports, such as:

- Travel or honeymoon vouchers: Abercrombie & Kent, British Airways Travel Shops and Bridge The World Travel all do them.
- Gift vouchers only: the jury's out on this, but if you genuinely think no-one will mind giving you M&S vouchers, it could be a great solution.
- Adrenaline sports or six months of fresh bouquets, a feng-shui consultation or a yoga course: at Bliss Gifts.
- Adopt an animal: at London Zoo, fostering a Sumatran tiger costs £3000; smaller animals are considerably less.
- Name a star: International Star Registry will give your nuptials a different level of permanency.
- Charity donations are a natural option if you have a special reason for requesting a donation to a special cause.
- A fabulous wine cellar: wedding lists are operated by Oddbins and the Revelstoke Wine Company.

Contacts

WEDDINGS ON THE WEB

There are numerous wedding websites, many of which are mentioned throughout the book and are rounded up here for easy reference:

Brides magazine: www.bridesuk.net

Confetti: www.confetti.co.uk

Cool White: www.coolwhite.com

Forever After: www.foreverafter.co.uk

Hitched: www.hitched.co.uk

I Do: www.i-do.uk.com

Get Spliced: www.getspliced.com

Web Wedding: www.webwedding.co.uk

Wedding Guide UK: www.weddingguideuk.com

Weddings: www.weddings.co.uk

WEDDING MAGAZINES

An ongoing, visually inspiring resource. Most come out every other month.

Brides: Best for fashion, style, pretty ideas and their once a year address book, which is also online at www.bridesuk.net

Wedding Day: Best for inspiring real weddings

You & Your Wedding: Best for a modern approach

Martha Stewart Weddings: US title, available in major UK newsagents. Gorgeous, inspiring weddings and ideas, also online at www.marthastewart.com

OTHERS

Abercrombie & Kent: 0845 070 0603; www.abercrombiekent.co.uk

Ask Jeeves: www.ask.co.uk

British Airways Travel Shops: 0845 6060747; www.britishairways.co.uk

Bliss Gifts: 01784 470369; www.blissonline.com

Bridge The World Travel: 020 7911 0900; www.bridgetheworld.com

Britart: 020 7392 7200; www.britart.com

Future Forests: 08702 411932; www.futureforests.com

International Star Registry: www.starregistry.com

London Zoo: 020 7449 6262; www.londonzoo.co.uk
Oddbins: 020 8944 4400; www.oddbins.com
Revelstoke Wine Company: 020 8875 0077; www.revelstoke.co.uk
Yellow Pages: www.yell.com

chapter
nineteen

and now that it's over...

Despite the out and out inevitability of this moment – when your realise your wedding is now a thing of the past – it can be a terrible shock. If you feel instantly miserable, you're not alone: go straight to the end of this chapter. If you're fit for practicalities, these may keep you busy just long enough to smooth the passage into a wedding-free life.

CLEARING UP

Unless you're in a hotel or organised wedding venue, you're going to need to clean up and clear out the morning after. Plan well ahead to avoid the worst possible scenario: sweeping the dance floor alone with your hangover! Bring in teams of helpers and rewarding sustenance.

Flowers can be put to good use:

The day after

'We had loads of volunteers: in fact the clearing up that I'd been dreading turned into one of the most fun parts of the wedding weekend. That really made us appreciate what great friends we had – and made us feel extra-loved, too!' Bride, 35.

***Sir Paul McCartney & Heather Mills** landed a reported £50,000 bill for a massive wedding clear-up at their wedding castle: the combination of lorries and rain turned the grounds into a 'quagmire'.*

- Ask the venue management if they can suggest a good home. Many have links with hospitals or hospices – or contact one yourselves.
- Ask the church where you married if they'd like any flowers from the reception, too. Even if they don't need them themselves, they too may have links with a charity.
- Flowers in vases will be fresh enough for a wedding the next day; liaise with the organisers and share costs where you can.
- Give them to your guests on the day (*see* page 144)

COURTESIES

The wedding itself is rich with thank yous and personal gestures, but there are still more to make after the event.

- **Cake** should, by tradition, be sent to all guests who could not attend. Modern cakes may not be the kind that will travel or keep, and alternatives such as a favour or photograph may be even nicer to receive. If you want to keep a tier of fruit cake for a christening, as is traditional, spike it with brandy and wrap it in greaseproof paper, then foil.
- **Thank yous for wedding gifts** should go out promptly after the wedding – if not before. Traditionally, they should be a simple card, entirely hand-written, from the bride (unless a gift is specifically sent to the groom). Sharing the task is a good way to cross the 'your friends/my friends' divide.

- **Thank yous** to helpers will have been given at the wedding. However, they've probably bent over backwards for you, so after all the work they've put in, it's natural to send an additional note of thanks, when you get home.

CHANGING YOUR NAME

The dilemma is whether...

THE WIFE TAKES HER HUSBAND'S NAME, WHICH:
- Is traditional.
- Is symbolic of the commitment you've made.
- Draws the least attention: it's what everyone expects.
- Is arguably no more sexist than keeping her father's name.
- May make her husband happy!
- Is practical: a shared name is generally easier to handle with legal or financial documents.
- Means she'll have to notify everyone.
- Means admin relating to your shared children is more straightforward, from birth to schools, and beyond.

OR THAT YOU BOTH TAKE THE WIFE'S NAME, OR A DIFFERENT NAME ALTOGETHER.
- Most advantages and disadvantages of the above apply. If you decide both of you will use the wife's surname, or a double-barrelled one, it should ideally be done by deed poll or statutory declaration.

OR THAT YOU BOTH KEEP YOUR ORIGINAL NAMES, WHICH:
- Is a contemporary route.
- Respects a woman's (and of course a man's) independence.
- Suits people with a career established in their unmarried name.
- Can confuse in some circumstances.

OR THAT YOU CHANGE TO A MARRIED NAME, BUT KEEP YOUR UNMARRIED, PROFESSIONAL ONE, WHICH:
- Is a natural compromise.
- Is confusing at times.
- Can be kept simple, by using your maiden name *only* for work. Overcome hitches by:

- Arranging for your bank to accept cheques or other payments made both in your maiden name and your married name.
- Telling travel organisers that you must travel in your married name.
- Liaising with your employer's human resources and payroll departments to ensure that all insurances, contracts and other legal matters take account of your new status.

A woman may change to her husband's name, or keep her own, without any further action. For other variants, it is technically possible to change your name simply by notifying all concerned parties, arranging for relevant documentation to be changed, and making a public announcement, such as at your wedding reception, or in your engagement announcement. A deed poll is not obligatory under law, but is clearest and often safest. To find out more, go to Deed Polls Online.

Legal and practical implications of new marital status or a new name
IMPORTANT NOTE: MEN TOO!
Do remember that the fact that you are now married may be as significant as a new name, and for that reason, notification in some instances is as important for newly married men as it is for women.

WHAT YOU MUST DO (BECAUSE IT'S AFFECTED BY LAW):
- Be clear and consistent about the name(s) you use. Ensure that there is no deliberate attempt to mislead. Whilst being scatty and disorganised isn't illegal, it'll give you peace of mind to know that your ducks are all in a tidy row should any problems arise.
- Notify the DVLC of your new name, and change your driving licence and car registration document.
- Notify the Inland Revenue or Department of Social Security of your new name and marital status, especially if you are claiming any allowance that relates to your single status. This applies to men as well as women.
- Notify any other relevant body to whom you are under legal obligation.
- Make a new will, because marriage automatically renders any previous

ones invalid (unless they specifically state that they are made with a forthcoming marriage in mind). This is particularly important if you have children or stepchildren.
- Ensure that when you travel, the same name appears on all documents and tickets.

WHAT YOU SHOULD DO (BECAUSE IT'S IN YOUR OWN INTERESTS):
- Your new name: notify bank, building society, insurers, credit company, Department of Health, utilities and anyone else who may need to know.
- Your marital status: notify any organisation for whom it is relevant. For instance, your medical insurance may provide free cover for a spouse.
- Re-register children's births: if you have shared children born before you were married, it is in their interests to re-register them as children of your marriage.
- Attend to matters relating to the surnames and inheritance of any stepchildren.

WHAT TO DO WITH YOUR DRESS

If you wore a trouser suit or simple evening dress, you're laughing. Wear them and enjoy them as much as you can. For a traditional dress, however, you could:
- **Sell it:** Act quickly, because it will sell much better if it's only a few months old. Have an outlet lined up and take their advice on cleaning (many prefer to do it themselves). If you plan to sell it privately and plan to advertise in the press, check out printing lead-times. Outlets are in Chapter Fourteen.
- **Keep it as it is:** Classic wedding gowns are so exceptional, why not just keep it? You can take it out and look at it occasionally, and your daughter might wear it one day. First, have it cleaned by a wedding dress specialist, as early as possible. If you have stains on your dress, check how to clean them first with the manufacturer/experts: dry-cleaning fluid fixes some stains. Preserve your dress properly: the Bridal Gown Preservation

Company will collect nationwide, clean and pack your dress for long-term storage; or do it yourself after cleaning by packing well in a generously sized, breathable (not sealed plastic), acid-free box. Support sleeve and bodice shapes with colourless, acid-free tissue, and interleave folded layers with tissue too. If you hang it, cover with cotton, not plastic. Store in a dry, temperate room.

- **Change it:** Dyeing or altering won't suit every outfit, but a good dressmaker (or the original designer) may be able to take out the train, take off decoration, or otherwise re-purpose: Designer Alterations specialise. Dyeing should be undertaken with great caution: even done professionally, colours are limited and the effect rarely 'good as new'. What's more, it's done at high temperatures, so delicate fabrics will be spoilt.
- **Wait and see:** Keep as it is for now (cleaning and storing as above); if you decide to transform it into an evening dress or christening robe for your child later, the option is there.

AFTERWARDS: THE BIG CRASH

If you get away with a mild hangover and a fond farewell to your tiara, you're one of the lucky ones. Lots of brides, and a few grooms, hit a serious black spot that takes a long time to pass.

What happens
'Physically, a wedding sets you up for a big dive,' says psychologist Lori Bisbey. 'You've built up enormous amounts of adrenalin which will plummet immediately afterwards. You may have drunk too much and had little sleep. You're simply not in good shape to deal with the emotional adjustment as the transition from one life to another hits home.' 'You get a reality check,' adds psychologist Ben Fletcher. 'You've built up a fantasy life in your head and come down to earth with a thud.' You may literally grieve for the difference between your expectations and the reality, especially if you feel you've compromised on your wedding. Extreme as it may sound, you could feel any of the following in a gut-wrenching, wake-in-a-panic kind of way:

- That things weren't perfect and there's just nothing you can do about it now.
- That the wedding is really over. For good.
- That your dress is ruined (the fact that it cost a fortune won't protect you from stains or rips).
- Homesick: that the family you grew up in isn't your home any more.

Aftershock

'As the day came to an end, I realised something: it was a wonderful day, a happy day, but it wasn't really "for us". We'd wanted everyone to be happy and we'd worked really hard, and now it was over. I felt deflated and disappointed.' Bride, 29.

'Once it was over, I wanted a second chance. To do it all again. As if that had been a very nice dress rehearsal, and now I was ready to do it for real. I found it hard to accept that that was that.' Bride, 33.

'We stayed around for a week after our wedding, then went away for a romantic weekend. We had a two-week honeymoon six weeks after that. The timings were perfect: we didn't feel we missed anything, and we had time alone and something to look forward to as well.' Bride, 27.

'The vicar said something which I couldn't get out of my head: that during the ceremony, when my father passes my hand over to my husband's, it signals the moment when I say goodbye to my old life and embrace a new one. But I just kept thinking, "I like my life as it is. I don't want to say goodbye to it."' Bride, 29.

'I woke up the next day at 5am, and started obsessing about the things I'd forgotten to do or say. That went on for about a fortnight. It was like a kind of torment.' Bride, 35.

'For weeks after the wedding, I used to wake up in the night in a panic.' Bride, 24.

'When we got to check-in at the airport, I literally collapsed, sobbing. I felt overwhelmed by a kind of homesickness. I cried all the way to Mauritius on the plane. My poor husband!' Bride, 29.

- That the photos – the only means you have to hold on to the day – are not good.
- That it went too fast – and you missed it.
- That you didn't talk to everyone – or even anyone.
- That you suddenly fancy every person you meet of the opposite sex.
- That you hate saying 'husband' or 'wife' and you're supposed to love it.
- That you're arguing more than ever in the entire history of your relationship.
- That instead of being romantic and special, you spend your entire honeymoon wishing you were at home with your mates.
- That you were drunk, embarrassing, heckled the speeches ... or worse.

How to beat post-wedding blues

As well as trying to believe that all of the above are suprisingly common reactions that will pass, you could:

- Before the wedding, arrange (or ask someone else to arrange) a small gathering of your closest friends to take place a week or so after your honeymoon. Swap photos and stories and plan the next big event!
- Remember to keep a foot in the real world throughout all the planning. The fantasy will end so abruptly, it really does help if you're still vaguely acquainted with reality.
- Plan in advance how you'll spend the day after your wedding.
- Even if your friends and family are around for post-wedding celebrations, don't apologise for wanting a little time alone.
- Go back to the church. Most couples don't, which seems a shame. The place will have happy memories, and it's just the kind of continuity you need.
- Now's the time to reflect on how lucky you were to catch this woman/man! Focus on the fact by listing ten things each of you wants from the first year of marriage – from a picnic in the park to your first anniversary plans.
- Enjoy the sheer relief that all the work and tension is now history and that you have all the happy memories in their place.
- Make your peace with imperfection. Do it before the wedding, if you can.

Read Richard Carlson's *Don't Sweat the Small Stuff … and it's all Small Stuff* (Hodder & Stoughton). Schmaltzy it may be, but it helps. Don't beat yourself up over the things you didn't have time for, forgot, or went wrong. For each thing that wasn't perfect, one hundred things were. Think about them instead.

- Focus on a new project; ideally one you dreamed up before the wedding.
- Write down the ten things you gained from the wedding – besides a husband and some nice presents. A fitter body? Lovely nails? Gorgeous hair? A gift for public speaking? Work out how you're going to cultivate or maintain them on a long-term basis.
- Make an occasion of present-opening together. Write down who gave you what and a note or two about your memories of them at the wedding. It'll help make for touching thank-you notes.
- Work systematically on your memories – a photo album, written account of the day, or a box of mementos. *See* Chapter Seventeen for more on capturing your memories.
- Read your message book – or, on second thoughts, don't. That's a *real* tear-jerker!

Money-wise: What to expect
Dry-cleaning: £60+
Dress cleaning and preservation: £100+ including collection

Contacts
The Bridal Gown Preservation Company: 01924 891 495;
    www.bridalcare.co.uk
Designer Alterations: 020 7498 4360; www.designeralterations.com
Deed Polls Online: www.deedpollsonline.co.uk

index